Silent Hunters

German U-Boat Commanders of World War II

Edited by

Theodore P. Savas

Silent Hunters:
German U-Boat Commanders of World War II
edited by Theodore P. Savas

Copyright © 1997 Theodore P. Savas

Includes bibliographic references and index

ISBN 1-882810-17-1

Savas Publishing Company
1475 S. Bascom Avenue, Suite 204,
Campbell, California 95008 (800) 848-6585

To my wife Carol

and my Children,
Alexandra Maria and Demetrious Theodore,

for whom my love knows no bounds

Table of Contents

continued

Table of Contents (continued)

Illustrations and Maps

Contributors

Erich Topp is a former U-boat commander and one of WWII's leading tonnage aces. He retired from the West German Navy as a Rear Admiral in 1969. His reminiscences were published as *Odyssey of a U-Boat Commander: The Memoirs of Erich Topp* (Praeger, 1994).

Timothy P. Mulligan, a native of Baltimore, received his doctorate in history from the University of Maryland in 1985. Since 1972 he has worked at the National Archives, where he has specialized in captured German and related records, particularly in the field of German Navy records. His publications include two books, *The Politics of Illusion and Empire: German Occupation Policy in the Soviet Union, 1942-1943* (New York, 1988), and *Lone Wolf: The Life and Death of U-Boat Ace Werner Henke* (Westport, 1993), and numerous articles. He is currently preparing a general account of U-Boat sailors during World War II.

Gaylord T. M. Kelshall is the curator of the Chaguaramas Aviation Museum in Trinidad. He is the author of *The U-Boat War in the Caribbean* (Naval Institute Press, 1992).

Eric C. Rust, the son of an officer in the Kriegsmarine, is associate Professor of History at Baylor University in Waco, Texas, and the author of *Naval Officers under Hitler: The Story of Crew 34* (Praeger, 1991).

Jordan Vause is the author of *U-Boat Ace: Wolfgang Luth* (Naval Institute Press, 1991), and *Wolf: U-Boat Commanders of WWII* (Naval Institute Press, 1997), a recent selection of the Military Book Club.

Dwight R. Messimer, a Lecturer at San Jose State University, holds a Master's degree in history from that school. He has written several books on German and American military naval topics spanning both World Wars. Two of his recent books, both published by Naval Institute Press, include *The Merchant U-Boat*, about the German blockade runner *Deutschland*, and *Escape*, an account of the mass breakout from the American officer's POW camp at Viggingen, German in 1918.

Editor's Preface

I wouldn't have made a good submariner.

Just the thought of climbing inside a cramped welded steel tube and submerging beneath an unforgiving sea sends a chill down my spine and sets my heart pounding. Sure, there was lethal danger on the ground, but an infantryman operated in a familiar world, his feet firmly fixed on accustomed terrain. Perhaps riding in the fuselage of the airplane more closely relates to the submariner's experience, but a crewman is still surrounded by air he can breathe. And, lest we forget, there's that rip cord he can yank to soften his drop back to earth.

But what of the adrenaline-fueled terror when your enemies find you, when their pinging asdic beams lock onto your slow moving and blind boat two hundred meters below? What was it like to be trapped deep beneath the sea while depth charges exploded all around you, your boat blackened and flooding, and you unable to fight back? Can you instill in a commander the ability to remain calm and clear headed during such unholy times, as oft demonstrated by the likes of Erich Topp or Otto Kretschmer, or is such a leader born and not made? And where does a man's mind wander when his submarine creaks and groans as she takes her last plunge toward the distant ocean floor?

My step-father experienced life and death as a young marine in the South Pacific. After reading one of these essays he informed me that he had often wondered whether he could have handled the stress of serving on a submarine. Knowing well what he had undergone during his war, I was stunned by the revelation. Thankfully most of us will never have to endure such a thing. It is our lot to appreciate and experience the world of the U-boat and her crew vicariously, through the words of those who stood in the conning tower beneath the white cap, manned the headset in the radio shack or kept the engines running smoothly.

The fascination and admiration—and for some, loathing—for the submariner knows few bounds. Interest in the subject cuts across generational lines and is not limited by one's training, education, profession or past experiences. Interest in this topic is growing on both sides of the ocean, as evidenced by the recent success of Clay Blair's mammoth and definitive *Hitler's U-Boat War: The Hunters, 1939-1942* (New York, 1996). The genre has witnessed the publication of a plethora of books and articles, some good, some not, and many with an agenda to push or axe to grind. Unfortunately—and much like the American Civil War, an area with which I am intimately familiar—most of these works have focused on but a handful of subjects, the well-known aces whose stories have been told and retold.

But in the shadows of these aces reside hundreds of others who conned their boats out of Kiel, Wilhelmshaven, Narvik, Trondheim or France's bases on the Bay of Biscay, and will never receive more than a few lines in a book, an annotation in a footnote or a casual nod from a genealogist. Some of these hundreds, like Victor Oehrn, Fritz Guggenberger and Karl Merten, returned from their patrols and led productive, even sedate, lives thereafter. Many more, Engelbert Endrass and Ralph Kapitsky among them, left their families and friends and never returned. And one, Heinz-Wilhelm Eck, was captured on his maiden patrol and eventually executed as a war criminal. Most of them deserve a better fate, if not in life then certainly in the eyes of history.

I am not an expert on the U-bootwaffe and make no such pretensions. Indeed, I am an attorney by training and have spent only a handful of days on the rolling surface of the sea, none during wartime. But the authors whose essays grace this collection are scholars in the field, recognized authorities on the German U-boat war. My role as editor was primarily in securing their talents for this project, while they selected the subject officer. The criteria I set forth for selection of these men were simple: choose a U-boat commander who has not received the scholarly treatment he deserves, one who either accomplished his record incrementally during several patrols or someone whose experiences were somehow unique and worthy of study.

They say truth is in the details. Yet, for fifty years much of the detail of German's U-boat commanders has remained, like the submarines they commanded, hidden by the fog of history. This volume hardly claims to be definitive, but there is much to learn from the thoughtful contributions of these essayists. It has been a pleasure working with them, and I am proud to have played a role in bringing them together.

Theodore P. Savas
San Jose, CA
March 1, 1997

Acknowledgments

I am pleased to acknowledge several individuals who assisted me with the development of *Silent Hunters*. I apologize if I overlooked someone.

The genesis of this book took shape one evening in the summer of 1995 in Jordan Vause's living room. It was there that I broached the subject with him, and after some discussion he readily agreed to participate, deeming it both worthwhile and interesting. Jordan's readiness to loan books, discuss U-boat history amidst a house full of frolicking children (his five and my daughter), not to mention that he and his lovely wife Carmel host wonderful Christmas parties, has made him a valued friend.

Baylor University's Eric C. Rust, who graciously offered his considerable talents in translating and footnoting Erich Topp's "Castor Mourns Pollux," also cheerfully volunteered to pen the Introduction. In addition Eric carefully reviewed the manuscripts, pointing out mistakes and inconsistencies that have saved me considerable embarrassment. I am indebted to him for his enthusiasm and assistance throughout this project.

Between sessions of writing music for various A&E programs and working on his forthcoming Civil War book on the Port Royal expedition, the indefatigable Patrick Brennan took the time to read portions of the manuscript, including the Editor's Preface. After experiencing Admiral Topp's angst-filled memoir on the life and death of Engelbert Endrass, Pat scored a hauntingly beautiful theme to accompany the reminiscence.

Lee Merideth, who produced the index, also read the manuscript and offered valuable suggestions. Our friendship has been long and his advice sound. Lee is always there in a pinch, and my gratitude is deep.

Others deserving mention include: Bill Wyman, who scanned many of the images in this volume, often late at night and with but a moment's notice (no doubt the frosty Pete's Wicked Ales provided some incentive!); Mona Lisa Prussia, of Prussia Graphics, who provided needed technical assistance and lively storytelling, as she always does; and Michele Hoppe, who assisted in several ways and whose passion for flying airplanes is, ultimately, my loss.

And finally, my family. My daughter Alexandra (my "Zane-Zane"), sees far less of her papa than she deserves and yet consistently displays a level of patience well beyond her five years. Our hours of rough-housing on the living room floor, hiking in the hills and reading beneath a cozy blanket in front of the fireplace have seriously diminished over the past several months—time neither of us can ever have back. Her understanding (and even encouragement) as she routinely saw me off after dinner to either my library or office brought both a smile to my face and a heaviness to my heart.

My wife Carol ("the long-suffering mother Carol," as my historian-friend Robert K. Krick often refers to her) has toiled largely in silence while I have labored on this and too many other projects. She has willingly picked up the resultant slack that necessarily follows when one of the household partners turns attentions elsewhere, and for that I am very grateful. The birth of my son Demetrious during the evolution of *Silent Hunters* more than doubled her workload on the home front. Yet, while I was "away at sea" my best friend continued to labor on. . .and my debt to her continues to escalate.

Introduction

As you approach Kiel Bay, Germany's major port and naval base on the Baltic Sea, you will notice on your port bow a huge brick structure in the shape of a stylized submarine conning tower soaring 236 feet into the skies above the bay and its gently rolling hinterland once carved out by glaciers during the ice age. This is Germany's Naval Memorial, erected in the interwar period at Laboe where Kiel Bay widens to become one with the Baltic Sea beyond. A daunting symbol from afar and a haunting place to visit close-up with its subterranean halls and chambers containing paintings, inscriptions, wreaths, battle flags, ship models and battle mock-ups, the Laboe memorial stands as a shrine to those who served Germany at sea and paid for that service with their lives. To this day German naval units dip their colors in respect as they pass the memorial on their way in or out of the bay, and warships flying foreign flags do likewise as a courtesy one seafaring nation customarily extends to another.

A few miles up the bay at Möltenort, still on your port bow and diagonally across from the Kiel Canal's Baltic terminal, you will encounter another memorial set close to the water's edge on a peninsula. It is much smaller and less loud and obvious than the one at Laboe, in many ways more intimate, more personal, more silent—not unlike that branch of the German navies whose legacy is being remembered here: the U-boats. The memorial at Möltenort pays tribute not so much to the abstraction of heroic wartime duty as to the specific, individual sacrifice of each boat and each crew member that failed to return. Today bronze tablets and markers list U-boat after U-boat and man after man who went down as they fought literally on all seven seas in the two World Wars. If the Laboe Memorial inspires awe vis-à-vis the magnitude of the sailors' collective achievement and ordeal, a stay at Möltenort moves visitors with a humbler, subtler reminder of every single life cut short before its time—almost 30,000 in World War II alone. The Vietnam War Memorial in Washington, conceived on the same principle, daily yields a similar effect.

The men whose stories are told in the present volume naturally knew the memorials at Laboe and Möltenort well and passed them perhaps a hundred times in the course of their naval training and shipboard careers. In the late 1930s and early 1940s recollections of World War I were still vivid, meaningful and immediately applicable to contemporary developments. Indeed, more than one young officer must have wondered about the odd similarities between the U-boat war 1914-1918 and the latest conflict then unfolding: the same enemy, the same mission, the same strategy, virtually the same technology, and of course the same esprit de corps that had set the U-boat service apart from and—in its own self-assured estimation—above the rest of the fleet. Would all this also mean the same result, the same terrible toll in human lives and unrewarded effort that the earlier war had exacted?

When hostilities opened in 1939, their end and outcome, mercifully from a German point of view, lay clouded in a distant future. Guarded optimism ruled the day, even as the German Navy knew it was once more the underdog compared to the Royal Navy and had no alternative, especially after 1941, but to wager everything again on the submarine card—essentially to buy time for the Army and Luftwaffe to win the war elsewhere. And so the silent hunters slipped out of their shelters along Europe's shores—from Norway's North Cape all the way to Salamis in the Mediterranean and Constanta in the Black Sea—to be swallowed up in the vastness of the sea and to stalk their prey with the same dogged-ness and deadliness that had marked the U-boat campaign a generation before.

Since 1945 most aspects of this struggle have been told, written down and made the subject of documentaries, motion pictures and television programs, from both the Allied and the Axis points-of-view, a thousand times over. Not a year goes by without major new efforts to ascertain the facts and fathom the meaning of the drama that unfolded on the high seas and beneath them, from the sinking of the *Athenia* on September 3, 1939, to May 1945, when the surviving U-boats and their crews hauled down their battle ensigns and surrendered to the Allies.

Silent Hunters: German U-Boat Commanders of World War II, seeks to contribute to our understanding of that drama in several important ways. First, it presents in considerable detail the stories of six German U-boat commanders whose extraordinary wartime records are not exactly unknown in the English-speaking world but have never received the kind of intimate exposure in biographies, autobiographies as well as scholarly monographs and essays that others like Kretschmer, Prien, Lüth, Topp, Suhren, Metzler, Schaeffer, Werner, Cremer or Henke have enjoyed over the years. In fact, only Heinz Eck's entanglement in the *Peleus* affair and his subsequent trial as a war criminal received coverage in an English-language book back in 1948—a work long out of print on a subject virtually forgotten except by those who make the U-boat war their area of interest and expertise. In another instance, Karl-Friedrich Merten's recent lengthy memoirs are available, but only to those with access to the German language. In short, *Silent Hunters* rescues from relative obscurity a handful of men whose stories should do much to enlighten those who desire a broader and clearer picture of the war at sea.

Secondly, besides adding breadth to our knowledge of the U-boat war, the essays in this collection add much needed depth and context. They replace bleak and blank stereotypes with subtler images, leaving room to explore the spectrum of human emotions, expressions, connections and decisions that is always there but necessarily ends up under the table when writers try to catch the "big picture" or follow some murky agenda, be the motivation one of accusation, apology or glorification. Such limitations largely fall away in this volume as the reader relives the precise moments when Erich Topp and Engelbert Endrass became Castor and Pollux; when Fritz Guggenberger's pleasant sojourn off Rio de Janeiro turned into instant disaster; when Karl-Friedrich Merten felt compelled to attack former comrades to save the honor of his service; when Victor Oehrn hatched a scheme that would bring great glory to someone else; when Ralph Kapitsky realized that he and his boat would not make it home; or when Heinz Eck faced and failed the test of his life on a sultry, tropical night in the wastes of the Central Atlantic.

Moreover, these essays were written by experts—every one a published and respected author in the field of German naval history in general and the relentless U-boat war in particular. They combed the archives, interviewed and corresponded with survivors, compiled, compared and assessed secondary sources on the events in question, and then wrote their essays in the full awareness that considerable controversy and debate continues about the nature of U-boat war and about the men who fought it.

Lastly, this book reminds those of us who were not yet alive when the silent hunters engaged in their deadly game of just how central World War II has remained in the lives and memories of those who experienced it. History will remember Engelbert Endrass always as Günther Prien's First Watch Officer at Scapa Flow and as Erich Topp's best friend. For Americans, Topp remains the man who sank the *Reuben James* on Halloween 1941, no matter what else he might have done in his long and distinguished career since. Fritz Guggenberger, were he still with us, could never shed the image of the U-boat ace who sent the *Ark Royal* to the bottom of the Mediterranean. Heinz Eck would have ended the war along with millions of others in an Allied POW camp and then taken up some benign post-war career had it not been for the imponderable coincidence that made U-852 cross the path. of a Greek freighter off the African coast in 1944, the one bound for the Indian Ocean, the other for the New World.

In more than a superficial sense, they and all the others became both creatures and captives of the war forever.

Eric C. Rust
Baylor University

Silent Hunters

Engelbert Endrass, wearing his Knight's Cross, welcomes Erich Topp back after a successful war patrol in 1941. *Courtesy of Erich Topp*

Erich Topp

In Memoriam Engelbert Endrass

Castor Mourns Pollux

What is yours will be gone. Your kin will die,
And you yourself will die like them.
One thing, I know, will live forever:
The deeds of the dead in all their glory.

– From the Hávamál

I wrote these pages in the lonely wastes of the Atlantic when all
hope had vanished that Engelbert Endrass might return alive from his
last patrol.

*   *   *

Again the boat is heading west through the stormy Atlantic. This, our 15th patrol, is like all the others. We had our misgivings about the 13th, but that is now a thing of the past. The sea has become the only place that makes me feel at home since I know that you, Bertl, are out here with me, below me in the depths of the ocean. May the sea with its vast, overarching eternity fill in me the cheerless emptiness that has been haunting me since you died. I do not complain. When a child is suffering pain, tears can be a consolation. That does not work for me. Wherever I reach with my eyes and ears, with my thoughts and spirit—you are there. And yet, you are no more. What remains is the knowledge that we reached the zenith of our lives together. It is a feeling grand and bitter at the same time.[1]

Heavy seas wash over the bridge. A belt keeps me tied to the rolling, swaying platform. Above me unsteady stars, their image blurred through the driving spray and the salt that burns my eyes.

The stars have moved off far away and withhold their usual radiance. You, too, experienced this cosmic harmony when eternity is at your touch and makes your heart swell as if it is about to burst, when you feel as one with what is around you and inside you. Call it what you want: in those moments I was closest to you, Bertl. The awareness of our friendship became the great source of strength with which we mastered all of life's challenges. It was *our* bond to eternity.

No one could have said it better than you before you went out on your last mission:

"Fate, if you love us, allow both of us to survive this war. But if you want to be merciful, please let me be the first to go."

High above, Castor and Pollux still shine brightly, that pair of twins whom the gods placed in the sky as an eternal symbol of friendship between two men. "Castor and Pollux"—that's how they used to call us, they who knew us well. And are they not amazed and furious now that Castor did not plunge into the depths when Bertl died?[2]

You yourself found the answer to all this in the last words you wrote to me, words filled with a premonition of what was to come: "God does not give us back the good times we enjoyed, but he keeps the earth turning so that those who care can continue to pursue their happiness."

I don't want to, but I hear the voice of my slain brother and take it as a legacy and challenge to live, to sail the seas and to do battle with the enemy until he is vanquished.

That's how we did our 15th patrol.

We had reached a position NW of Cape Finisterre on our way out into the Atlantic when aerial reconnaissance reported a convoy bound for England from Gibraltar. U-Boat Command ordered ten boats in the vicinity to close in. Homing in on the aircraft's radio signal I was soon able to make contact with the convoy itself. Our wolf-pack was named "Group Endrass." Careful shadowing allowed us to guide the other boats toward the prey. By nightfall we had the convoy surrounded. Bertl's name and memory inspired the entire operation: every thought, every action we dedicated to his legacy.

The fight was fierce. The convoy was closely guarded by destroyers and other escorts carrying the latest weapons and equipment. They sank three of our boats, while two others returned to base badly mauled. We ourselves made three separate attacks and sank six ships. Your spirit, Bertl, gave us strength and protection.[3]

One Saturday long ago at the Naval Academy, three ensigns—Klaus, you and I—got together to go sailing. We belonged to that huge group of officer recruits who had recently descended on the institution. We loved the water and the sea and spent every spare minute in the boats. City life, busy and glittering, meant little to us.[4]

We sailed down the bay to Sønderborg, bought eggs and butter, ate more whipped cream than was good for us, laughed and talked a lot, paid our compliments to the girls, and, in general, decided that we were made to be friends.

That night we cruised back and forth on the outer bay where it meets the Baltic. By early morning we decided to turn around when the wind began to freshen from NW. With long tacks to WSW we endeavored to make it back, but any gains were soon lost due to the boat's tendency to drift sideways. The wind became a storm. We shortened sail, but apparently not enough. Around noon, just as we were rounding the tip of Holnis Peninsula, a sudden downburst hit us with full force. I let go of the main sail so Klaus could try to pull it down while Bertl did likewise with the jib. But before we had a chance to do any of this, a second mighty gust caught the bulging main sail and pushed us irresistibly toward the shore. The rudder, unable to withstand the pressure, broke in two; the anchor, unprepared, was of no use. Before we knew it we had run aground. I swam ashore to get help while my two friends tried to save and salvage as much as possible. Hours later—wet and bloodied, disheveled and with torn clothes, but proud, our eyes shining brightly—we finally relaxed as a motor launch towed us back home.

In those moments we found each other. What the events of the previous day had failed to achieve, what many shared hours of talking, listening and idle fun could never have produced, those minutes of immediate danger and mutual dependence accomplished instantaneously. We sought each other, felt radiant as we began to appreciate our sense of inner understanding, and were happy.

Our paths thereafter often kept us apart. We served on different cruisers as we learned the business of being officers. Typically, when the time came to determine who among us had the better record as ensigns, each of us wanted the other to take first place—not because we lacked leadership skills or could not make up our minds, but because each of us was convinced the other was indeed a better and more deserving recipient of that honor.

When we three took leave of each other after this interval we did so with the solemn oath: "No matter what, we shall meet again in the U-boat branch."

During subsequent assignments on surface vessels or ashore we felt like prisoners behind barbed wire. I recall how evening after evening Klaus and I would sit together on the verandah of the officer casino at Friedrichsort to breathe the fresh sea air after suffering all day on the dusty barracks grounds. We would watch the boats of the Weddigen and Saltzwedel Flotillas return from their exercises at sea—small, dark silhouettes cast onto the water by the last rays of the setting sun. An unspeakable yearning seized us to hasten the day when we, too, would be a part of them.[5]

At last even you, Bertl, were released from the hated desk job which you despised with all its bureaucratic detours and inertia, its lifelessness and lack of challenges, so much indeed that you were almost ready to throw it all down and quit.

The day Bertl and I were assigned to the Wegener Flotilla we marked in red in our calendar and celebrated with red champagne until we were immersed in the dreamland that marked the world of submariners. That was in October 1938. At last we could wield the sharpest weapon in our navy's arsenal. Whatever the future had in store for us, we would be out there in the vanguard of the action. We grew even closer together in those months of tough and thorough training exercises, against the backdrop of impending and inevitable international conflict. The daily challenges left us no time for ourselves and very little opportunity to indulge our friendship. I remember how we sometimes huddled together in our "cells" aboard the old hulk *Hamburg* that served as our accommodations in those days. In the winter, water would condense on the overheated metal walls and drip down, provided the heating system worked, as it often would to the point of glowing menacingly in the dark. At other times the system failed completely and everyone spent the night shivering in the icy cold. In the summer, the sun-baked walls would heat up the air inside to such high temperatures that, by contrast, the Sahara would have been considered a pleasant place. Then there was the water supply system with its incessant thumping and clattering, reminiscent of machine-gun fire during an enemy attack, making life miserable in all the cabins that lined the "cheerless lane" as we commonly called the passageway outside.

But in the end we laughed about these vicious evils of everyday life, made fun of them, and ultimately ignored them. We hated wasting our nights or Sundays with paperwork in preparation for the next day's activities—paperwork that came back to us from our superiors with endless requests to insert a comma here or provide more precise figures there so that we had to type the whole report all over again. But all this nonsense vanished when we stood on the bridge of our boats as they steered out to sea in line ahead under a brilliant sky. Then, careful so that our commanding officers would not notice, I would signal to you: "Watch Officer to Watch Officer—Let them all go to Hell!" And you would reply: "Watch Officer to Watch Officer: Not only that. Let them do double time!"

The outbreak of the war found us in our assigned positions out in the Atlantic.

Late one night, after our second patrol, Bertl came to talk to me. We had spent the evening with Klaus, but there had been an awkward atmosphere of suspense. Indeed, Klaus had retired early for the night, much against his usual custom.

"I have to tell you something, Erich, I can no longer keep it to myself. Prien will go on a special mission. It has something to do with the enemy's capital ships. It's a matter of all or nothing, them or us. Klaus and his boat will be out on a similar raid."[6]

I asked, "Emsmann?" Bertl nodded. Silence. Then I said, "Bertl, I envy you." Bertl replied, radiating confidence: "Everything will be fine." And none of us had the slightest doubt about it.

We in *U 46* were near the Shetland Islands when the story of Scapa Flow broke. Prien had regained the open waters, everything had gone off without a hitch. Besides Prien, Bertl and the men of *U 47*, there was at least one other individual who could not have been happier, and that was I.

And Klaus? For a long time we heard nothing at all. After all, we assured ourselves, it does happen that a boat's radio transmitter fails. But, on a mission like his, no news usually meant bad news. One day, when we had already given up hope, an enemy broadcast announced that the bodies of three U-boat men had washed ashore in the Straits of Dover. Their names matched those of Klaus' boat. We refused to believe it. There had to be other possibilities. Captivity perhaps? Rumors circulated of boats returning from patrol with half-starved crews and fuel tanks nearly empty. After all, we submariners are used to waiting and being patient.

Our missions take us far afield, into the North Sea and out into the Atlantic. We are often separated from our comrades for long periods of time. Having to be forever alert, and being bound up in the boat's routine, keeps us from giving our friends and their fates too much thought. But they stay with us in our consciousness, even if they are not physically present. Sometimes you hear nothing at all from them. Sometimes their boats are mentioned in radio traffic. Then you feel as close to them as if you could reach out and shake their hands. Months pass, half a year. Our bases are widely separated; one does not run into one's comrades as often as in peacetime. And yet, we remain true to one another. During an attack suddenly your image, my comrade, arises in my mind, if only for a second. Your example, perhaps your death, inspires me to take greater chances than I normally would. And when our paths cross again after all, we slap each other on the shoulder and exchange knowing glances as if we somehow had to apologize for the long separation, as if we wanted to assure ourselves that we were indeed still alive. Yes, Klaus, we know what waiting is all about.

Long after the broadcast about those men washed up on the beach, and long after the International Red Cross had informed us that they knew of no prisoners from your boat, it suddenly struck me that I would never hear you laugh again. My comrade Klaus, you are no more, your place is empty. You were the first to go. You won't be the last. My grief for you is mixed with pride.

We who remain alive continue to seek out the enemy. We suffer casualties, but their places are quickly taken by others. There is something unique about this camaraderie among U-boat men. Many things contribute to it: the length of the missions; the physical challenge; the never-ending routine; the tenacity with which one endures the hours when sudden death can come at any moment during a depth charge pursuit, hours when one feels so terribly helpless without even a chance to fight back. These experiences leave a lasting mark on a submariner.

Anything trivial falls away. What remains is the naked human being, the genuine comrade.

Bertl, now I want to recall a little more about you, my friend. And when I have finished doing so, everyone will know why I call you a true friend in contrast to the superficial way in which most people use that word.

If I wished to give an indication of your courage and your readiness to take on challenges, all I needed to mention would be Scapa Flow or the nearly 250,000 tons of enemy shipping you sent to the bottom of the sea. But such praise would suffocate you who never made a great deal about it.[7]

I once had an opportunity to observe a sculptor at work. What impressed me the most was the way he selected from a great pile of rough-hewn rocks those best suited for his ideas and his work. He did it quickly and with such a sure hand that one got the impression that no other rocks but those chosen could possibly be transformed into a piece of art. He never asked my opinion for reassurance. His self-confidence required no confirmation by others.

In exactly the same way you were chosen to be a U-boat commander. Everything inside you worked happily and organically together toward the one goal without you really being aware of it. Only among your closest comrades would you share your experiences and concerns; if there was a crowd you would be suspicious of their hunger for sensational stories rather than the truth.

But whenever you were in a story-telling mood—in your calm and never exaggerating way, always with a knowing eye for the precious limitations that mark all human beings and their creations—you were as though a gift for us, casting a spell upon us thanks to the intensity of your experience and the genuineness of your existence. You never belittled the dangers we have to live with; nor would you ever fail to show respect for our foe. After all, a storm was a storm, and depth charges were depth charges. When recounting such moments you were honest in admitting how pale you and your men had grown as you sought each others' eyes during those moments of crisis. For you knew that it is a false kind of courage to meet death with a fake smile on your face. If someone had mentioned your personal courage you would have wondered what that person was talking about. You would have looked at him with suspicion and you would have decided right away that he did not really belong to us. But you also would have been kind enough not to rub it in. You knew that convoy nights, the ecstasy of hunting unsuspecting prey, or even the agony of underwater pursuits, are experiences not given to everyone. Others will never understand that traditional words and values do not apply to those situations.

Yes, you were modest. For you there was only one all-encompassing revelation, or call it truth, and that was the sum total of the conclusions you drew from your war experiences. Those conclusions made you into a human being and reduced all ponderables to something very simple and profound. The war and its challenges elevated you above your ordinary environment so that you could see and understand it better beyond all logic, for with logic you can prove anything, and beyond all ideology, for everyone of us sees a different face to which one prays. To be human, to feel responsible for oneself and for one's influence on others—that was your essence: straightforwardness, integrity, balance, and circumspection. This attitude is reflected most notably in your war diary:

1045: Without warning, three aircraft prepare to make a bombing run.

1048: Emergency dive. Aircraft dive from cloud cover. The first dropped four bombs. Boat's stern badly damaged.

While running submerged we discovered that the port shaft and rear hydroplane have been damaged. No. 5 torpedo tube flooded and leaking because outer cover and casing gone. Trim tank, No. 1 diving cell and watertight stern section also flooded.

Decide to rest boat on sea floor for a while.

Water penetration in stern section too much for pumps to handle. Urgent need to raise boat. Boat refuses to stir. Slowly increase air pressure on diving cells. Nothing. —

Full pressure on all cells. After long minutes boat slowly lifts off and shoots toward the surface at 40 degree angle.

No aircraft in sight.

During the attack Seaman Plaep was severely wounded by a bomb fragment.

Those are your simple words. I heard the same report directly from your lips when the attack was fresh in your memory, your voice vibrating with the emotion of the moment. And then you took away all tension and suspense by looking hard at us comrades and commenting, "Well, the good Lord must have wanted us to go on for a while longer."

When you had safely returned and taken the boat into the dry dock, we saw the huge hole, the demolished stern section, the bent shaft. The shipyard people shook their heads and admitted, "Can't believe they made it home like that." Their words showed how proud they were of the boat they had built and of the man who commanded it.

I can hear the bombers screaming down from the clouds. Before anyone can react to the watch officer's desperate, last-minute warning, the bombs explode on top and all around the stern. Fatally wounded, the last man staggers through the hatch before it is pulled shut. The boat rears up under the blast of the explosions, then drops like a rock to the bottom. While everything is being done to save the boat, the commanding officer looks on helplessly as the wounded sailor bleeds to death before his very eyes. The water level inside the boat rises incessantly, adding lethal weight by the minute. The moment rapidly approaches when no human will can possibly force the boat back up. Carefully, compressed air is being directed to the diving cells to restore buoyancy. But not too much, because the boat cannot afford to break through the surface where the bombers are waiting for the coup-de-grace. Jets of water keep penetrating the pressure hull and inundate the boat. "Boat refuses to stir," you wrote. "Slowly increase air pressure on diving cells. Nothing." After those words there is a long dash in your diary. Every submariner knows what that means: minutes of agony that can add streaks of silver to a shock of blond hair and drain all blood from one's face. Those moments can carve runic letters into your forehead, lines that will never go away and will make you look forever aged beyond your years.

"Full pressure on all cells. After long minutes boat slowly lifts off and shoots toward the surface at 40 degree angle." That is your last chance, your last desperate attempt to avoid instant catastrophe. Better to die manfully under a hail of bombs than to be slowly squashed to death on the bottom of the sea. Those minutes of unspeakable suspense seem like hours. Your entire burning will to live is focused on a tiny glimmer of hope.

Then the boat lifts off and shoots to the surface. Your relief of having escaped one mortal danger gives way to apprehension as to what will happen next. Will there be more bombs, more explosions? Will it be the end?

The Commanding Officer pulls open the hatch to take a quick look around.

"No aircraft in sight."

Anyone who can detect in your war diary the hidden drama and suspense that has been known to make war-hardened men collapse mentally and physically, will realize what I meant when I referred to your modesty and straightforwardness.

June 6, 1941. Weather is deteriorating. Storm force 9 to 11. Powerful seas engulf the boat. A tanker comes in sight. Even under the prevailing conditions an attack at short range may be successful. Decide to go for it. It is difficult to keep the boat at periscope depth.

1005. No. 3 torpedo on its way. Explosion after 34 seconds. Cannot use the periscope at first because of the swell, but a few minutes later manage to get a glimpse for a second or two. The tanker's hull looms immediately ahead. It must have run a complete circle. Emergency dive. Too late. When we reach a depth of 16 meters the tanker plows into us. No damage to the pressure hull, but neither of our two periscopes is working. We open distance a little and surface. The hatch to the bridge is jammed and cannot be opened from the inside. We dive again, blind as we are.

1200. Back to the surface. We quickly open a hatch on the deck. The First Watch Officer climbs through it. Hatch immediately closed again because heavy seas keep washing over the upper deck. The officer manages to open the conning tower hatch from the outside. The bridge looks like a junkyard, but no crucial damage except for the periscopes. We are forced to return to base.[8]

June 8, 1941. We sight a tanker.

1210. Alarm. We begin our attack with only one of our periscopes partially operational.

Fire two torpedoes. Both hit the target.[9]

2205. Steamship sighted. Prepare to engage with artillery.

0010. Open fire. Enemy does not return fire even though vessel is armed with two guns; instead crew lowers lifeboats.

0045. Cease fire.

0217. Vessel sunk.[10]

Under the heading, "General comments concerning the patrol", the U-boat commander adds: "The collision with the tanker was due primarily to the poor weather and the difficulty to keep the boat at periscope depth. Under such weather conditions the question arises if one should attack the enemy or let him go. I decided to attack."

These entries reveal, as seen through your honest eyes, what it means to weigh risks in submarine warfare. You felt no need to emphasize your aggressive spirit and your ability to make decisions, not even when you chose to engage two additional enemy vessels even though your boat was damaged, one of them armed with two guns. You take such qualities for granted. Your report is unadorned and to the point.

During many convoy battles you were fortunate to command a handful of men who felt deep affection for you and close attachment to one another. One of them wrote home these lines before he sailed with you on your last mission:

"Dear loved ones! Should you learn one day that our boat has not come back, there is no need for you to keep up hope. We are blessed to be able to serve under such a marvelous commanding officer. We are agreed that none of us will fall into the hands of the British. We want to fight and win together; or else, if it cannot be helped, to die together."

This splendid affirmation of Germanic faithfulness in life, war and death provides a glimpse of the power of your spirit that we comrades found so comforting, that induced your men to give their very best under all circumstances, and that drove you to seek out the enemy without hesitation.

And then there was *our* mission.

Under the brilliant sky of a late summer afternoon our two boats lay side by side in the locks of St. Nazaire. Everyone in the base knew how inseparable the two of us had become, and therefore the fact that we put to sea at the same time meant something special for everyone.

Our boats were decorated with flowers over and over. The sun reflected off the water and showed the pier crowded with people, happy faces everywhere.

Before we got under way, I assembled my men on the upper deck and said to them: "You know that Lieutenant Commander Endrass is a good friend of mine. Make absolutely sure that we don't have to be ashamed of our record when our two boats return together from this patrol."

We picked up speed and left the locks in line ahead while a brass band played appropriate tunes, cheers echoed back and forth and last messages were exchanged. Then the night swallowed up our boats and we were on our own.

Four days later, at night, I sighted a convoy and alerted Endrass' boat then on patrol not far away. After being driven off several times I managed to attack and sink a destroyer. As the enemy vessel went down, its own depth charges exploded and created a fireball that Endrass saw from the distance and used to home in on the convoy. At dawn our two boats rendezvoused. We exchanged information and laid our plans. For four days and nights we clung to this convoy, never once losing it out of sight.[11]

The enemy escorts knew their business well. Corvettes would suddenly approach and fire at us from out of the sun. During the day they forced us to dive; at night they illuminated us with flares and kept us away from our prey. But they also realized that we were two tenacious wolves circling their flock. Whenever we found an opening we would pounce and try to go in for a kill. They added destroyers to the screen. We even attacked the destroyers to relieve the pressure. In return they dropped depth charges on us. Enemy aircraft added to our problems. They even tried to use a Q-ship as a decoy, but we remained aloof and would not fall for the bait.

When one of us had lost contact with the convoy, the other would hang on all the more tenaciously. If one was under pressure from the escorts, the other would counterattack to distract the enemy. This battle raged over a distance of 700 miles, the equivalent of the distance between Paris and Moscow, until the convoy entered the Irish Sea. We commanding officers did not get any sleep during those days. Always knowing exactly what the other would do under the circumstances gave us a sense of security and made us strong. The harmony of our actions and reactions was a thing to behold. For both of us, those four days and nights represented the most wonderful experience the U-boat war had afforded us until that time. It was the high point of our U-boat careers. We both used those very words when we returned to base together. This sense of comradeship and understanding outweighed all the excitement of our welcome home, the congratulations, the flowers, the hugs, and all that. It still figured prominently when we reported to U-boat Command, and everyone present could hear it in our words and see it in our eyes.

Whenever we were together, it was always a high time, always summer. And this last summer, the one before you went out again never to return, is indeed irretrievable, unforgettable. Everything we did, we did together. For four weeks we lived with two bodies but just one soul. Every heartbeat confirmed it, whether we were in Paris and immersed ourselves in its overflowing vitality that we had missed so much out in the Atlantic, or whether we enjoyed the comfort of the house we shared in La Baule les Pins. We lived like kings and felt as if the world lay at our feet. After all, we had gone out in our tiny boat into the wastes of the ocean, just we and a few other men, mere nothings when compared to the eternal skies above us—and yet, we had defied the storms and the sea. A world power shook under our blows. You are the commanding officer. You lead your boat either to victory or demise. When you are victorious, you return to the rejoicing of those you left behind. The fairest girls will wave to you, the fullest glass is yours to enjoy. You return as a king, enriched by the gratitude of the fatherland. If you did win but failed to come back, you did so at the zenith of your life and fate spared you the agony of decline. In that sense fate had reserved a truly royal gift for you. The best are mourning your death.

That is how we lived. We loved our lives without deceiving ourselves as to what might be the other extreme, the last moment, the end. We anticipated death, just as we expected challenges and fulfillment in life. We hoped, however, that death would spare us, and if not, that we would meet it together. Fate has not been so kind.

Then came the day when you went out on your last mission. Little seemed different from earlier farewells, and yet there was a shadow hanging over it. "It is not like the other times," you said, "a good part of me I leave behind." I knew what you meant, Bertl, and it bothered me. Usually you had been the first who wanted to go out again, who could barely reign in his impatience on the days before the boat was scheduled to sail. You were the one who radiated happiness and fulfillment when you stood on the bridge of your boat wearing your leather gear, eager to cast off. At that point you cut off everything that held you back, your eyes fixed only on what lay ahead. It was not only the cold and icy December day that made you quieter than usual. "Be sure to follow me as soon as possible," you told me, as if you somehow sensed you needed me out there.

A few days later it is my turn to sail. Our operational instructions take us to different parts of the Atlantic. Christmas goes by, we say good-bye to the old year and welcome the new one. At night I often sit and listen to Radio Belgrade playing "Lili Marlen." Yes, Bertl, we had pledged to do that daily as often as possible as a means of feeling close to our loved ones. It was a symbol of unity, a festive act of remembering and having faith in a future which could only be better. Monique used to sing that song for us.[12]

My dark premonitions grew and reached the point of frightful certainty when there was no news at all, when none of the many radio frequencies we monitored carried a message from you. Day after day I refused to believe it. But your silence became more oppressive to me by the minute and threatened to knock me down as if a giant had punched me with his fists. I hoped and hoped, yet realized that the odds were lengthening. As long as possible I held on to my self-delusion because it made me feel better.

We were the first boat to return from the new area of operations off the Eastern Seaboard of United States. I knew our staff ashore had planned a big reception with lots of people and commotion. I avoided the whole thing deliberately by making base four hours ahead of schedule. Nobody was there to greet us when we entered the locks and made fast. I could not hold back any longer and, besides inquiring innocently about wind and weather, asked the supervising engineer at the locks when Endrass had sailed on his last patrol. He could not remember the date, but it had been a long time ago. That ended my doubts once and for all.

The boat has reached the protective concrete shelter. Comrades come by to greet me and extend their congratulations. All of them are looking at me inquiringly and somewhat longer than usual. I know what they want to ask me: Don't you know that your best friend is dead?

I refuse to accept their challenge, refuse to tear to shreds the last vestiges of my self-delusion. Nobody says a word about Bertl. They don't want to spoil my joy of seeing old friends again and to feel solid ground beneath my feet—a sensation every submariner cherishes when returning from a long patrol. "Thanks, comrades, I appreciate it. It's

An evening at the "Scheherazade" nightclub. From right to left: Engelbert Endrass, Monique, Erich Topp and friends. *Courtesy of Erich Topp*

good to be back." I willingly take my part in this tragicomedy, tell them all about the mission, about the ships we sank right off the U.S. coastline, about good and bad weather we encountered, about my splendid crew—anything to avoid the big question.

Later we sit in the huge reception hall. We have already lifted our glasses to celebrate our safe return, my formal report is long over. Finally I break the silence and ask the flotilla commander point-blank:

"Bertl won't come back?"

"No."

"No news?"

"None."

"I knew it."

The silence seems deeper than before. My last words hang in the room, hard and final. That's it. This is not the place or time for long speeches. I leave the room and am alone.

Face it, I tell myself, that your friend Bertl will never come back, that you will never again enjoy his sense of humor or hear his laughter. Face it that nothing can replace his loss, that nothing can outweigh the richness of our memories which allowed us to reach both the zenith and the nadir of our lives together. Face it that there is no common future the way we had imagined it so brightly. Face it that he is resting now somewhere out in the same Atlantic we used to traverse together so many times when hunting the enemy.

Weeks later I find myself again in the immense expanse of the Atlantic, the only place I can now call home. Your picture hangs in front of me. Next to it is a copy of your last letter to Monique, my friend, a letter that is like a legacy to me:

We have begun to discover each other, but this process is far from finished. Thousands of people only know their own heart, they float and drift through life. People need to love and understand one another: that is the only way to learn what another human being is really like. That is what fills your memory. . .My thoughts are with you. I am profoundly grateful for everything you have given me, while I am trying to think of what I can still do for you. Think of the faith of which you spoke last. . . no matter what. . .

Besides going down in history as the great commanding officer who made the world take notice, you are the great human being who lavishes his rich inner life upon others, who will remain unforgettable to all who knew you.

Engelbert Endrass and guests in the French villa he shared with Erich Topp in 1941. *Courtesy of Erich Topp*

Karl-Friedrich Merten
National Archives

Timothy P. Mulligan

Karl-Friedrich Merten
and the Prussian Tradition

"We couldn't have been sunk by a nicer man."
– Survivor from the *City of Cairo*

In a naval officer corps that prided itself on its modern and middle-class character, and in a combat service often distinguished by mavericks, Karl-Friedrich Merten constitutes a link to the military tradition synonymous with the emergence of modern Germany. A man of medium build, fair skin, piercing blue eyes and a dazzling smile, Merten emerged as one of Karl Dönitz's top submarine aces during a long and distinguished career in the *Reichsmarine* and *Kriegsmarine*. Yet for all of his accomplishments, Merten has received little historical attention. Only the posthumous publication of his memoirs, with invaluable insights into his character and background, has helped redress this imbalance.[1] If Adolf Hitler fought World War II—as characterized by a German aphorism of the time—with a Prussian Army, a National Socialist Luftwaffe, and the Kaiser's Navy, Merten can be said to exemplify both the first and the last.

To British and American readers the Prussian tradition invokes many images, the worst of which became familiar as propaganda stereotypes in both world wars: excessive obedience to authority, a veneration of the military and its values, a rigid social structure dominated by an arrogant aristocracy and the subjugation of individual freedoms. But for

German officers it represented a military ethos that blended idealism and stoic courage, unassuming modesty and selfless dedication, personal integrity and a willingness to sacrifice. "To be a soldier, especially an officer," wrote a young Claus Schenk Graf von Stauffenberg, "means to be a servant of the state, to be part of the state. . .The military forces and their pillar, the officer corps, represent . . .the true embodiment of the nation." The symbol of this tradition in World War I might have been U-boat ace Lothar von Arnauld de la Perière, descended from a French Huguenot family that had first served in the army of Frederick the Great and who established still-unsurpassed records for vessels sunk by a submarine commander (194) while earning praise from adversaries for his daring and chivalry in the treatment of survivors.[2]

But lineage was not required for membership in the tradition. Karl-Friedrich Merten's family claimed neither lands nor title. Indeed, they could only trace their roots to 17th-century Pomeranian farmers, successive generations of which gradually rose to middle-class prosperity. Merten's father, also named Carl-Friedrich, studied law at various institutions throughout Germany, then served as a lieutenant in the elite *1. Garde Regiment zu Fuss*, the Kaiser's personal guard. Shortly before his son's birth on August 15, 1908, in Posen, West Prussia (now Poznan, Poland), the elder Merten had been elected there to the post of *Erster Stadtrat* (Town Councilor). Five years later he was appointed *Bürgermeister* (Mayor) of the city of Elbing, where he would remain—eventually promoted to *Oberbürgermeister* (Lord Mayor)[3]—until his refusal to join the Nazi Party in 1934 led to his resignation.[4]

Young Karl-Friedrich's upbringing was strict but fair, and marked by the occasional trouble normal for a high-spirited boy, yet he was to know little of a peaceful, carefree childhood. Before his seventh birthday he experienced the deaths of a sister and brother. By then his society had already paid the costs of the first year of World War I. Elbing's contribution to the war effort consisted of its sons and the products of its Schichau shipyards, located on the Elbing River that fed the Frisches Haff, a narrow bay to the north. The river's depth limited the shipyard to such shallow draft warships as fleet torpedo boats, but these vessels sufficed to arouse what would prove to be a lasting nautical interest in Karl-Friedrich.[5]

In the war's last year, at the age of 10, Merten entered a Royal Prussian cadet institute in the Pomeranian town of Köslin. These schools served as a direct pipeline to the military, graduating adolescents with much the same sense of discipline and duty as that received by West Point and Sandhurst cadets at a later age. His parents considered the move to a military academy only one of several options, but allowed Karl-Friedrich the ultimate decision. Thus the young Merten himself made the first of several choices that eventually led to the bridge of a U-boat. The standard introductory speech that welcomed him and his fellow pre-teenaged comrades to the academy in April 1918 might have been composed with the future U-boat service in mind:

> Gentlemen! You have chosen the most beautiful profession there is on this earth. Before your eyes you have the highest aim there can be. Here we teach you to reach that aim. You are here to learn that which gives your life its ultimate meaning. You are here in order to learn how to die.[6]

The young Merten thrived in the atmosphere of firm but not overly harsh discipline, which sharpened and strengthened the rough-hewn character forged in childhood. After two years—with the war ended, the monarchy deposed, and a republic proclaimed—the Royal Prussian academy became a state *Realgymnasium* (equivalent to an advanced high school emphasizing modern languages, natural sciences, history and geography), accompanied by changes in the curriculum and teaching staff. With this symbolic passing of a Prussian institution and tradition, the 12-year-old Merten unknowingly witnessed what would be his own fate.

Yet at the time these changes signified little in Merten's own life, for while attending the academy he resolved to become a naval officer. In his final year at school he submitted his application, passed his physical examination and visited the naval district office in Königsberg (now Kaliningrad, Russia), where he was interviewed by then-*Korv.Kapt.* (Lt. Commander) Rolf Carls, who would eventually be recommended by Grand Admiral Erich Raeder as his successor as Commander-in-Chief of the Navy. Before Christmas 1925 Merten learned he had been tentatively accepted as an officer candidate. Immediately after graduation he reported to Kiel on April 1, 1926, swore an oath of allegiance to the German Constitution and began the final, grueling battery of physical, mental and character examinations guaranteed to eliminate all but the best qualified.

A few statistics demonstrate the exclusivity of the inter-war naval officer corps. Limited by the terms of the Versailles Treaty to a maximum strength of 1,500 officers among 15,000 total personal, the *Reichsmarine* actually remained below authorized levels. During the 1924-27 period, the navy in fact reduced the number of officers each successive year, from 1,357 to 1,215. Even as economic prosperity returned to Weimar Germany, service in the navy attracted large numbers of potential recruits. In 1926, some 44,100 applied to join, of whom a mere 635—a minute 1.4%—were accepted. Out of the 6,000 officer applicants who reported to Kiel in April, only 104 survived the final weeding-out process: 3 as administrative officers, 21 as engineering officers, and 80 as executive officers (*Seeoffiziere*). Among the last was Karl-Friedrich Merten.[7]

The selection process was not entirely objective. Naval officer candidates usually represented the well-educated and relatively privileged strata of society, characteristics shared with most modern navies. "We were mostly sons of active or reserve officers, and more than a few were sons of former officers of the Imperial Navy," observed Merten, whose own father retained reserve officer status in the army. This homogeneity of background and values shaped the character of "Crew 26" (the German Navy designated a class of midshipmen by year of entry rather than year of graduation) as it would for the German naval officer corps as a whole.[8]

Merten spent the next four and one-half years in a complex education and training program that contrasted sharply with that of his American counterparts at Annapolis. Where the latter spent most of their four years in classrooms, German *Seekadetten* divided their term among various shipboard training assignments and academic instruction. Merten's experiences outline this emphasis on seamanship and practical skills:

April-May 1926: "boot camp" basic training at Stralsund
May-October 1926: ordinary seaman aboard sailing ship *Niobe*
November 1926-March 1928: world cruise aboard light cruiser *Emden*,
    including visits to the American West Coast
April 1928-March 1929: classroom instruction at the naval
    academy Mürwik, located just outside the Schleswig port of Flensburg
April-July 1929: Torpedo- and Communications School Mürwik
July 1929: Mine Warfare School Kiel

August-September 1929: infantry weapons training, Stralsund
October 1929-February 1930: Naval Artillery School Kiel
February-October 1930: active duty as ensign aboard old battleship
Schleswig-Holstein

It should be noted that Merten and his comrades received no submarine training, a limitation imposed by the navy's lack of operational
U-boats. The varied but balanced development program, however, produced well-rounded executive officers who could learn quickly and adapt
to any naval branch as the need arose. The fruits of the system can be
seen in Crew 26's contribution of 19 U-boat commanders during World
War II, five of whom—Merten, Richard Zapp, Harro Schacht, Wilhelm
Rollmann, and Hans-Gerit von Stockhausen—won the coveted Knight's
Cross (*Ritterkreuz*) of the Iron Cross for their achievements. Ten of the
19, however, fell to death or capture before war's end.[9]

At the end of his apprenticeship the young *Leutnant zur See* (ensign) stood an undistinguished 47th in his class, a ranking that did not
affect his standard rotation of assignments at sea and on land. Merten's
training emphasized gunnery skills, a prerequisite for command of surface warships yet to be permitted or built. In particular, his training
emphasized large-caliber and anti-aircraft (flak) artillery. He had also
demonstrated a capacity for teaching, which would remain a hallmark
of his naval career: After a year's duty in interior communications and
firing control aboard the light cruiser *Königsberg*, Merten served for two
years as an instructor to new midshipmen at the Naval Gunnery School
Kiel. There followed two years as a watch and gunnery officer aboard
torpedo-boats (in the German Navy approximately equivalent in size to
destroyer escorts), then an extended tour as gunnery officer aboard light
cruiser *Karlsruhe*. By late 1936 Merten—now married and with the
rank of *Kapitänleutnant* (Lieutenant)—was well on his way to a successful if unremarkable career.

Events outside the navy, however, had begun to alter the government and society that Merten served. Adolf Hitler's nomination to
Chancellor in January 1933 marked the end of the Weimar Republic
and the beginning of National Socialism's epoch in Germany and
Europe. The first ominous signs of change for the armed forces occurred
in 1934, as the oath of loyalty to the German Constitution was replaced
by an oath of unconditional obedience to Hitler himself. Like other

components of German society, the navy—redesignated the *Kriegsmarine* in May 1935—would discover too late that it had surrendered control of its destiny.[10]

Merten's initial reactions to Hitler, candidly recorded in his memoirs, reveal a political shortsightedness characteristic of the German military at this time. Although his father opposed the Nazis' intolerance and racial policies, Merten and many of his comrades found their energetic nationalism appealing and ignored larger political issues. The celebration of Hitler's triumph on January 30, 1933, deeply impressed him: "We were overwhelmed. . .and evaluated the event for what it was, a national upheaval," wrote Merten. "Never again in my life would I be so swept up as at that moment." Hitler's approval of the murders of his own SA leaders in the summer of 1934 (known as the Röhm Putsch after the SA chief and principal victim, Ernst Röhm) aroused few deep concerns: "From the insular perspective of the Navy, order seemed to be restored on the national scene," explained Merten in his memoirs. "At the time I was convinced of the truth of all official statements. . .I could not and would not believe that Hitler knew of the excesses that occurred." Such expressions reflect the political limitations inherent to the Prussian military tradition, as well as a professional 'tunnel-vision' by which some historians characterize the navy.[11]

Indeed, Hitler's rise to power and the general recovery of the German economy brought material benefits and prestige to the navy. Expansion of the service began even before Hitler renounced the arms limitations of the Versailles Treaty, seemingly validated by the Anglo-German Naval Agreement of June 1935. *Kriegsmarine* warships participated in international duties and represented German interests during the Spanish Civil War. The navy's growth culminated in an ambitious shipbuilding program aimed at restoring Germany's position as a world sea power, but construction had barely begun before it was cut short by war's outbreak in September 1939.[12]

Merten participated in the Spanish actions as second gunnery officer aboard the *Karlsruhe*, June-December 1936, and as flak artillery officer aboard light cruiser *Leipzig*, December 1936-April 1937. In October 1937, he took command of *Geleitboot* (fast sloop) *F-7*, beginning "the happiest period of my naval career," Merten later recalled, for after 11 years of service, he had at last fulfilled the dream of independent command. It would last only 16 months, however, before external events began to affect assignments. Orders in February 1939 transferred him to another instructional course in large-caliber artillery as the international situation deteriorated.

In June 1939, Merten became training officer for the October (1938) class of officer cadets for a planned cruise to Central America aboard the pre-dreadnought battleship *Schleswig-Holstein*. In the end the voyage would prove to be much shorter but far more fateful. The aged warship departed in August for a scheduled ceremonial visit to the autonomous Baltic port of Danzig, the disputed status of which served as the pretext for Hitler's attack on Poland. At 4:47 a.m. on September 1, 1939, *Schleswig-Holstein* fired the first shots of World War II against the Polish fortified depot at Westerplatte. Merten, directly involved in the targeting of specific positions, experienced his first action in what would prove to be a week-long operation to reduce the fortifications.[13]

The German navy's employment of a warship commissioned in 1908 to open hostilities indicates its limited capacity to wage a naval war in 1939. Grand Admiral Erich Raeder had been assured by Hitler of Great Britain's neutrality in the event of a war over Danzig. When Raeder learned of the British declaration of war on September 3, the navy commander-in-chief commented that German surface forces were

Kapitänleutnant (Lieutenant) Karl-Friedrich Merten and midshipmen of Crew 39A aboard the Schleswig-Holstein, shortly before that aged warship fired the first shots of World War II. *U-Boot-Archiv*

"so inferior in number and strength to the British Fleet that. . .they can do no more than to show that they know how to die gallantly." Merten felt astonishment at Hitler's "political dilettantism" in failing to anticipate such developments, but with his "consciousness of duty" he prepared for the unequal struggle.[14]

Merten remained aboard *Schleswig-Holstein* through April 1940, training the next year's class of officer cadets while participating in minor actions. During this period the small *Kriegsmarine* achieved its greatest victory in securing the conquest of Norway, but at grievous cost to its surface units (one heavy and two light cruisers and ten destroyers sunk, other warships damaged). Merten's assignment as a training officer reflected both his instructional skills and advancing age, but he was determined to see combat. He realized that his best chance lay in the U-boat service. While still performing his training duties he went outside channels to petition the organizational chief of the submarine service and his former superior on the *Karlsruhe*, Adm. Hans-Georg von Friedeburg, for a transfer. Although his favorably-disposed comrade carefully avoided any promises, Merten soon received orders to report to torpedo school on May 1, 1940.

The future U-boat ace's ensuing experiences demonstrate the strength of the Prussian military tradition in its reliance on the character of its officers. Despite his prior specialization in naval artillery and unfamiliarity with submarines, torpedoes, and communications security, five months' intensive training brought him up to speed in all those subjects. One of his instructors provided the following assessment of Merten at the conclusion of his training:

> A very self-confident and self-reliant officer who is both ambitious and sensitive. He participated enthusiastically in the training course. Through his inclinations and performance he has acquired much knowledge. His calm and assured handling of a submarine, including submerged maneuvers in the face of contrived difficulties, testifies to his seamanship. His attitude has demonstrated that he is a combat-ready officer who is suited for command of a combat U-boat.[15]

Merten's training performance so impressed his superiors that they recommended he serve only a "confirmation" patrol as a commander-in-training before receiving his own boat. This reflected highly individualized evaluations in the selection of submarine commanders. Although most initially served extended apprenticeships as U-boat watch officers, some received commands directly after training. Thus, Merten and other *Konfirmanden* (a German term for youths awaiting religious confirmation, borrowed by the navy) represented an interim category. The virtually identical casualty rates among the three groups suggests that this subjective selection yielded equal results.[16]

In September 1940, Merten reported to the recently established U-boat base in Lorient, France, where he was assigned to U-38 under *Kaptlt.* Heinrich Liebe. Merten's new commanding officer, a member of Crew 27 and a submarine officer since 1935, had just earned the Knight's Cross after sinking nearly 90,000 tons of Allied shipping. Even before Liebe returned from leave, however, Merten availed himself of the opportunity to listen to evening conversations of such top U-boat aces as Günther Prien, Heinrich Lehmann-Willenbrock, and Reinhard Suhren in the *Prefecture*, the former French naval barracks. Merten's "confirmation" consisted of a winter patrol in the North Atlantic, a two-month ordeal that yielded the meager results of one ship sunk and another damaged. While not particularly successful from a tonnage-sunk viewpoint, Merten's maiden voyage furnished the future ace with what he later described as "a hard yet impressive primer" in the requirements and rhythms of U-boat command. The increasing tempo of the Atlantic battle left little chance to ponder these lessons, for the night that U-38 docked Merten boarded the train bound for Germany and his own submarine.[17]

Merten's new command was U-68, a Type IXC boat just being completed in the Deschimag AG Weser Shipyards of Bremen. Commissioned into service on February 11, 1941, U-68 represented a submarine class designed in the mid-1930's to perform such strategic missions as reconnaissance, minelaying, and even tactical command tasks. Once war came, however, the Type IX's substantial fuel capacity and cruising range of 11,000 miles made her the long-range workhorse of the submarine fleet. Slower to dive and more sluggish to handle than the smaller Type VIIC, the Type IX quickly proved too vulnerable to convoy escorts and therefore assumed the role of the "lone wolf," preying on unescorted shipping for extended periods in areas increasingly removed from the North Atlantic battleground. In this role she proved most effective. Although never amounting to more than 12% of the

U-boat fleet, Type IXC boats alone accounted for approximately 37% of all merchant sinkings.[18]

It is interesting to note that each of the two mainstays of Dönitz's U-boat force (Type VIIs and Type IXs) favored different age characteristics in commanders. Type VII boats, operating for relatively short but very combat-intensive periods in battling convoys, demanded the advantages of youth: energy, aggressiveness, quick reactions and optimism. To compensate for command inexperience, Dönitz substituted a tight control of group operations via radio communications. Type IX submarines, which averaged more than 100 days at sea on each patrol, required the virtues of maturity: patience, endurance, insight, coolness under pressure and independent judgment. The selection of Merten for his first U-boat command at age 32 reflected this matching of skills and mission. That only 15 of 203 new submarine commanders in 1941 were older than Merten underscores both his seniority and the predominance of Type VII boats (152 of 203).[19]

U-68 spent the next four and one-half months in the Baltic on shakedown cruises and training exercises. These sea trials were designed to test the vessel's seaworthiness and mold boat and crew into a single fighting unit. Through the gamut of engine and diving trials, torpedo firing practices, simulated emergencies and tactical exercises, Merten and his men grew familiar with one another and their vessel. They did not even appreciate that they had less time in trials and training (138 days) than the standards subsequently maintained (an average of 160 days through 1942-1943), as Dönitz cut corners in 1941 to build up as large a submarine fleet in as short a time as possible.[20]

Merten and his crew very nearly paid the full price for their inexperience on their first patrol, a month-long transfer passage from Kiel to Lorient via the North Atlantic convoy lanes. Within five days after her departure, U-68 had endured a severe depth-charge attack and narrowly escaped ramming by a British destroyer south of Iceland. Later, Merten fruitlessly chased an independent steamer, established but lost contact with a British convoy before he had a chance to fire, and claimed the "probable sinking" of a pursuing corvette though in fact he hit nothing. When internal damage to the main bilge pump left the boat with only limited diving capabilities, Merten broke off the patrol and headed back to France. Before he could arrive, however, the starboard diesel engine broke down and a young ensign fell ill with pneumonia. Exhausted and frustrated, Merten tied up to the dock in Lorient on August 1, his only unsuccessful cruise behind him.[21]

Dönitz and his operations chief, then-*Kapt. z. S.* (Captain) Eberhard Godt, did not blame Merten for his lack of success, for they had selected him for an important albeit controversial mission. In his briefing on September 7, Merten learned he was bound for South African waters, a strategic gamble to surprise Allied shipping there at the expense of potentially more profitable sinkings closer to home. During the 6,000-mile voyage to the objective, Merten and two other U-boats would be forbidden to attack targets after crossing the equator in order to preserve the element of surprise. In the end things did not work out as planned, but Merten became part of a sea epic.

Departing on September 11, U-68 experienced nothing more exciting than rigorous practice dives and gunnery drills for the first 10 days of her patrol. During the night of September 21-22, the U-boat joined another southbound submarine, U-107 under *Kaptlt.* Günther Hessler, Dönitz's son-in-law. Together the two boats attacked Convoy SL-87 north of the Cape Verde Islands. Merten and his crew laboriously earned their first success, but its extent is still disputed. According to Merten, U-68 torpedoed and sank three steamers, a claim accepted by U-boat Command and still credited by some historians. Careful post-war analysis has challenged and chipped away at Merten's claim, awarding two of the victims to a third U-boat that joined the action, U-103 under *Kaptlt.* Werner Winter. Only the 5,300-ton British steamer *Silverbelle* stands as U-68's unquestioned initial sinking. Subsequent attacks the next evening on a British destroyer and a tanker proved fruitless, ending Merten's second convoy action.[22]

It nearly proved his last. A few days later he proceeded to a secret rendezvous with the homeward-bound U-111, under *Kaptlt.* Wilhelm Kleinschmidt, at Tarafal Bay in Santo Antao, northernmost of the Cape Verde Islands. The purpose of the rendezvous was to restock Merten's exhausted torpedo supply. U-67, under *Korv.Kapt.* Günther Müller-Stöckheim, also arrived to transfer a stricken crewman for passage home. The British Admiralty, alerted to the rendezvous by recently decrypted intercepts of Merten's request for the meeting and subsequent replies, dispatched the submarine *Clyde* to surprise the U-boats. The attempt miscarried, but just barely. U-68 and U-111 had just completed the difficult and dangerous torpedo transfer when *Clyde*'s torpedoes

(Below) ULTRA intercept of a decrypted and translated German radio signal from
U-111 relating to U-68's near-fatal encounter with British submarine Clyde in Tarafal
Bay, Santa Antao (Cape Verde Islands), September 1941. *National Archives*

```
                    28 SEPTEMBER 1941 TOP SECRET ULTRA JAM JPC
    2155/28/297    TTEZ UKHQ     117       SERIES A


    FROM U-111
    1. ONLY PRESENCE OF NATIVES NOTICED THROUGH ROW BOAT.
    2.  0230 CAST OFF FROM MERTEN ((U-68)) WHO WAS AN-
    CHORED. 0328 MERTEN LAST SEEN IN FORWARD POSITION IN FRONT
    OF ENGLISH U-BOAT 4 MI. FROM COAST, BEARING 200, TRUE.
    THREE MINUTES BEFORE SHIP OF CLYDE TYPE, DIMMED OUT, AT
    600 METERS. BEHIND IT RECOGNIZED A SILHOUETTE. DID NOT
    MAKE OUT TYPE. MERTEN'S COURSE 260, CLYDE'S COURSE 180, MY
    OWN COURSE BEFORE SIGHTING 270. DETONATIONS. ((REST OF
    MESSAGE GARBLED))
                        1215/7/2/46
```

sped past the stationary U-boats. Unable to sink the Germans with her
torpedoes, the British submarine rammed and damaged U-67. Merten
did not even realize he was under attack until the torpedo fired at him
detonated harmlessly on the rocks ashore.[23]

To this point Merten's submarine service matched his career: solid
but undistinguished. Good fortune rather than merit seems to have
spared him the pitiless fate dealt other inexperienced commanders. His
profligate expenditure of torpedoes for rather meager results (17 torpedoes for one undisputed sinking) perhaps testified more to the unsuit-
ability of Type IXC boats in convoy actions than Merten's long-range
marksmanship. On the positive side of the ledger, Merten evidenced an
ability to extract the utmost from his crew, as demonstrated by U-68
remaining in action for nearly 50 consecutive hours during the attack
on SL-87. A keen analytical mind was also evident in the detailed
recommendations he appended to his war diary, ranging from proposals
for radar equipment and signal flares in convoy attacks to suggestions
for stronger types of rope lines in U-boat resupply operations.

Merten also mixed his strong, wry sense of humor—a key ingredi-
ent in binding captain and crew—with his official duties. Later in the

U-boat's career, floating cases from a victim were eagerly brought aboard only to reveal piles of weather protection coats. The crew prepared a formal business card for their commander as "Traveller in Oilskins and Wet-Weather Gear." When advised by his radioman that U-111 had erroneously reported U-68 as "probably sunk" by the surprise attack in Tarafal Bay, Merten quipped: "That's how it goes. One morning you wake up a dead man and don't even know it!"[24] Perhaps U-68's near escape indeed marked a resurrection, for from that point on her fortunes markedly turned and her captain's assets came to the fore.

One of these concerned his reputation for snatching and hoarding supplies and spare parts whenever and wherever possible. "Merten should adopt a hamster or vulture as his boat's emblem," U-67's chief engineer jested.[25] This trait had led Merten to request the torpedo resupply from U-111 in the first place. For the same reason, he asked to rendezvous with the damaged U-67 to refill his fuel tanks from that homeward-bound submarine. With this accomplished on October 2, Merten reconnoitered an empty Georgetown harbor on Ascension Island before proceeding to St. Helena, Napoleon's final place of exile. The port of Jamestown held only a single ship, the 8,145-ton British oiler *Darkdale*. Despite the shallow waters, Merten daringly dispatched the large ship literally under the guns of the port's defenses in the early hours of October 22. The sinking of the *Darkdale* marked the first U-boat sinking of an Allied ship below the equator.[26]

Merten continued southward toward Walvis Bay on South Africa's Atlantic coast, sinking two more British merchantmen on the way: *Hazelside* (5,297 tons) on October 27, and *Bradford City* (4,953 tons) on November 1. The latter's sinking demonstrated that Merten, while he had come a long way, still had much to learn. Merten did not detect the *Bradford City* until U-68 was almost upon her, forcing Merten to dive and maneuver in order to achieve the best angle of attack. After firing his torpedo salvo he veered sharply to port, unaware that his target had done likewise. After hearing the satisfying detonation of a torpedo hit, Merten sought a view of his victim through his periscope. Undoubtedly what he saw must have been chilling: the looming hull of the *Bradford City* was only 40 meters distant and still closing with the momentum from her now-dead engines. Merten ordered all engines reversed but could not avoid a minor underwater collision that punched U-68 to the surface a mere 10 meters from the U-boat's prey. "Thank God the

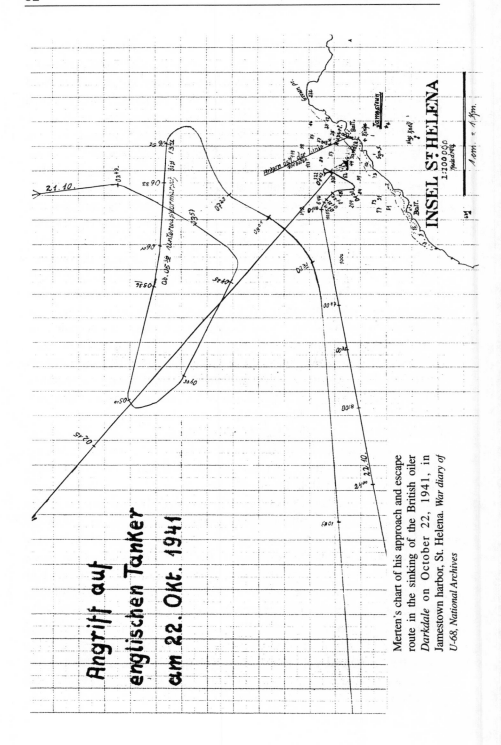

Merten's chart of his approach and escape route in the sinking of the British oiler *Darkdale* on October 22, 1941, in Jamestown harbor, St. Helena. *War diary of U-68, National Archives*

enemy manned their lifeboats instead of their guns," noted a relieved Merten in his war diary. Fortunate to have escaped with only minor damage to the bow, U-68 dove and motored to a safe distance to observe the *Bradford City's* final agonies.

Merten continued his cruise off South Africa but did not encounter any other targets, unaware that decrypted intercepts of U-boat messages allowed the British to divert shipping away from U-68 and other boats in the area. The principal enemy for Merten and his crew remained the draining tropical heat that wrapped the boat in an average (Fahrenheit) temperature of 91°, rising to as high as 140° in the engine room.[27]

On November 11, Merten received word that the Cape Town operation had been broken off, with orders to rendezvous for fuel and provisions with *Schiff 16* (*Atlantis*), the most successful German commerce raider of the war. The refueling on November 13-14, 530 miles SSW of St. Helena, briefly reunited Merten with an old friend and *Atlantis'* commander, *Korv. Kapt.* Bernhard Rogge. After the rendezvous U-68 departed to operate off the Congo. On November 22, as Merten proceeded to a meeting with the supply ship *Python* to take on additional torpedoes, he learned that *Atlantis*, while refueling *Kaptlt.* Ernst Bauer's U-126, had been surprised and sunk by the British cruiser *HMS Devonshire*. Determined to cut back his operations and provide assistance in any rescue efforts, Merten linked up with *Python* and *Korv. Kapt.* Hans Eckermann's U-A on December 1. To his surprise and relief, he encountered Rogge with the survivors of *Atlantis*. After further discussions with his unfortunate comrade, Merten renewed and almost concluded his fuel and torpedo resupply when *HMS Dorsetshire* appeared on the horizon. Merten immediately cast off the fueling lines and crash-dived, but U-68's newly-acquired weight of supplies and torpedoes left her out of trim, and he was unable to attain an attack position. When U-A missed the British cruiser with a torpedo spread, *Python* came under heavy and accurate fire from the British cruiser. Merten surfaced in time to see the *Dorsetshire* disappearing to the southeast and the German supply ship ablaze and sinking.

With both U-68 and U-A under Rogge's command, and with that officer aboard Merten's submarine, the two boats began a historic rescue mission. The 414 survivors of *Atlantis* and *Python* were divided up, each U-boat taking aboard 105 men, the rest placed in 10 lifeboats towed behind the submarines. A handful manned a motor launch used

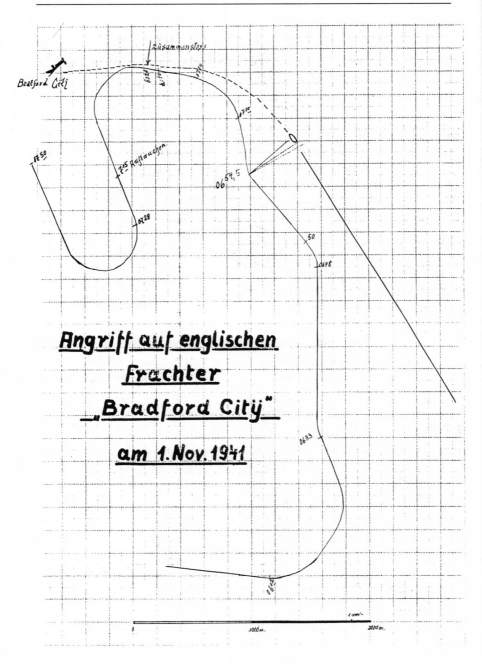

Merten's chart of his pursuit and sinking of the British freighter *Bradford City* on November 1, 1941, in the South Atlantic. *War diary of U-68, National Archives*

for communications. On December 2, this unusual formation commenced the hazardous return voyage to France, more than 5,000 miles to the north. U-129 under *Korv.Kapt.* Nicolai Clausen joined them the next day, followed by *Kaptlt.* Joachim "Jochen" Mohr's U-124 two days later. Mohr's perilously low fuel situation was alleviated by Merten's transfer of some of his own carefully hoarded supply. Four Italian submarines also arrived between December 14-18 to take on survivors, greatly easing the crowded conditions. U-68 delivered her survivors to St. Nazaire on Christmas Eve, tying up the next day in Lorient.[28]

Thus ended the longest-distance rescue operation undertaken during World War II. All 414 survivors and their rescuers returned home safely, a testament to German seamanship as well as to the relatively light Allied defenses at the time. Merten had played a crucial role in the rescue as a conclusion to a patrol that had lasted 116 days and covered a distance of 17,600 miles. Ironically, it would not be the last instance where Merten assumed the role of savior.

U-68's next two patrols followed the classic pattern of "lone wolf" operations for Type IXC U-boats in distant waters. After a long journey to its designated area, U-68 stalked unescorted, independently routed merchant ships while evading Allied air and sea patrols. Each patrol averaged 60 days, and during each Merten and his crew sank seven

---

```
                    6 DECEMBER 1941
     1134/6/213    EHPS SXMN    117    SERIES A        ((SOUTH-
BOATS FROM BDU)    OFFIZIER D


     1. IT IS INTENDED TO TAKE OVER TOTAL OF 60 SHIPWRECKED
ONTO 4 ITALIAN BOATS.
     2. TRANSFER PLANNED FOR PERIOD FROM 15TH-17TH DECEMBER
IN AREA OF OL ((ES)) WESTERN THIRD ((18-36n., TO 10-30 N.-
29-00 TO 25-13 W.)), STEER TO CENTER WESTERN ((PART OF
GRID)). ATTENTION MERTEN ((U-68)): STEER TOWARD RS 40
((ES? 40:14-33n., 26-39w.)).
     3. DELIVERY OF 900 DAILY RATIONS ((FOOD)) FOR EACH
GERMAN BOAT IS PLANNED.
     4. BDU IS COUNTING ON DAY'S RUNS OF 230 MILES.
                                          1600/6/3/46
```

ULTRA intercept of Dönitz's signal to Merten regarding the transfer and provisioning of survivors of raider *Atlantis* and supply ship *Python*, December 1941. *National Archives*

Allied merchant ships, a total of more than 90,000 tons. From February to April 1942, Merten operated in the region off the west coast of Africa in the area of Freetown and Sierra Leone. In May and June 1942, U-68 prowled new waters in the Caribbean, focusing especially on the Venezuelan and Colombian coasts and the eastern exits of the Panama Canal. On both patrols the U-boat suffered its principal damage not from depth charges or bombs but from other causes—a further testament to Merten's leadership in avoiding Allied defenses.

It was during these patrols that Merten's long-acknowledged skills as a teacher blended with the continued proof of his ability to learn. His marksmanship at the beginning of the third patrol remained question-

A tired but relieved Korv.Kapt. (Lt. Commander) Karl-Friedrich Merten on the bridge of U-68. This image was taken on the last leg of the longest rescue mission of World War II. *U-Boot Archiv*

able, with only two hits in his first six firings. Thereafter, however, it improved greatly, and Merten was able to record ten hits in fourteen launchings. His record continued to improve through his fourth and fifth patrols when, respectively, 15 of 21 and 14 of 19 torpedoes fired found their marks. Particularly remarkable were four hits achieved at ranges of 2,000 or more meters from submerged firings, and a fifth at a range of 1,000 meters without aid of the temporarily-disabled attack calculator. U-boat Command recommended a standard range of less than 1,000 meters for underwater torpedo attacks, and optimally between 400 and 500.[29]

Several occurrences made the latter patrol particularly memorable. Shortly after departing Lorient, defective exhaust valves forced U-68 to divert to El Ferrol, Spain, where a German depot ship repaired the damage with the enthusiastic approval of Spanish Navy authorities. The U-boat's closest brush with destruction came on June 10 from one of her victims, the British steamer *Surrey*, when her cargo of 5,000 tons of dynamite detonated as she plunged into the depths. The force of the underwater explosion caused "the strongest blow U-68 has yet experienced," Merten recorded, with damage to the rudder and torpedo firing controls and almost all breakables on board. Most important for Merten came a signal four days later with news of his decoration with the *Ritterkreuz*, celebrated by all aboard with an oversized, hand-fashioned Knight's Cross and a round of beers. The crew had reason to celebrate: Merten's patrol marked the most successful U-boat operation (in tonnage sunk) in the Caribbean throughout the war.[30]

For his fifth and final patrol, Merten returned to his objective of a year earlier, Cape Town. Dönitz's orders of August 1, 1942, called for U-68 to join four other Type IXC boats and a "milch cow" supply U-boat as *Gruppe Eisbär* ("Polar Bear" Group) to strike Allied shipping in the waters off South Africa. Once again, in order to achieve strategic surprise the boats were prohibited from attacking shipping below a certain latitude. Although the prohibition was implemented against Dönitz's better judgment, at least this time U-boat radio communications would not betray them: the addition of a fourth rotor to the 'Enigma' encryption device preserved German naval cypher security through most of the balance of 1942.[31]

The 6,000-mile voyage to the target area began on August 20. After crossing the equator, U-68 encountered and sank two independently-routed merchantmen on September 12 and 14. The first sinking yielded the recovery of the captain and chief engineer, both of whom were handed over to *Korv.Kapt*. Georg von Wilamowitz-Moellendorf's supply boat, U-459, during a refueling rendezvous on September 22 southwest of Walvis Bay. Merten proceeded jointly with U-172, under *Kaptlt*. Carl Emmermann, toward what the Naval High Command hoped would be a surprise attack on Cape Town's crowded Table Bay. Instead of heavy traffic, however, the two submarines entered the area on October 6 and found the brightly-lit roadstead almost empty of shipping. Requests for freedom of action to pursue more plentiful targets in the Cape Town approaches were denied, a restriction conscientiously observed by Merten but evaded by the more adventurous Emmermann. Finally receiving permission to attack at discretion beginning October 8, Merten dispatched six vessels in less than 27 hours. His total might have been even higher had not the steadily-deteriorating weather forced U-68 to break off pursuit of potential victims. By October 14, Merten and his crew were battling hurricane-force winds and rolling seas that smashed the U-boat's crockery. When a shift westward led to calmer waters but no targets, Merten commenced the long voyage home on October 30.[32]

En route to France Merten sank his last vessel, the British ship *City of Cairo*, 500 miles south of St. Helena on the night of November 6. Two single torpedoes sent what Merten believed to be an 8,000-ton cargo ship to the bottom within two hours. As they monitored the ship's distress call and watched the numerous lifeboats go into the water, however, U-68's crew realized they had sunk a passenger liner with women and children among its 125 passengers. Because of the recent *Laconia* incident and consequent non-rescue order by Dönitz, Merten could not undertake any serious efforts on behalf of the survivors. He did, however, go in amongst the lifeboats and assist them by megaphone in recovering other survivors still in the water. After providing the exact course to St. Helena, he departed with the comment, "Goodnight, sorry for sinking you."[33]

There was little celebration aboard U-68 that night in the belief that the odds against their victims' survival were too great. In fact, about 200 of the *City of Cairo's* 300 original crew and passengers survived. Most followed Merten's directions and were picked up near St. Helena 13 days later. One lifeboat became separated and drifted for 51 days before reaching the Brazilian coast, but by that time only two of the original eighteen people on board were still alive. In 1981 the saga of the *City of Cairo* and her passengers became the subject of a book and subsequent press stories in England. The public discussion prompted Merten to write the *Sunday Express* and provide his own account of the incident. An astonished Merten received over 200 letters from Britain in response, some from the survivors or their families, others from Royal Navy veterans expressing appreciation or interest for his efforts. Three years later the British survivors held a reunion in London and invited their erstwhile foe to attend. One of the survivors later observed: "We couldn't have been sunk by a nicer man."[34]

On November 17, 1942, Dönitz notified Merten by radio that he had been awarded the Oak Leaves to his Knight's Cross, only the 147th member of the German Armed Forces to be so honored. Nineteen days later U-68 tied up at Lorient and Karl-Friedrich Merten stepped off her gangplank for the last time. In only five patrols he and his crew had spent 373 days at sea, traveled nearly 65,000 nautical miles, played a major role in the longest-range rescue operation of the war, and sunk 27 Allied merchant ships totaling 170,248 tons, ranking Merten among the top six U-boat aces of the war.[35] Merten also shares in the credit for sinkings accomplished by his former watch officers, whom he tutored in the art of submarine command: *Kaptlt.* August Maus, Merten's first officer from the beginning through December 1942, recipient of the *Ritterkreuz* for sinking nine ships totaling 59,000 tons; and *Kaptlt.* Alfred Lauzemis, who served successively as second officer, first officer, and commander of U-68 throughout the boat's history, sinking five vessels before U.S. Navy aircraft sent both to the bottom on April 9, 1944.[36]

After a two-month stint in command of the 26th U-boat Flotilla in Pillau (now Baltiysk, Poland), Merten—promoted to *Fregattenkapitän* (Commander)—settled in as commander of the 24th U-boat Flotilla in Memel, where from April 1943 to March 1945, he trained future submarine commanders in what he learned to do so well himself: submerged torpedo firings. Ironically this period coincided with the effective defeat of the U-boat effort in the Atlantic, rendering much of this training academic. Merten's role in Memel is memorable in quite a different context, as he increasingly found his time taken up in disputes with the Nazi Party *Gauleiter* for East Prussia, Erich Koch. In late July 1944, when he learned that Koch had ordered 6,000 minimally-trained

Hitler Youth teenagers to man defensive positions outside Memel against the advancing Red Army, Merten took matters into his own hands and ordered the evacuation of the teenagers by sea. Loyalty remained a characteristic of the Prussian tradition; sacrificial fanaticism did not. With Dönitz's support he withstood the outraged *Gauleiter*'s wrath and coordinated that August the general evacuation with his flotilla of 50,000 civilians from Memel—arguably the most significant accomplishment of his German Navy service.[37]

Following the disbanding of his training command on March 12, 1945, Merten served as a liaison officer to Führer Headquarters in Berlin during the war's final month. In late April he proceeded with a group of officers to southern Bavaria, the proclaimed but illusory "Alpine Redoubt" that provided the setting for Merten's internment after Germany's capitulation. Unlike so many of his submarine comrades, Merten did not spend an extended period in captivity but was discharged from his 19 years of naval service on June 30, 1945, having attained the rank of *Kapitän zur See* a mere seven days before the German surrender. By April 1946, he had found work in the French-directed administration of the Rhine waterways salvaging wrecked barges, and after two years' employment had apparently settled into his new life.

But the past would not go away. On November 22, 1948, French authorities arrested Merten for his "illegal" sinking of the Vichy French tanker *Frimaire* in the Caribbean in June 1942. The sinking of this vessel, whose voyage was unregistered with German authorities and which was steaming unlit in a war zone, had prompted an energetic investigation by Dönitz at the time that exonerated Merten. After a six-month trial the French court concurred with this finding and released him.[38]

Following retirement from a successful postwar career in shipyard and ship construction firms, Merten began work on his voluminous memoirs. As some of his contemporaries and a new generation of Germans became more critical of Dönitz and the sacrifices of the U-boat campaign, Merten increasingly devoted himself to a passionate defense of the attitudes and values that had characterized his own service.[39] In one co-authored book, several published reviews, and personal correspondence he strongly attacked Dönitz's critics, dismissing their arguments as distortions and hindsight. Yet, when fellow ace and

Knight's Cross holder Erich Topp publicly criticized Merten's own writings, Merten responded with a personal appeal to meet privately and discuss their differences, rather than engage in open debate.[40] He also found time to complete his memoirs and assist historians in researching the submarine campaign.[41]

More than a life passed with Karl-Friedrich Merten's death due to cancer on May 2, 1993. A man of personal integrity and courage, Merten never perceived the need to reevaluate the conditions by which such attributes could be abused. Social and political values unreservedly accepted in his youth, blasted and twisted in the cauldron of two world wars, were discarded by a new generation seeking to redefine the German identity. In all probability the Prussian tradition that guided him, his comrades, and previous generations died quietly with its last representatives.

The precise meaning of that tradition will continue to occupy and frustrate contemporary and future historians. Their study will not be made easier by the case of Karl-Friedrich Merten, a dedicated and conscientious officer whose paradoxical legacy combined an extraordinary record of destroyed enemy shipping with a reputation among friend and foe alike as a savior of lives.

*   *   *

Ralph Kapitsky as a Mishipman at the Naval Academy at Flensburg.
Courtesy of Herbert Schlipper

Gaylord T. M. Kelshall

Ralph Kapitsky
Battle in the Caribbean and the Death of U-615

In March 1943, German U-boats tore apart convoy HX 229 in the North Atlantic. Their success was a direct result of the efforts of the shadowing U-boat, which doggedly hung onto the convoy while vectoring other boats into position. It was a frustrating job, made all the more so since the Allies knew their best chance to evade the growing threat was to eliminate the shadower. In this case, the shadower was U-615, and she paid dearly for her success. The destroyers *HMS Anemone* and *Harvester* caught the submarine and, over a span of ninety minutes, inflicted serious damage in a series of seven successive depth charge attacks on the submerged boat.

Nevertheless, U-615 doggedly hung onto the convoy until released from the arduous task and allowed to attack. The gathering dusk and heavy sea mist surrounded the surviving merchant ships. After two attempts in a long and difficult hunt, U-615 was finally in position. A torpedo tore into the ammunition-filled *Edward B. Dudley*, which disintegrated with its entire crew in a blinding flash. In order to see its quarry clearly, U-615 had crept close to the ship before launching the fatal torpedo, so close that it took a few moments after the explosion for the U-boat commander to realize that he had been hit by a piece of flying debris, which left his right arm numb.[1]

The daring commander of U-615 was Ralph Kapitsky, and the sinking of the Liberty ship *Edward B. Dudley* was only his third success, and thus he was not considered an ace in the accepted sense. As part of

Group Tiger during his second war patrol, Kapitsky attacked convoy ONS 136 in October 1942, sinking his first two ships in the process, the freighters *El Lago* and the large 12,000-ton *Empire Star*. But it was the heavy damage suffered by U-615 while shadowing convoy HX 229 in March of 1943 that was to have dramatic consequences for both its commander and her crew.[2]

*   *   *

Ralph Kapitsky was born on June 28, 1916, in the beautiful university city of Dresden to peace loving, respectable parents. Ralph would later write that he could not understand how his father, who was with the Deutsche Bank, could have sired two sons who would go on to follow military careers so at variance with their parents' life. Despite a youth dominated by a Christian education, sedate living, the opera and theater—Ralph once played the part of Mark Antony in *Julius Caesar* and later *Macbeth*—the two brothers found themselves in the service, motivated by the slogan "You are nothing, your country is everything."[3]

Ralph joined the Kriegsmarine in April 1935, while his brother Johannes joined the Wehrmacht panzer forces shortly thereafter. By October of that year Ralph was an officer cadet aboard the old armored ship *Schlesien,* and attended the naval academy at Flensburg. After brief service as a midshipman on the cruiser *Karlsruhe,* Ralph was transferred to the Luftwaffe later that year to be trained as a navigator and observer, and eventually as a co-pilot of naval aircraft of Coastal Air Group 806.

The start of World War II found his unit assigned to the invasion of Poland, with Kapitsky flying in a HE-111. After several bombing missions—which included, ironically, anti-submarine patrols—Kapitsky's aircraft was shot down and he was injured in the crash. His wounds did not prove serious, and he was able to take part in the Battle of Norway soon afterward. After the Norwegian Campaign, Kapitsky was trained as an observer and gunner, first in a Stuka and then in a JU-88. By July 1940, his squadron was based at Caen, France. Fortune smiled on the Dresden native, who flew and survived one hundred missions during the Battle of Britain. To his great joy, the Kriegsmarine reclaimed him in December 1940 and he was assigned to submarine duty. By July 1941, Kapitsky was serving with the 7th Flotilla as First Watch Officer on

U-615's officers take a break from training in the Baltic, June 1942. (Left to right): Oberleutnant Herbert Skora, chief engineer; Leutnant zur See Herbert Schlipper, First Watch Officer; Leutnant zur See Claus von Egan-Krieger, Second Watch Officer; Ralph Kapitsky, commander. With them is Leutnant zur See Hermann, a trainee. *Courtesy of Herbert Schlipper*

Horst Elfe's U-93. After completing two patrols on U-93, Kapitsky underwent rigorous training to prepare him for his own boat, U-615, a Type VII under construction at the Blohm and Voss shipyards at Hamburg. After a work-up in the Baltic, U-615 departed Kiel, Germany in March 1942 on her first operational war patrol around Great Britain to La Pallice, France, where Kapitsky was assigned to the 3rd Flotilla and from which base he would operate on his second and third war patrols.[4]

Forced to undergo lengthy repairs after the battles around convoy HX 229 in March 1943, Kapitsky and U-615 missed the slaughter of May 1943, when the Allies achieved their first decisive success in the war against the U-boats by sinking forty-one submarines. Admiral Karl Dönitz, Commander-in-Chief of the U-boats, was forced to recall his crews from the North Atlantic until they received the technical equipment necessary for them to face the Allied anti-submarine forces on equal terms. It was a major defeat for the U-boats and a loss of prestige

U-615 returns from her first patrol, a cruise to the North Atlantic. Ralph Kapitsky is on the left wearing the traditional white commander's cap, with IWO Herbert Schlipper standing next to him. *Courtesy of Herbert Schlipper*

for Dönitz, who looked upon the episode optimistically as but a temporary setback. Still, for reasons of morale and strategy, he could not cease operations completely after the May 1943 debacle. But where could he best utilize his depleted fleet of boats? During 1942, German submarines had achieved a string of solid successes in Caribbean waters, sinking more than three hundred and fifty ships in the poorly defended terminus of the North Atlantic convoy routes. Against Dönitz's objections, Adolf Hitler had ordered the U-boats reassigned from the Caribbean theater to oppose the Allied landings in Africa. Would the Caribbean region yield still more sinkings?[5]

The two important commodities flowing from the Caribbean were oil and bauxite, both of which were vital to the Allied war effort. Losses in this theater had earlier forced the Allies to reinforce substantially the Caribbean, but Dönitz felt that the inexperience of the defenders would allow his boats a chance to repeat their 1942 exploits in 1943. While the defenders had indeed been inexperienced and unorganized the prior year, by mid-1943 the Caribbean defenses were quite a different matter.

Three factors were operating against the U-boats dispatched by Dönitz to the Caribbean. First, in order to even get into the Atlantic, the boats had to traverse the Bay of Biscay, a death trap for U-boats effectively patrolled by aircraft of the RAF Coastal Command. Second, boats bound for the Caribbean needed tankers to refuel them during the lengthy voyage. Unfortunately for the Germans, the Allies had broken their naval codes and had effectively hunted the vital tanker U-boats to destruction. Third, the strength of the defending forces in the Caribbean had been significantly upgraded and organized, making the region not only a difficult but extremely dangerous area of operations.

Still, these considerable obstacles might have been overcome and the Caribbean theater turned once again into a fruitful hunting ground had it not been for a change in U-boat tactical doctrine. Instead of diving when approached by attacking aircraft, U-boats were ordered to stay on the surface and fight off the enemy with enhanced anti-aircraft armament. The policy, however, was fatally flawed. Once the U-boat stayed on the surface to fight, it could not dive without providing the aircraft an undefended and helpless target. Nor could a U-boat outlast an aircraft. Pilots quickly learned they could simply stay out of range and call for reinforcements, at which point coordinated attacks from the air would saturate the boat's defenses. The "Fight Back" Order doomed the 1943 Caribbean offensive to failure.[6]

The first boat to sortie from the French ports on the Caribbean operation was Günther Müller-Stöckheim's U-67 on May 10, and the last boat to return was the emergency tanker U-760, which was so badly damaged that on September 8 it entered a Spanish port and was interned. Sandwiched between, forty-four U-boats were committed to the Caribbean and a further eight to the Brazilian theater. Of these fifty-two boats, thirty-three—a staggering 64%—were lost. The defeat of the 1943 Caribbean Campaign was an even greater disaster for the U-boats than May 1943.[7]

Lieutenant Commander Ralph Kapitsky's U-615 was one of the boats assigned to the 1943 Caribbean offensive. Kapitsky sailed from La Pallice on June 12 in company with Herbert Rasch in U-257 and Bernhard Zurmühlen in U-600, relying on the mutual protection of the combined firepower of the three submarines to see them safely across the Bay of Biscay. Just two days out the group was attacked over a period of several hours by Whitley bombers of RAF Coastal Command. The aircraft inflicted damage on all three boats, with each suffering men killed and wounded. During the melée U-615's AA armament scored the only German victory of the day when it brought down a Whitley bomber. That the boats managed to survive at all was due more to luck than anything else: there were several similar battles being waged in the bay simultaneously, and thus the RAF could not concentrate on them.[8]

During a lull in the attacks, the three U-Boat captains held a conference. They were aware that if they continued on the surface, the RAF would eventually swamp them with coordinated attacks. Therefore they decided that they would separate and continue the passage submerged. As U-615 prepared to dive, her crew carried below the body of Third Watch Officer Hans Peter Dittmar, who was killed on the bridge during one of the attacks. The submariner, a veteran of Gunther Prien's famous attack on Scapa Flow in U-47, was making his tenth patrol. It was unnerving for the crew to have the dead body aboard in the cramped quarters of the U-boat, especially since Dittmar had been one of the most popular persons aboard U-615.

The balance of the journey beneath the surface of the Bay of Biscay proved uneventful. When out of reach of the aircraft, U-615 committed Dittmar's body to the deep and began her run to the Caribbean on the surface. The next hurdle Kapitsky faced was the always dangerous task of refueling at sea. The heavy toll of U-boat "Milch Cows" (large U-tankers used primarily for supply and refueling purposes) was creating a logistical crisis in the mid-Atlantic. The loss of tanker U-118, for example, compelled U-Boat Command to improvise and juggle the refueling schedules of several boats. Forced to assume U-118's assignments, Konstantin Metz' U-487 topped off her tanks from three outbound boats (U-170, U-535 and U-536) whose orders were canceled. The logistical fuel knots in the mid-Atlantic also compelled U-Boat Command to order Kapitsky's U-615 to take fuel directly from U-535. The transfer of twenty tons of fuel by an ordinary fire hose from one boat to another was a slow and tedious operation, made even more so by the presence of an American carrier group that was hunting Metz' tanker, which was operating nearby. While this time-consuming operation was underway the crews of U-615 and U-535 could hear the exploding depth charges that were ripping apart U-487. Both boats kept a watchful eye and had to be ready to quickly disengage and dive if the hunters appeared.[9]

Once the refueling was completed, Kapitsky turned U-615 toward the Caribbean while U-535, her operational patrol cancelled, headed in the opposite direction for France. She never made it. Caught by British aircraft in the Bay of Biscay, the U-boat was sunk with all hands on July 5. In the meantime U-615 completed an uneventful passage across the Atlantic and entered the Caribbean by slipping between the islands of Antigua and Guadeloupe. Kapitsky had received a comprehensive briefing on the Caribbean before embarking on his patrol, but from the start he demonstrated that he was an unconventional commander. The normal U-boat entry points to the Caribbean were the Windward Passage, the Mona Passage, occasionally the Anegada Passage or the Galleon's Passage—but never the Guadeloupe Passage. The latter course was too long, too shallow and under the nose of the anti-submarine squadron based in Antigua, which was responsible for watching Vichy French Guadeloupe. No other U-boat in the Caribbean war is recorded as having used this entry point to the operating area.[10]

Once inside Kapitsky turned south for Trinidad. His assigned operating area was off Curacao and like other U-boat commanders, he had been warned about getting too close to Trinidad. The adjacent Gulf of Paria was a major training area for U.S. Navy ships, as well as the terminus of the North Atlantic convoy routes. In February 1942, Albrecht Achilles in U-161 had resolutely penetrated the Gulf of Paria, sinking two ships in Trinidad's Port of Spain harbor. As a result of this audacious attack, the island was vastly reinforced and had become a major anti-submarine base. The defenders spent the rest of the war waiting for U-161 to return. U-boats made it a point to keep clear of Trinidad—particularly in 1943.[11]

But the temptation proved too great for Ralph Kapitsky. The daring commander took U-615 south to Trinidad and penetrated the Gulf of Paria for a look around. After he crossed the controversial minefield that the British and Americans spent the war arguing about, bottom-mounted sonars picked up U-615's propeller noises, followed by the magnetic loops detecting his crossing. Within minutes Kapitsky had satisfied his curiosity and slipped back out to assume his assigned position off Curacao. The brief penetration had left a disturbed hornet's nest in his wake. Unbeknownst to Kapitsky, for days after he left anti-submarine forces on Trinidad were still hunting him.

The island of Curacao was where convoys that originated in Trinidad picked up oil tankers which, via New York or Halifax, would eventually reach Britain or Russia. The area was crawling with tanker traffic, but unlike 1942, when it had been a favorite operating area of the U-boats, it was now heavily defended. It was also the home base of the Liberator bombers of the 8th anti-submarine squadron. Kapitsky soon discovered it was virtually impossible to operate off Curacao. Even though he sighted considerable tanker traffic, strong surface escorts and heavy air cover kept him submerged and unable to obtain adequate firing positions.[12]

Although Kapitsky's patrol around Curacao was frustrating, his perseverance eventually paid off. On July 28, the 3,000 ton Dutch tanker *Rosalia* crossed his bow and he sent her to the bottom ten miles south of Curacao with two well-aimed torpedoes. Reaction to the attack was immediate and vicious. On the following day Kapitsky was caught on the surface by a Liberator 60 miles northwest of Curacao, and the plane's four depth charges gave the boat a severe shaking up. Kapitsky had believed that the area northwest of the island might offer some respite from the non-stop air activity, but he was mistaken. After moving U-615 east of the island, Kapitsky inadvertently ran into convoy GAT 77 on its way to Trinidad. Unfortunately for the U-boat, Kapitsky's periscope was sighted as he was making his approach, and once again

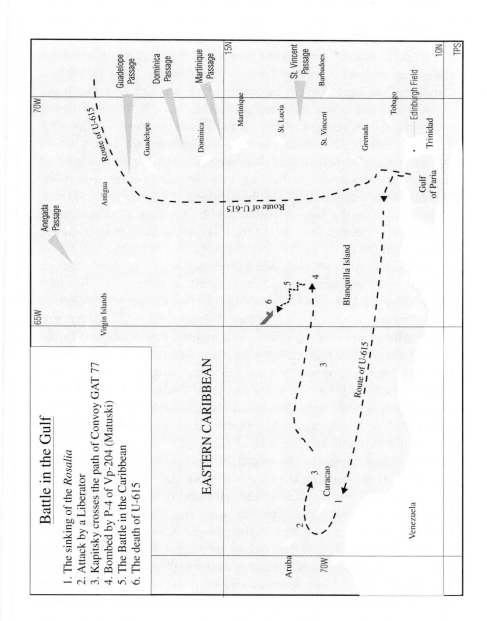

Battle in the Gulf

1. The sinking of the *Rosalia*
2. Attack by a Liberator
3. Kapitsky crosses the path of Convoy GAT 77
4. Bombed by P-4 of Vp-204 (Matuski)
5. The Battle in the Caribbean
6. The death of U-615

EASTERN CARIBBEAN

Route of U-615

Anegada Passage

Guadelope Passage

Dominica Passage

Martinique Passage

St. Vincent Passage

Virgin Islands

Antigua

Guadelope

Dominica

Martinique

St. Lucia

St. Vincent

Barbadoes

Grenada

Tobago

Edinburgh Field

Trinidad

Gulf of Paria

Blanquilla Island

Curacao

Aruba

Venezuela

70W

65W

70W

15N

10N

TPS

the boat was subjected to a depth charge attack. Frustrated and exhausted, Kapitsky determined to give his crew a rest and moved northeast of the island into the open area off the convoy routes.[13]

While U-615 was evading the probing enemy off Curacao, the 1943 Caribbean offensive was sputtering to a conclusion. For a month the Caribbean had been witness to dozens of vicious clashes between the U-boats and defending aircraft. Pursuant to the "Fight Back" Order, many of the U-boats had stayed on the surface to battle it out—with disastrous results. Twenty-two boats were operating in the Caribbean theater during this period, and all of them were blanketed by heavy air cover. Daily battles were being fought throughout the area, and many U-boats were being sunk or badly damaged. The German crewmen were discovering the hard way that a U-boat simply could not carry enough AA ammunition to defend itself against the non-stop, relentless attacks from the air.

Although the Americans were also losing aircraft in these encounters, they had so many squadrons assigned to the theater that they could afford to lose some of the machines to protect the merchant ships. During the entire month of July U-Boats sank only three tankers, two freighters and two schooners, at a frightful cost in return. In the mid-Atlantic, U.S. carrier groups were destroying the limited number of U-boat tankers almost as soon as they were assigned to their operational areas. In addition to the destruction of a valuable asset, their loss also determined how long operational U-boats could stay at sea. Without the "Milch Cows," many boats were left at sea thousands of miles from home without enough fuel to reach port. As a result, U-boat Command had no option but to call off the Caribbean offensive. Even this decision did not stop the slaughter, since the RAF was waiting in the Bay of Biscay to pounce on the returning boats. Of the nineteen U-boats that survived the offensive, only two, Stahl in U-648 and Carlsen in U-732, made it back to the French bases undamaged.[14]

The order recalling U-615 arrived on August 1. Kapitsky dutifully turned the boat's bow eastward and made for Galleon's Passage between Trinidad and Tobago. His aborted attack on convoy GATT 77, however, had revealed his presence to the Americans, who were determined to sink the offending U-boat. A combined air and sea search of the area between the Dutch islands and Trinidad was launched with the specific intent of finding U-615. Four days later on August 5, the destroyer *USS*

Biddle obtained an asdic contact and delivered a depth charge attack, but U-615 managed to avoid the explosives and slipped away. The *Biddle's* discovery, however, narrowed the parameters of the search area, and relays of Mariner flying boats were now quartering the region northwest of Trinidad. Near midnight on the same day, Lt. J. M. Erskine, flying Mariner P-6 of VP 204, obtained a radar contact forty miles northwest of Blanquilla Island. Flying over the contact, Erskine released a pair of flares which illuminated a U-boat running eastwards on the surface. He attacked with a pair of high explosive bombs in a fast descending spiral, but after the bright flashes faded, the submarine was still on the surface heading east.

The audacious Kapitsky had decided to gamble that evening. He had been heading east at the leisurely pace of 6 knots, so that no appreciable wake would give away the boat cutting its way across the ocean's surface. The aircraft had surprised him, but it was a dark, rainy night and Kapitsky believed that the aircraft would lose him once the flares died out. He was wrong. Within a short time Kapitsky found himself directly in the path of an attacking Mariner—without an anti-aircraft gun manned. Erskine passed directly over the U-boat, but three of his four depth charges hung up in the bomb bays. The fourth charge hit the water one hundred and fifty yards ahead of the boat's bow. Kapitsky turned U-615 hard to starboard and hit the crash dive alarm. By the time Erskine could get back into position U-615 had disappeared, but he still put one depth charge thirty yards ahead of the swirl, which shook the diving U-boat.

Even though the submarine had narrowly escaped destruction, the Americans were jubilant over the discovery. They had pinpointed the boat's exact location, and Erskine's signal to Chaguaramas Naval Air Station generated an immediate response, as Mariner P-6 took off to join the hunt. The two VP-204 Mariners dissected the area, while down below Kapitsky slowly ran eastwards underwater, hoping for a chance to surface and make better speed. At 2:00 a.m. P-6 obtained another radar contact and attacked. After the depth charges went off the flight crews were appalled to see a two masted inter-island schooner in the light of a flare. The vessel was in the wrong place at the wrong time, and though she survived, her crew received a considerable shock from the unpleasant experience. The clever Kapitsky had surfaced and used the schooner as a decoy, operating for a short while within its radar shadow before eluding his pursuers once again.[15]

The mistaken attack on the sailboat and the realization of Kapitsky's ruse only served to annoy the Americans and increase their desire for revenge. A Harpoon anti-submarine bomber of VB-130 from Edinburgh Field in Trinidad joined the Mariners in their pursuit of the quarry. From Antigua in the north to Dutch Guiana in the south, anti-submarine squadrons turned out in force. They had been triangulating U-boat signals for some time and realized that the Germans were pulling out of the Caribbean. Although they knew they had won, it only increased their desire to destroy the dreaded underwater machines. Between Puerto Rico in the north down the chain of eastern islands to French Guiana, there were twenty-one anti-submarine squadrons operating, as opposed to only three during 1942, when to the U-boats the Caribbean had become known as the Golden West. Kapitsky was operating in a very hazardous environment, close inshore and moving in the direction of the largest U.S. Naval anti-submarine base in the world. And the Americans knew he was there.[16]

At dawn on Friday, August 6, the Americans made a tactical mistake. With four convoys operating close to Trinidad and another about to depart, air cover was necessary to protect the merchant ships. As a result, only one aircraft, Mariner P-4 of VP-205, was assigned to take over from the three airplanes that had carried out the all night task of holding U-615 under the surface. Many of their aircraft were operating east of Trinidad hunting the retreating U-boats, and it was deemed a priority to use most of the remaining planes to guard the convoys. Nevertheless Mariner P-4, flown by Lt. A. R. Matuski, with two other officers and eight enlisted men aboard, took over the search for U-615. Their preliminary hunt failed to turn up any sign of the U-boat, and Matuski flew west to his base line for a creeping search to the eastward. Kapitsky, desperate to ventilate his boat with fresh air and re-charge his batteries, watched the Mariner flying boat through his periscope as its disappeared westwards. His opportunity had arrived. The long gray shape of U-615 rose from the depths and the diesels took over from the electric motors, drawing ocean air through the boat and charging life back into the drained batteries.[17]

U-615's commander knew he needed a maximum charge on his batteries for the hazardous run past Trinidad, which meant he would have to spend a considerable amount of time running on the surface. Using his abundant firsthand experience as an aircraft navigator, as well as his knowledge of anti-submarine procedure, he attempted to calculate exactly how long it would take the flying machine to return, and how far eastwards he could run at maximum surface speed, timing his stay on the surface to coincide with the return of the airplane. Kapitsky was good at his craft, and his calculations were remarkably accurate. Unfortunately, he miscalculated by about ten seconds.[18]

At 1:30 p.m. Kapitsky judged he had pushed his luck enough and that the flying machine would soon be back in the area. A normal dive was ordered. In the easy atmosphere of a precautionary submergence, unhurried by attack, no one saw the Mariner on the horizon. The bridge watch disappeared below and the conning tower hatch was closed. U-615 began her last dive.

Lieutenant Matuski probably fixed the U-boat on radar and cut a corner, obtaining visual contact soon afterwards. Using cloud cover to conceal his approach, he set up his attack. The conning tower of U-615 was just dipping below the waves when the Mariner swept overhead and bracketed the helpless boat with four depth charges. The shattering blasts threw the boat out of control and caused heavy damage, and she began to plummet downwards into the depths of the sea. Kapitsky fought to regain control of U-615 and blew her ballast tanks to arrest the descent. Badly wounded, U-615 was out of control. Her terrified crew watched in horror as the boat continued to sink to more than eight hundred feet, well beyond her designed crush depth. With her hull groaning from the immense pressure, the U-boat finally reversed her downward plunge and began to ascend. After what seemed like an eternity, rising ever faster, she broached the surface in a welter of foam. Overhead a jubilant Matuski radioed Chaguaramas, informing them that he had attacked and a damaged a submarine. He noted that the U-boat was down by the stern and proceeding very slowly.[19]

Indeed U-615 was badly damaged. The interior of the U-boat was utter chaos. Her lubricating oil tank had burst open and the precious oil had flowed down into the bilges, where it mixed with tons of sea water coming in through damaged stern glands. Without lubricating oil, both diesels were out of commission. The starboard electric motor had also shorted out, leaving only the port motor to move the crippled U-615 at barely two knots. Equipment was scattered everywhere, pipes had burst, bulbs were smashed, electric circuits shorted. Even if U-615 had been left alone, her crew would have been hard pressed to get her operating again. But they were not left alone.

The Mariner pilot had radioed for help, but like most young pilots Matuski did not wait for it. Instead, he set up another attack run on what he considered to be a beaten U-boat. U-615's AA armament had been increased before she sailed from La Pallice, not as dramatically as some of the other boats, but enough to provide a lethal barrage. Her deck gun had been removed, while the after end of the conning tower had been widened and extended so that she would carry two single 20mm cannons instead of the original one. They were mounted, however, without any gun shields. Her potential to increase the odds of inflicting lethal blows against aircraft was found in the rectangle around the hatch, where four MG 34 infantry machine guns were mounted. A normal MG 34 could fire up to nine hundred rounds per minute, but U-615 mounted two twin short barreled versions, called the 81Z. Thus, in theory at least, the six machine gun barrels in the battery could put up a barrage of five thousand four hundred rounds per minute—in addition to the nine hundred rounds per minute combined rate of the two 20mm cannons. U-boats could not carry enough ammunition to feed these guns for very long, but when they all opened fire together, the effect could be catastrophic for the target. There was another major drawback to this type of armament: the machine guns were only effective at three hundred yards or less, which meant the gunners had to wait under fire for the target to close to point blank range before their own weapons could be used.[20]

As soon as U-615 surfaced Kapitsky ordered his gunners onto the bridge. The scrambling crewmen reached their assigned positions in time for Matuski's second attack. Eight minutes after the first radio message, Chaguaramas received a second garbled transmission which said "P-4 damaged—damaged—Fire," followed by an ominous silence. Nothing more was ever heard from Mariner P-4. Days later another Mariner on patrol reported a broken wingtip float, an uninflated dinghy and a cardboard box floating well to the westward. The debris was all that was left of the third Mariner that VP-205 had lost during the July 1943 battles.[21]

It was at this point in the ongoing battle that the warrior Ralph Kapitsky obviously was came to the fore. U-615 was so badly damaged that she could never safely dive again, and at two knots on a single electric motor without any means of recharging the batteries, her life span was obviously drawing to an end. In addition, she was taking on water, and only the heroic efforts of her mechanics working feverishly below decks held the bow above the surface, with her stern just awash. Under similar circumstances most U-boat commanders would have abandoned ship. But Kapitsky refused to do so. Instead, he ordered all the AA ammunition piled on the bridge and personally directed the gunners, while urging his crew below to contain the water flooding into the boat and repair what they could.[22]

Even before the second radio message from Mariner P-4, the duty reserve crew under Lt. L. D. Crockett, VP-204, had been alerted. The airplanes from Crockett's squadron, however, were either already airborne or badly damaged from the frequent and bloody July clashes with the U-boats. Undaunted, Crockett borrowed Mariner P-11 from VP-205, which was the only available machine at a base that housed five squadrons of flying boats. Within minutes Crockett was airborne in the Mariner and heading for the site of the developing crisis, one hundred and eighty miles northwest of Trinidad.

During the hour or so that it took Crockett to get to the scene of the fight, Chaguaramas was hurriedly recalling aircraft to refuel and back up P-11. The other anti-submarine bases in Trinidad were also informed of the situation and they, too, began recalling and reassigning aircraft. For months, sometimes for more than a year, these flight crews had crisscrossed the Caribbean looking for U-boats. Although their patrols had turned the area into an extremely dangerous theater for the submarines, many of the pilots had never seen one, let alone sunk one. Now, at last, they had caught a U-boat that could not get away, and there were many volunteers who itched to get involved.

While Crockett was approaching in the Mariner and the several bases were planning the U-boat's demise, the Germans were feverishly attempting to stabilize their floating platform. Kapitsky managed to raise the stern of U-615, bringing the boat back to something approaching an even keel. Pouring lubricating oil by hand, one diesel engine was coaxed into life, though only for short spurts. As many of the crewmen labored, the gunners kept a sharp lookout for the expected American attack. At 3:30 p.m., Crockett found U-615.

L. D. Crockett had some experience fighting U-boats. Just three weeks earlier, as the captain of a VP-204 Mariner, he had watched helplessly as his co-pilot died with a 20mm shell in his stomach, fired from Horst Dietrichs' U-406. With Crockett's attention focused on coaxing his badly damaged Mariner back to home base and saving the lives of the rest of the crew, U-406 made good its escape. Although he had an intense desire for revenge, Crockett was a cautious, experienced pilot who resisted impulses to rush rashly into an attack. Instead, he circled the damaged U-615 from three miles out at three thousand feet. The crippled boat was proceeding very slowly northward, a cloud of blue diesel smoke trailing above its wake. On his second circuit he could see a few puffs of smoke as 20mm shells self-destructed immediately behind the Mariner. Surprised by the accuracy of the long distance shooting, he pulled P-11 even further away from the still dangerous U-boat. Having passed a full appreciation of the situation to Chaguaramas, Crockett decided to carry out his attack.[23]

Kapitsky and his men watched the Mariner circling their crippled boat, fully aware that this was the beginning of the end. We will never know whether Kapitsky questioned his decision to continue the fight knowing he could never save U-615. Apparently his sense of duty was stronger than his desire for mere survival. Kapitsky was determined that his boat was going to go down fighting. When the Mariner P-11 began its attack run, Kapitsky brought his gunners to the ready. Crockett was trying a high level attack from fifteen hundred feet with explosive bombs. It was a cautious assault on the boat, intended more to keep the submarine busy while he waited for reinforcements than to bring about its destruction. At almost a mile the twin .50 caliber machine guns of the nose turret began walking their bullets towards the U-boat, while Crockett judged his position by eye, intending to bomb without the benefit of a bomb site.[24]

U-615's guns remained silent even when the heavy American bullets began hammering the U-boat. Kapitsky was holding his fire, waiting until the Mariner was within effective range. At three hundred yards he gave the command and all eight barrels of his anti-aircraft battery erupted. Mariner P-11 was repeatedly hit by the wall of fire, but Crockett was still able to drop his bombs, which exploded off the U-boat's port quarter. Although U-615's crew felt the surge from the blast, it did little if any harm to the boat. The same was not true for the Mariner. Besides the many holes in the aircraft and smashed equipment, a 20mm shell had ripped a huge hole in the starboard wing root, causing a spectacular gasoline-fed fire. Crockett realized that sooner or later the fire would reach a main fuel tank, and P-11 would disintegrate. He did not harbor a death wish, but if in-flight immolation was to be his fate, then the U-boat would also have to die.

Kapitsky slowly turned U-615 to starboard and watched in amazement as the huge Mariner, instead of flying out of range, came spiraling down toward the boat. Unbeknownst to Crockett, as the aircraft swept downwards Navy Machinist A. S. Creider had hauled himself up into the wing root, where he began tackling the source of the fire. Crockett pulled out of his dive at two hundred feet, boring straight in towards the U-boat, which was now heading south. Trailing a long column of smoke and flame, the Mariner shuddered under the impact of numerous cannon shells and machine gun bullets as it closed the distance. Hitting back with its own heavy machine guns, Crockett passed right over U-615 and bracketed the U-boat with four MK-44 depth charges. As the pilot hauled the badly damaged aircraft around, he could see four tall towers of water spewing up around U-615.[25]

Once again chaos reigned aboard the U-boat. The depth charges had opened up numerous cracks in the hull and water was pouring in. Down below in the dark cigar-like hull, terrified sailors were working up to their knees in seawater, and the boat's stern was once again beneath the sea. This time, however, the boat's bow was well out of the water, a particularly precarious position for a U-boat. If the nose of a submarine rises too high, water contained in the forward ballast tanks will empty into the sea through the open bottoms of the tanks, making the submarine highly unstable and liable to slide underwater stern first. Concerned about the boat's dangerous angle, Kapitsky shouted orders down the hatch to assist the dazed men working below, who were feverishly attempting to properly trim the boat. Meanwhile, his gunners kept a wary eye on the Mariner as it sped away. Aboard the aircraft, Creider had miraculously brought the fire in the wing root under control. Although the machine was riddled with holes and the pilot could no longer transfer fuel, it was still flyable.[26]

By this time the sinking boat could only make two knots with a rudder jammed hard a starboard, which meant that U-615 steamed in a continuous circle. Despite his desperate condition and the fact that the crippled boat was but one hour's flying time from the dreaded anti-submarine bases on Trinidad, Kapitsky still refused to surrender. Instead, his shocked and battered men continued to attempt to restore some semblance of order as only a veteran crew who loved their commander could. As his men feverishly moved about their tasks, the badly damaged Mariner was still circling the U-boat just out of range. There would be no time to effect major repairs, for Kapitsky knew that this was a sign reinforcements were on the way. Forty-five minutes later, Harpoon B5 of USN anti-submarine squadron VB-130 [pilot unknown], out of Edinburgh Field, arrived on the scene.

Determined to be in on the kill, Crockett in his battered P-11 took overall command of the attack and arranged for both aircraft to come in together. The Harpoon was armed with four fixed forward-firing .50 caliber machine guns, which delivered 2,000 rounds per minute. When combined with the fire from the nose turret of the Mariner, U-615 would be saturated with flying metal—just before the Harpoon delivered what its crew hoped would be the coup-de-grace with her depth charges. The airmen anticipated that the two aircraft attacking simultaneously would divide the fire of the U-boat. Crockett's plan ultimately worked, although not quite the way he expected.[27]

At Crockett's signal both aircraft, the Mariner on the right and the Harpoon on the left, turned towards U-615. Kapitsky could see the two machines move lower until they were hugging the ocean at full speed, just fifty feet above the surface. He wisely reminded his gunners to ignore the damaged Mariner and concentrate on the Harpoon, which carried the depth charges. At long range the two aircraft began hosing their heavy machine gun bullets into the U-boat. Kapitsky allowed his 20mm guns to return fire, holding back his machine guns until the range had tightened. While the German gunners manfully held their positions while braving the storm of bullets, both sides saw their plans thrown askew by the speed of the Harpoon. At two hundred and eighty knots, way over the top speed of the Mariner, the Harpoon began to leave the flying boat behind. In fact, the Harpoon was so fast that it left the German tracer fire trailing behind it and flew straight through the fire of the Mariner's bow guns without being hit. As the Harpoon flashed over U-615, four depth charges plummeted down, once again bracketing the U-boat. The Harpoon was long gone and the German gunners were seeking protection from the expected blast of the depth

charges when Crockett safely passed over the U-boat in his battered
P-11.

Although the attack was delivered perfectly, U-615 was probably
saved by the fact that she was on the surface. Had she been diving or
underwater, the explosions would have broken her apart. Strangely, instead of hurling the U-boat upwards, the simultaneous detonation of all
four charges had the unusual effect of forcing U-615 underwater. The
gunners were immediately washed overboard, while Kapitsky and the
lookouts, tethered to the submerged boat, were sucked beneath the sea.
As the water subsided and U-615 rose back above the surface, her
gallant gunners swam back to the casing and clambered aboard, where
they once again manned their guns. Survivors claimed that U-615 was
underwater for a full fifteen seconds—a quarter minute that must have
been completely terrifying to those roped to the bridge and trapped
inside. Crockett could see that U-615 had been hard hit by the Harpoon's charges, and he hauled his flying machine around in a tight turn
intending to deliver the killing blow with his single remaining depth
charge. To his surprise, the gunners were back aboard and his approach
was met by a withering hail of fire. He quickly turned P-11 out of the
way, rejoining the Harpoon at a safe distance.[28]

While her gunners were still full of fight, U-615 was barely alive.
Below decks the U-boat was a complete wreck. Everything breakable
that had survived the previous attacks was now smashed, and only the
single electric motor was operable. Lighting was a thing of the past, and
water stood in places waist deep. A few gallant members of the engineering staff gingerly worked the remaining motor, while the rest of the
crew, unoccupied now that damage control efforts were useless, clus-
tered in the control room and conning tower directly above. The bridge
was occupied by Kapitsky, his First Watch Officer Herbert Schlipper, six
gunners and an unusually large number of loaders, who worked non-
stop to keep the magazines of the weapons full.

Even the most optimistic crew member knew that U-615 was sinking, and that other than freeing the jammed rudder, which they accomplished, there was little else to be done to save the boat. Kapitsky and
his men may well have recalled their three previous patrols, when at
times it seemed all was lost. This was true especially on their second
patrol, when they had spent Christmas 1942 facing the worst North
Atlantic gales of the century, with engine breakdowns plaguing them in

hurricane force winds. Their current predicament—riding a U-boat that was nothing more than a slowly sinking platform for a battery of guns, while being attacked by aircraft—was infinitely worse. Yet not once, either at the time of the sinking or in the years since that traumatic afternoon, did any of them question Kapitsky's decision to keep fighting. The crew of U-615 stood behind their commander with boundless faith in the fact that he was doing the right thing. Kapitsky himself may have questioned his decision as he stood on the bridge and followed the course of the desperate battle. Before the trip to the Caribbean he had confided to his diary his doubts about the Nazi Party and Hitler's leadership. He even went so far as to discuss these matters with friends. Kapitsky's duty, however—and allegiance—was to his country. He was a free thinker, a leader of considerable ability and a veteran warrior with considerable air and sea combat experience. Now, however, he found himself fighting a soldier's battle. Unable to maneuver his boat as a naval vessel, he was simply the commander of a besieged fortress, determined to go down fighting against considerable odds.[29]

U-615's commander was also facing a warrior of considerable ability in Lieutenant Crockett. The redoubtable pilot was still on the scene, flying a machine that the average flyer would long ago have retired from the fight. Just as Kapitsky was determined to go down fighting, Crockett intended to see the end of the U-boat. The fight had developed into one of brutal endurance and iron courage, and the Mariner pilot was intrigued by this submarine that refused to die. While the scenario continued to play out, Crockett kept up a continuous running commentary with Chaguaramas, where the staff was also fascinated by the fight being put up by the lone U-boat. Aircraft were being vectored to the scene of the fight from all over the Trinidad theater, and the pilots were eager to be in on the kill. At the three largest airbases in Trinidad—Chaguaramas, Edinburgh Field and Waller Field—pilots impatiently waited on armorers and re-fuelers to get their aircraft combat ready. In many ways, this personal duel between Kapitsky and Crockett was developing into a clash of titans.

Kapitsky may have wondered why the battered circling Mariner remained on scene and why a pilot would jeopardize himself and his crew when so many reinforcements were so close, perhaps not accepting the fact that he was also doing the same thing—without any hope of reinforcement. In any case he had little time for contemplation because the Mariner and Harpoon had only completed two circuits of his boat before the next aircraft arrived on scene. Released from convoy coverage, Mariner P-8 of VP-204, flown by Lieutenant jg. J. W. Dresbach, had raced to the scene of the battle.

Once again Crockett took control and coordinated the attack. The Harpoon on the right and Crockett's battered P-11 on the left were to come in slightly ahead of P-8, attacking from the south. All three aircraft changed places several times in order to confuse the U-Boat's gunners as to which of the attacking machines actually carried the depth charges. On Crockett's order the three planes turned toward U-615. At long range the two outermost aircraft began firing their deadly .50 caliber bullets at the U-boat. This heavy fire was soon joined by guns from the P-8. The attack order solidified, with the faster Harpoon storming toward U-615, followed closely by P-11 and then P-8. The fire from their guns created a sea of mini-geysers around the stricken U-boat, and eventually hammered the hull and battered the conning tower. Although Crockett's elaborate and well developed plan seemed to be working, his diversion failed.

Kapitsky, who had been carefully tracking the new Mariner P-8, directed his gunners to hold their fire and concentrate only on the third attacker—the one in the center. They remained at their weapons as the U-boat rattled and clanged from the sounds of striking machine gun bullets. Kapitsky stood with his men in full view of the action, ensuring that every gun was trained on Mariner P-8. As Crockett's Mariner P-11 swept overhead, its waist gunner, followed by the twin tail guns, rained bullets onto the U-boat which opened fire on P-8. The combined fire of the U Boat's guns shattered the nose of the Mariner and a 20mm shell slammed into Lieutenant Dresbach. The fatally injured Dresbach's last conscious act was to release his depth charges, which he accomplished just moments before his corpse slumped forward onto the control column. P-8's co-pilot, Lt. jg. A. R. Christian, struggled with the controls while trying to hold Dresbach's body back, shouting for the crew to remove the dead pilot from of his seat.[30]

The depth charges, released fractionally early by the dying pilot, fell about ten yards astern of U-615. The blast from the four charges, which detonated twenty-five feet underwater behind the boat, kicked the stern completely out of the water and smashed the recently fixed rudder and aft diving planes, hurling everyone off their feet. By the time P-8's crew managed to drag Dresbach's body out of his seat, the nose of the Mariner was a twisted mass of torn aluminum and smashed perspex, and the cockpit was covered with blood. White hot anger boiled inside Lieutenant Christian at the sight of his dead companion. Instead of trying to evade the U-Boat's pointblank fire, he hauled the big flying boat around in a tight upward circle. Ignoring Crockett's shouted radio commands to withdraw, Christian maneuvered P-8 across U-615 again, releasing two bombs in the process. The explosives, dropped from high above the boat, detonated harmlessly three hundred feet off the U-boat's port side. Christian's decision once again pitted the Mariner against U-615's AA battery, as the crews of the two other aircraft watched helplessly from a distance. Somehow the Mariner managed to avoid serious injury the second time around and P-8 flew out of range of Kapitsky's spitting guns. Christian turned for home with his dead pilot and four seriously wounded crew.[31]

In both the attacking aircraft and the operations room in Chaguaramas, there was incredulous dismay followed by intense anger. Everyone thought that this coordinated attack by three aircraft would finish off the stubborn U-boat. No one could understand how it had survived. The offending undersea intruder was effectively thumbing its nose at the mighty U.S. Navy—a navy that had just defeated a major U-boat offensive against the Caribbean Theater. Convoys were stripped of their air cover and every available machine was directed to proceed to the scene of the battle. In addition, three surface ships were detached from near Grenada, and the new destroyer *U.S.S. Walker* was ordered out of the Gulf of Paria at full speed.

The withdrawing aircraft provided a brief respite for the men on U-615. Whatever relief they may have felt watching Christian's Mariner leave the scene, however, was dashed away when they realized that their commander had been hit during the attack. A prone Ralph Kapitsky was lying slumped on the deck, his shredded leather garments initially hiding the grievous wound he had suffered. A heavy caliber bullet had smashed into the U-boat commander's upper thigh near the hip. The wound was bleeding profusely and it was impossible to apply a tourniquet to halt the loss of blood. Kapitsky lay in a grotesque pose, with one of his legs completely dislocated and thrown up and back across his chest, a grimace of intense pain masking his face. There was nothing that the crew could do about his wound other than administer morphine to ease the pain.

One of the 20mm gunners was also lying on the deck. The boat's senior mate, Helmut Langner, had suffered a grievous wound when a fifty caliber bullet smashed through his knee. Langner was the gunner who had brought down the Whitley bomber in the Bay of Biscay. The disabled mate struggled into a sitting position and called for rope, which he used as a tourniquet on his thigh to stop the bleeding.[32]

Kapitsky was conscious and lucid despite his terrible wound. He even joked with his men while they propped him against the periscope standard. First Watch Officer Herbert Schlipper attempted to have both Kapitsky and Langner taken below, where they might lie on their cots in greater comfort, but both men refused. They wanted to die on the bridge, in action. Realizing he could no longer effectively lead his men, Kapitsky turned over command of U-615 to Schlipper, and asked that he pass along his last regards to his parents. It is significant to note that even though Schlipper was now in command, he too elected to fight on, as Kapitsky wished him to do.

While the last attack by P-8 had been in progress, Lt. Cmdr. Hull, in Mariner P-2 from VP-205, arrived on the scene. Hull's machine was part of a third squadron employed in the battle to sink U-615. Lieutenant Crockett had ordered him to wait until Christian's P-8 had finished its attack. Although annoyed that a mere lieutenant would attempt to tell him what to do, Hull nevertheless held off. Crockett had a vested interest in U-615 and he intended to maintain control of the situation. Once Christian left the scene with his dead and dying crew in an aircraft that was little more than a mass of holes, Crockett set up another coordinated attack, this time with Hull's Mariner P-2 in the center position. Once again the three aircraft barreled in toward U-615, and once again the attack failed. Because of a mechanical malfunction, the depth charges were released when the Mariner's bomb doors opened, and they exploded harmlessly six hundred feet astern of the U-boat. Despite Crockett's plea not to attack again, an upset Hull turned his Mariner—in a stunt similar to Christian's second attempt—and climbed up to fifteen hundred feet for a high level bombing run. The explosives landed harmlessly five hundred feet from the U-boat. Hull, however, was not as fortunate as Christian had been the second time around, and Crockett and the pilot of the Harpoon watched helplessly as P-2 was ravaged by the U-Boat's guns. The fire penetrated the aircraft and seriously wounded some of its crew, forcing Hull to turn and head for home. Shortly afterwards the pilot of the Harpoon announced that he was low on fuel and had to head for home as well. Probably feeling like he had come full circle, Crockett and his battered Mariner P-11 were once again alone with the U-boat that refused to die.[33]

Reinforcements were not long in arriving. Next on the scene was Lt. Jg. Wallace Wydean's U.S. Navy Airship K68, from squadron ZP-51. The giant blimp had been almost at the end of what was known as a Golden Triangle patrol when Wydean, hearing of the battle to the westward, had elected to join it. Though he was keen to make an attack on U-615, Crockett ordered him to hold off. Almost every aircraft that had attacked U-615 had been badly chewed up, with the only plane able to avoid serious damage being the fast Harpoon. The U-boat's gunners would have taken enormous delight in clawing apart the slow moving airship, which could only make about seventy knots. Only once in the Caribbean war had a blimp attacked a surfaced U-boat, and the airship was destroyed in the attempt. Reluctantly obeying his senior officer, Wydean, representing the fourth squadron to join the epic struggle, kept the airship out of range.[34]

By now it was late evening. Darkness was falling, the sea had turned rough, and to Crockett's dismay, the weather was growing worse by the minute. August was the height of the Caribbean hurricane and wet season, and U-615's battle with Trinidad's anti-submarine aircraft was taking place in a sector notorious for the development of frightful nighttime thunderstorms. What is commonly referred to as a "tropical wave" was pushing through the area, and it was becoming increasingly difficult to see the tiny silhouette of the U Boat's wallowing conning tower and still stay out of range of its guns.

As night fell a representative of the fifth squadron to take part in the action appeared on the scene. The aircraft was a B-18 bomber from the 10th Bomber squadron, operating out of Edinburgh Field. The B-18 was a hybrid aircraft with a shark nosed fuselage mated to the wings of the DC-2 airliner. Too slow for bombing raids, it was quickly superseded by the legendary B-17, but it carried a useful bomb load and was suitable for anti-submarine work. Many B-18s had been destroyed at Pearl Harbor during the Japanese surprise attack of December 7, 1941. After-

ward, the remainder were concentrated in the Caribbean, where for a
time they constituted the major anti-submarine weapon. By mid-1943,
the B-18 was being phased out and replaced by the B-24 and B-25, but
there were still quite a few of them in operation during the 1943 U-boat
offensive.[35]

Crockett set up his last attack just as the light was fading. As the
two aircraft set up and began their coordinated run at the submarine,
U-615 simply disappeared from view. Kapitsky's replacement, Herbert
Schlipper, had managed to maneuver the crippled boat into a rain storm
which, together with the gathering darkness, effectively swallowed the
U-boat. The frustration of the attackers was beyond description. They
set up a crisscrossing search grid and regularly dropped flares, but it was
little use in the deteriorating weather. Shrugging off the appalling conditions, the giant airship K68 nosed into the clouds and rain close to the
water, with Wydean relishing the fact that he was now useful to the
operation. As the search continued, more Mariner flying boats arrived
in the area, all anxious to be in on the kill.

By 8:00 p.m. the hunters had still not located the elusive U-boat.
The attackers had other problems as well. Since none of the aircraft
were showing lights, there was a danger of collision as they flitted into
and out of rain showers. Lt. Cmdr. Joster's Mariner P-15, of VP-205,
arrived on scene and he took control of the growing operation. The first
thing he did was order Crockett to take P-11 home. The disappointed
pilot had no choice. He was low on fuel in a badly shot up aircraft with
wounded crew aboard who needed medical attention. How Crockett had
been able to operate without even a compass in the airplane was a
wonder. But by this stage of the operation he had become a liability, and
just getting home would be a significant achievement. He managed it in
the appalling weather by finding the Venezuelan coast visually and
creeping eastward at very low level. All afternoon damaged flying boats
had been coming home to Chaguaramas. When they landed they had to
be taxied straight to the ramp, since none of them could float for very
long. The ambulances had been busy ferrying the wounded crew and
the dead to the naval base hospital, and so it was to be with P-11 when
she arrived.[36]

Northwest of Trinidad the epic struggle continued, and at 9:15 p.m.
the giant airship finally located U-615. The boat was visible between
two rain squalls, and Wydean vectored the B-18 bomber into an attack

run. Once again, and for the last time, an aircraft came barreling in at low level against the submarine. And once again, fire from an attacking aircraft peppered the U-boat, whose gunners responded with a deadly barrage. The B-18's depth charges plummeted into the sea and the hammer blows of the explosions rocked the U-boat. The charges were close, but not close enough to send U-615 below the waves. By the time the B-18 was able to turn for another run, U-615 was gone. Schlipper had managed once again to find temporary sanctuary in another rain storm.

Wydean had been so eager to be in on the kill of U-615 that he had neglected to tell anyone that even an airship needed fuel, and now he was running critically short of the precious liquid. Only after the B-18 attack did he confess the shortage, and Lt. Cmdr. Joster ordered him to return to base immediately. The airship didn't make it. Wydean ran out of fuel and had to attempt an emergency landing on Blanquilla Island, which wrecked the machine.[37]

Below the searching aircraft a macabre scene was playing out on the crippled U-615. Propped against the periscope housing, Kapitsky still clung to life. Lightning flashed through the skies and thunder cracked as the storm continued unabated. The sight was a tragic one as the mortally wounded commander greeted his crewmen individually and said his farewells as they came up from below. Somehow the wounded commander managed to retain a sense of humor. When Engineering Petty Officer Stefan Lehner stood before him, Kapitsky joked that, because of their present prospects, nothing would come of his recently completed training course as a chief machinist. He shook hands farewell with each of his crew while the accompaniment of humming aircraft engines, methodically searching to find them, played in the distance. Only the weather hid them from their numerous attackers, and by this time the sky was full of them. There were no fewer than twelve Mariner flying boats overhead, all hunting for U-615. The search had evolved into the largest anti-submarine operation of the war conducted against a single U-boat. At regular intervals the senior officer would order all the aircraft to simultaneously drop flares, lighting up one hundred square miles of sea, but the weather still hampered them and U-615 remained in the shadows.[38]

By now the crew of U-615 was assembled on the casing. For safety reasons, Schlipper had Kapitsky, Langner and one other wounded man placed into a two-man life raft. The small craft was resting on the U-boat's deck, but because of U-615's slow speed on its dying batteries and the need to stay in the rain showers, it was not always possible to keep the boat's bow heading into the rough sea. As a result, a bigger than usual wave washed the life raft and the two seamen who were attending it off the casing and into the water. Within seconds the raft and its three wounded occupants, with two sailors clinging to it, disappeared in the rain and darkness. Schlipper maneuvered U-615 as best he could in a frantic attempt to find the raft. For an hour they searched until, ironically, they spotted it by the light of the flares that the Mariners were dropping. As the U-boat approached the lifeboat, Seaman Richard Suhra dived overboard to try and secure it, but he in turn disappeared in the rough sea and was never seen again. After a strenuous operation the raft was finally recovered and hauled back onto the U-boat, where it was made secure. Even after enduring this, Kapitsky was still conscious and able to joke about his plight, commenting to Schlipper that he was now qualified to receive the silver wound badge.[39]

Ralph Kapitsky died at 1:00 a.m. on August 8, 1943. The commander of the U-boat that had fought the greatest battle of the war against aircraft passed away against the background sound of snarling hunter's engines overhead, complimented by lightning and rolls of thunder, with the lashing rain soaking everyone. The sailors of U-615 sewed his body into a hammock with a weight between his feet. To the singing of the traditional naval hymn, the words of which were unheard in the fierce wind and rain, his remains was committed to the deep in a solemn and intensely moving improvised ceremony. Even as the body of their much beloved commander slid over the side, U-615's gunners stood to their weapons, waiting and watching. They were still ready to fight.[40]

But the epic battle was over, for the hunters never found U-615. She was dead regardless, slowly sinking as the water level below climbed and the last power drained from her batteries. There was nothing that could be done to repair the boat and indeed she was still afloat only because her engineers were slowly bleeding the last of her high pressure air into the ballast tanks. From the moment Lieutenant Erskine had found her and his Mariner had delivered the first attack, U-615 had taken a fearsome beating and had survived thirteen separate depth charge and bomb attacks. Even for a Hamburg-built boat—which many U-boat crews considered as the best constructed submarines—she had proved to be exceptional, equal perhaps to her indomitable commander.

As dawn approached with U-615 dead in the water and the waves washing over her, Schlipper ordered her battle ensign raised. He sent engineer Oberleutnant Herbert Skora, Petty Officer Claus von Egan and the boat's Mate Abel back down into her control room to prepare to flood the boat. They could still hear the angry swarm of hunters overhead, although by this stage they were widening their search patteren in the belief that U-615 had eluded them and was escaping.

As the final scenes were playing out on U-615, the new Fletcher Class destroyer *USS Walker*, under Lt. Cmdr. Townsend, was racing to the scene in the hope of finishing off the U-boat. Other surface ships were also drawing near, and additional aircraft were being made ready to take over at daylight. At 5:25 a.m., just as the first touch of dawn was lighting the eastern horizon, Schlipper fired a red flare. The burst of light was seen from the bridge of the *Walker*, which immediately altered course and headed in that direction. In the gathering light the U-boat's crew could see the topmast of the destroyer racing toward them. The end had indeed arrived. On Schlipper's command the engineering crew opened the sea cocks and flooded the boat before joining the remainder of the lifejacketed crew in the water. They watched silently as their gallant boat slid beneath the surface and made her final dive to the ocean floor 10,000 feet below, just to the west of the underwater Aves Ridge. "She sank under us," was how one survivor described it. The last thing her crew saw was U-615's war flag as it dipped below the waves.[41]

At 5:55 a.m., the gunner's control director on the *Walker* passed word to the bridge that a U-boat was submerging directly ahead at a range of twenty thousand yards. If what the men in the tower saw through their powerful range finder was actually a U-boat, it was the last glimpse by the Allies of U-615. The *Walker* raced ahead and found a group of survivors floating in the water. Cutting her engines, she came to a stop alongside them. There were forty-three Germans bobbing in the sea. There was also one corpse in a lifejacket. When the dinghy had been swept off the casing of the U-boat, the medical kit was lost as well. As a result, Petty Officer Helmut Langner died from his painful knee wound. The *Walker* lowered a scrambling net for the U-boat's survivors, but the water was rough and the task was difficult. Only two men had climbed the side of the destroyer before a powerful explosion was felt.

The detonation coincided exactly with a report from Mariner P-9, of VP-205, that it had just seen a U-boat submerging to the west of the *Walker's* position.

This curious set of circumstances may never be adequately explained. The explosion was probably one or more of the torpedoes going off in U-615 as she sank and the enormous water pressure crushed the torpedo pistols. But the Mariner's report of a U-boat west of the *Walker* was never adequately explained. Perhaps the air crew had seen a final glimpse of U-615 and had misreported the direction, although this is unlikely. Another U-boat, Eberhard Dalhaus' U-634, was in the Caribbean but she was some distance away, heading north to make her escape out of the Mona Passage.[42]

Fearful of a torpedo attack, the *Walker* pulled up the nets and made speed, leaving the remaining survivors in the water while racing westwards to where the Mariner was circling. Directed by the aircraft, the destroyer carried out two depth charge attacks, the results of which were inconclusive. After a half-hour of fruitless searching, the *Walker* gave up and returned to the remaining survivors of U-615, who by that time had given up hope of rescue. A total of forty-three men were fished out of the sea, as was Langner 's body.[43]

Even though all the facts of the battle were not known and the pieces of the puzzle had not yet been put together, the *Walker's* crew was aware that the men in the water were from a U-boat that had put up a tremendous fight. As a result, U-615's survivors were treated with great courtesy by their captors. To the U.S. Navy, however, the *Walker's* plucking of the Germans from the sea was by no means the end of the affair. The engagement had been too hard fought and U-615 had eluded destruction under the most adverse combat circumstances. U-boats running on the surface had been routinely broken into pieces by a single well-placed depth charge attack. How had U-615 managed to avoid such a fate? Eventually many convinced themselves that either U-615 had escaped, or they had been fighting several U-boats.

And so the hunt for U-615 was intensified and lasted for another three days. It was difficult for the U.S. Navy to accept that one lone U-boat had caused all that trouble, and it was three days before the *Walker* landed her forty-three survivors in Chaguaramas for temporary internment in Trinidad's prisoner of war camp. In the meantime, Petty

Officer Helmut Langner had been buried from the deck of the American destroyer with full military honors.[44]

*   *   *

Ralph Kapitsky is not listed as one of the great U-boat aces of World War II. In his four war patrols he only sank four merchant ships, but his importance is far greater than his meager showing in the tonnage war. The Dresden native and former Luftwaffe pilot fought an epic battle that was unique in the annals of a world war in which he played but a small role. He stood his ground and continued to fight long after many U-boat commanders would have abandoned such a lopsided affair, thereby establishing himself as a fearless leader of men. But what, if anything, did Kapitsky achieve by his apparently hopeless defiance of the odds?

By early August 1943, American airmen had just won a major campaign against the U-boats. The titanic month-long struggle decided who controlled the vital Caribbean choke point, the terminus of the North Atlantic convoy routes. The American pilots were aware that they had won. They enjoyed the smell of their hard-bought victory and were dominating the retreating U-boats. Losses in time of war are always higher when a military force is defeated and then tries to retreat from the field of battle. So it was with the U-boats. Admiral Dönitz's submarines had found the Trinidad Sector an impossible operating area because of the complete dominance of the theater by aircraft. It was so bad that one of them, Hagenskötter in U-466, had actually radioed U-boat headquarters that the sector was as dangerous as the Bay of Biscay. In actuality it was more hazardous than Biscay. The latter body of water was nothing more than a transit route through which the boats had to navigate, while the sea off Trinidad was an operational area where the boats were expected to stay on station and attack shipping. But by the summer of 1943 the U-boats were unable to position themselves to sink shipping, and for a month all they had been able to do was survive—at least some of them.

When the boats began to retreat, the American pilots became even more aggressive. As a result, none of the boats that were trying to get away were able to put much distance between themselves and the anti-submarine bases. They surfaced only to charge their batteries, and even then such an act often proved fatal. The eastward progressing U-boats were targeted for destruction by relays of aircraft hunting individual boats. It was a situation that could end only one way, with the eventual destruction of each boat. It is at this point in the story that Kapitsky's actions impacted events.

The protracted struggle around U-615 only lasted for one long day, but the fight was so fierce that it generated a massive anti-submarine operation spanning a full five days. Kapitsky's battle was also on the main convoy route, an area that was extremely sensitive to the Allies. It simply could not be ignored, nor could the potential for catastrophe be downplayed. Thus the presence of a U-boat in that area generated an immediate and overwhelming response from the Americans. Kapitsky's tenacious fight caused the Americans to switch the center of gravity of their anti-submarine effort from east of Trinidad to the northwest. Thus twelve large Mariners were assigned to simultaneously hunt the lone U-boat. When the Mariners ran low on fuel, fresh aircraft took their place. These aircraft were pulled from convoy duty, patrolling operations—and the hounding of other retreating U-boats.[45] Kapitsky's tireless effort and the consequent reallocation of Allied anti-submarine resources provided a lull in the relentless attacks against the other withdrawing boats. The decrease in air patrols allowed them to surface and race eastward to relative safety. U-190, U-309, U-415, U-510, U-634, U-648 and U-653 owed their escape from the Trinidad death trap to U-615 and her crew.

Although Ralph Kapitsky almost certainly never realized it, he and his men had waged one of the most distinguished rear guard actions of any war.

*   *   *

Fritz Guggenberger relaxes after a war patrol. *U-Boot-Archiv*

Eric C. Rust

Fritz Guggenberger
Bavarian U-Boat Ace

"I'll be the one wearing blue jeans," Fritz Guggenberger had told me on the phone when I inquired how I might recognize him at the train station of Garmisch-Partenkirchen, where he had promised to pick me up for an interview. Sure enough, when I stepped onto the platform in Garmisch after a lovely train ride south from Munich through the foothills of the Bavarian Alps under a lazy summer sky, there he was in his jeans, just as tall, lanky and athletic as I remembered him from the old pictures snapped almost half a century before. As he waved at me and we shook hands, I still could hardly believe that this was the same man, holder of the Knight's Cross with Oak Leaves, who had undertaken no fewer than fifteen war patrols in German submarines during the war, and on one of them had sent the British fleet carrier *Ark Royal* to the bottom of the Mediterranean; the commander who had barely gotten away with his own life when his last boat, U-513, went down near Rio de Janeiro; the man who had helped organize the largest POW escape on American soil from his camp in Arizona, and later risen in rank to Rear Admiral in the new West German Navy and a high NATO command position before retiring to this breathtakingly beautiful spot in the German Alps, an hour's drive from where he had been born. What a life, what a story!

That was in 1982, and the recollections of my meeting with Fritz Guggenberger have remained vividly with me ever since. Still in his jeans, he took me to lunch in a first-class restaurant on the Eibsee, in elevation the highest German lake in the shadow of the snow-covered Zugspitze, Germany's tallest mountain, where we dined on trout and began a wide-ranging talk which we later continued at his comfortable home in town. There he introduced me to his charming wife Liselotte, and after coffee, cake and a long conversation covering Guggenberger's rich experiences and career I took leave of him later that night to return to Munich. On the train ride back I recall asking myself why the German Navy had traditionally hired so few Bavarians. If all were only a little like Guggenberger, the country would have been splendidly served.[1]

Friedrich Karl Guggenberger, "Fritz" or "Fiedje" to his friends and comrades, was born in Munich on March 6, 1915, the posthumous son of Friedrich Guggenberger, an Imperial naval officer, and his wife Marie, née Brug. His father, a lieutenant commander, had died on August 28, 1914, at the very outset of the First World War in the Battle of Heligoland Bay when British forces under Admiral Beatty surprised and sank the German light cruisers *Mainz*, *Köln* and *Ariadne* in the North Sea. His mother, two months pregnant when her husband died, moved back to Munich to give birth to her son and eventually was remarried to a physician, Dr. Karl Oehrl, who practiced family medicine in the small town of Weikersheim some 30 miles south of Würzburg on the Tauber River. Here Guggenberger, along with his three siblings, spent his childhood and adolescence in an orderly, sheltered and thoroughly bourgeois household and atmosphere.

Those were the years when Germany's Weimar Republic tried to get off the ground despite its many birth defects. Guggenberger's family rejected the Versailles Treaty as a historical injustice and also noticed how the advancing Industrial Revolution threatened the traditional lifestyle of the region's many small and independent wine growers, causing noticeable social tensions. While attending third grade, Guggenberger experienced the terrible hyper-inflation that almost wrecked Germany's economy in 1923. Later he remembered many frank and open discussions in his stepfather's house centering on political and intellectual issues of the day. As so many other youths in the 1920s, Guggenberger joined the Wandervogel movement, with its emphasis on community activities, nature worship, rebellion against stuffy bourgeois norms and appeal to a mystical-romantic and profoundly nationalist view of German history.

By 1925 Guggenberger qualified for the Gymnasium, Germany's élite secondary schools which still today prepare their graduates for advanced university studies as well as military and other professional careers. Since Weikersheim with its 1200 inhabitants was too small to have its own Gymnasium, Guggenberger commuted first to Bad Mergentheim (1925-1930) and then to Tauberbischofsheim (1930-1934) in the neighboring state of Baden-Württemberg. Here he found students of similar socio-economic backgrounds, several of them Jewish, and teachers whom he would remember as open-minded, deeply interested in developing the minds of their charges, and politically close the Catholic Center Party. While excelling in most subjects, Guggenberger had some trouble with foreign languages, and despite a lifetime spent far away from his native Bavaria, he never much sought nor ever quite managed to lose his distinct southern accent.

Guggenberger never doubted that one day he would become a naval officer like his father. His mother encouraged him in this pursuit, especially since the Great Depression made a secure and respected naval career all the more alluring. If rejected by the Navy, Guggenberger might possibly have studied forestry, or medicine like his stepfather, but joining the Army never occurred to him as an alternative to service in the Navy—even though his grandfather had been a general. He easily passed his physical exam in Würzburg and the so-called "psycho-technical" test in Munich, thus qualifying for a career as a regular naval officer (*Seeoffizier*) rather than as a specialist with officer rank such as naval engineers or weapons, administrative, and medical officers. This meant he could advance to command ships, squadrons and fleets and even attain flag rank if his career should be a successful one. Conversely the Navy must have been delighted to gain someone of Guggenberger's caliber—bright, enthusiastic, politically reliable, physically fit, and already part of a military and naval dynasty. Moreover, as a Bavarian and Catholic, Guggenberger added desirable variety to an officer corps in which six out of every seven members were Protestant and came from regions north of the Main River.[2]

On April 8, 1934, having just graduated from his Gymnasium (Oberrealschule) in Tauberbischofsheim and celebrated his nineteenth birthday the previous month, Fritz Guggenberger began his basic military training along with 317 other naval officer cadets on Dänholm Island near Stralsund on the Baltic coast. He and his comrades became known forever after as "Crew 34," the class of naval officers who had entered the service in that year. Crew 34 would eventually contain some of Germany's most successful and highly decorated U-boat aces of World War II, including Erich Topp, Jochen Mohr, Engelbert Endrass, Carl Emmermann, Helmut Witte, Adi Schnee, Günther Müller-Stöckheim, among many others. They knew each other not merely from their common experiences in the U-boat branch but from the very outset of their naval careers.

Boot camp is rarely a pleasant experience. Guggenberger recalled his three months of basic infantry training as "hard," but he was also fortunate in that his drill sergeant seemed more lenient and understanding than those in charge of other groups who made their men suffer to the point of utter mental and physical exhaustion. By June 1934 Guggenberger and his friends transferred to the *Gorch Fock* for three months of hands-on nautical apprenticeship on a working sailing vessel, a three-master that took the cadets on an extended tour of the Baltic Sea. Guggenberger later thought of those days as his "most miserable command" because of the insulting and frequently dangerous chicanery he and others had to endure constantly from their superiors, officers and petty officers alike. It was also aboard the *Gorch Fock* that Guggenberger, like everyone else in his Crew, took a new service oath on August 2, 1934, when Adolf Hitler assumed the office of Reich President upon Hindenburg's death. The new service oath bound the German Armed Forces in personal loyalty to Hitler.[3]

A highlight of every cadet's course of instruction is the midshipmen's cruise, which carried Guggenberger's half of Crew 34 for nine months in the light cruiser *Emden* around Africa into the Indian Ocean as far east as Trincomalee in Ceylon (Sri Lanka) before returning through the Suez Canal and the Mediterranean. Even though Guggenberger fell ill with malaria and later typhus while in Africa, a twin punch that knocked him out for six weeks with high fever, he did enjoy learning about life and responsibilities on a warship. On this cruise the *Emden's* commanding officer was none other than Karl Dönitz, the future creator and leader of Germany's submarine force. Perhaps not surprisingly, a relatively high percentage of Crew 34's officers would later serve and excel under Dönitz in World War II as submarine commanders and chief engineers.

While the *Emden* had made her way to the Orient and back, the other half of Crew 34 visited both coasts of the Americas in the light cruiser *Karlsruhe*. In June 1936 the two vessels delivered their charges to the Marineschule Mürwik, Germany's naval academy on Flensburg Bay just south of the Danish border, where they experienced nine months of theoretical training in the classroom. Guggenberger, bright and academically well prepared, had a "great time" at the venerable institution, whereas many others in his class struggled to master the sixteen demanding subjects in their curriculum. Predictably, while he did extremely well in such areas as navigation, seamanship, tactics and naval history, Guggenberger received his weakest grades in the required foreign languages—English and French in his case—and did certainly not volunteer to tackle a third modern language as several others in his class chose to do. Even with his language handicap, Guggenberger ranked thirteenth in his class out of the 165 new second lieutenants in the regular naval officer branch (*Seeoffiziere*), a distinction he could take much pride in and which traditionally meant choice commands and more rapid promotion in the future.[4]

Already at the Marineschule and during the subsequent short practical courses for junior officers covering applied navigation, communications, shipboard and coastal artillery, infantry, torpedoes and mines, Guggenberger expressed his desire to join the rapidly expanding submarine force as his future field of expertise. Besides the popularity and public esteem the U-boat branch enjoyed since its spectacular successes in World War I, Guggenberger felt attracted by the spirit of camaraderie among submariners that he could not expect if posted, say, to a battleship, cruiser or a destroyer, let alone an assignment ashore. There was also the prospect of an independent command early in his career. But the Navy's personnel managers, at least at first, had other plans for this promising young man from Bavaria. Half a year after graduating from the Naval Academy, in September 1936, Guggenberger found himself back aboard the cruiser *Emden*, this time not as a green midshipman but as one of several cadet officers in charge of training the next batch of officer aspirants, those of Crews 35 and 36. While this assignment gave Guggenberger two additional and generally exciting cruises to the Far East as well as valuable experience in mastering challenges in such diverse areas as diplomatic representation, weaponry and navigation in unfamiliar waters, it did not seem to advance his dream of real, "front-line" naval service. Even upon returning from his third voyage on the *Emden* in April 1938, Guggenberger received a further instructor assignment as a group officer at the Marineschule Mürwik—undoubtedly a prestigious posting for a young officer, but again essentially a desk job rather than a shipboard command on an "active duty" man-of-war. One can imagine how frustrated and envious he became toward his Crew comrades who had foregone exotic adventures in the Orient in favor of years of practical service in the fleet or the naval air arm.

Still at the Naval Academy and by now a first lieutenant, Guggenberger experienced the outbreak of World War II. The mood on September 3, 1939, when England and France declared war on Germany, was somber and fatalistic, very different from the joyful exuberance that had marked the beginning of World War I in 1914. Most seemed to feel that this war had been started without much concern for its consequences, a charge that could be leveled against Hitler as well as against the other players in this drama, such as Stalin, Mussolini, Daladier and Chamberlain. Whatever the war's deeper causes and implications, one thing was certain for Guggenberger: his service was needed at the front as soon as possible. Within a month of the outbreak of war, by October 2, 1939, he found himself posted to the U-boat Training Command in Neustadt to enter a world very different from the one he had known since joining the Navy five years before.

In retrospect Guggenberger himself seemed amazed how brief his introduction to the submarine service was before he was entrusted with the responsibilities of an I.W.O. (First Watch Officer) the No. 2 man in charge of a frontline boat. In fact, he spent merely eight weeks in Neustadt to familiarize himself with the new weapon and another month at the Naval Communications School in Flensburg-Mürwik next to the Naval Academy in a special course for U-boat watch officers. On January 2, 1940, he assumed his new assignment as I.W.O. aboard U-28 of the 2nd U-Boat Flotilla. Guggenberger's solid experience in seamanship, navigation, supervising subordinates and excellent performance in his previous positions much facilitated this rapid and successful transition.

U-28 belonged to the class of ten so-called Type VIIA U-boats. They had been built in 1936 and 1937 to serve as forerunners for the popular

A pre-war picture of U-28, on which Guggenberger served his apprenticeship as a watch officer in 1940. *U-Boot-Archiv*

and slightly larger Type VIIB and VIIC "Atlantic" boats, of which Germany would construct well over 600 during the course of the war. A "medium-size high-seas boat" originally developed from the UB III design of World War I, U-28 and her nine sisters (U-27, U-29 to U-36) displaced 626 tons on the surface and 745 tons submerged. Their maximum surface speed reached 16 knots, thanks to two diesels with 2310 HP combined, while their electrical engines for underwater propulsion produced 750 HP and speeds up to 8 knots. The boats were 215 feet long, a little over 19 feet wide and had a draft of 45 feet at periscope depth. Armament consisted of five torpedo tubes as well as the standard 8.8-cm deck gun and one 2-cm automatic anti-aircraft gun. The boats could carry a total of 11 torpedoes, and while the size of the crew at 44 was the same as that in subsequent Type VII versions, Type A had a more limited range of only 4,300 nautical miles at an economical speed of 12 knots.[5]

When Guggenberger joined the crew of U-28, the boat had already sunk four allied merchantmen totaling almost 25,000 tons in two regular patrols around the British Isles and one mine-laying mission between September and December 1939. Her early successes were conducted under the leadership of a veteran skipper, Lieutenant Commander Günter Kuhnke of Crew 31. In fact, all indications are that Kuhnke and Guggenberger complemented each other well as a team, with Kuhnke supplying experience and perhaps a certain hesitancy to run unnecessary risks in this early phase of the war, while Guggenberger added youthful energy and a somewhat more aggressive spirit when it came to seeking out the enemy. Guggenberger would later comment that in his experience early skippers like Kuhnke were sometimes overly "cautious" perhaps because their training had been so intense and their knowledge of details too intimate for them to appreciate opportunities rather than dangers and limitations. Later in the war, according to Guggenberger, commanding officers tended to be more at ease in calculating and taking risks and also showed superior resistance to the physical and mental stresses that naturally came with the job.

As part of the 2nd (Saltzwedel) Flotilla, U-28 was based in the port of Wilhelmshaven on the North Sea before the entire squadron and its staff transferred to Lorient on the Bay of Biscay after the defeat of France in 1940. In fact, U-boat Command Headquarters itself at this point was just outside Wilhelmshaven in the countryside at Sengwarden. As if U-boat warfare with fewer than expected operational units was not challenging enough, the winter of 1939-1940 turned out to be extremely harsh, demanding on materiel and men alike and rendering navigation hazardous, especially in coastal waters. Even the Kiel Canal connecting the North Sea with the Baltic remained virtually impassable for a time. Nevertheless, on February 18, 1940, U-28 was ready to sail on another minelaying and combat mission, Guggenberger's first active patrol.

After laying twelve mines in the Firth of Forth outside Edinburgh, U-28 proceeded around Scotland to waters southwest of the British Isles. There, on March 9, she encountered, torpedoed and sank the freighter *P. Margaronis* (4,979 tons) of Greek registry in a night attack. While the merchantman was not part of a regular convoy, Kuhnke and Guggenberger must have suspected her of carrying contraband so close to the enemy shore of Cornwall, possibly even with a distant Allied escort and air cover. At any rate, they never positively ascertained the ship's identity and reported her size as approximately 6,000 tons. Two nights later a similar fate befell the Dutch vessel *Eulota* (6,236 tons) near the southwest entrance to the English Channel. This time U-28 reported its victim as a tanker of about 10,000 tons. Given poor visibility in bad weather and long, dark winter nights, such overestimation of one's actual successes was neither uncommon nor usually intentional among submariners. After this encounter U-28 returned home to Wilhelmshaven, reaching her base safely on March 23, 1940.[6]

The year 1940 was generally a good one for German submarines in the Eastern Atlantic and its adjacent waters. Allied countermeasures had not yet attained the level of organization and sophistication they would reach later in the war. Many Allied and neutral vessels still sailed singly and unescorted between ports and thus became easy prey for Germany's hunters of the sea. Between April and June Germany vastly improved her geostrategic situation by defeating Denmark, Norway, the Low Countries and France in a campaign to which her Navy contributed significantly—especially in making possible the conquest of Norway through sea-lift capabilities. Even though a considerable number of German surface units were sunk in the course of these operations, and the U-boats were temporarily crippled by a technical defect in their torpedo firing mechanism, the net result of Hitler's bold move was to gain operational bases both in Norway and France with direct access to the Atlantic shipping lanes. No longer would German submarines waste valuable time traversing the North Sea en route to their patrol areas north and west of the British Isles. At the same time Hitler's spring campaign of 1940 virtually made the Baltic sea a German lake, thus giving U-Boat Training Command an ideal and undisturbed place to test and prepare new boats for frontline duty.

Kuhnke, Guggenberger, II.W.O. Ernst-Ullrich Brüller (Crew 36) and the rest of U-28's men played only a marginal role in these momentous events. Their late return from their minelaying mission precluded participation in the Norwegian venture and the boat did not put to sea again until May 5, bound once more for its familiar hunting grounds southwest of the British Isles. After weeks of idle patrolling, U-28 finally encountered and sank the 40-year-old unescorted Finnish steamship *Sarmatia* (2,417 tons) in a daylight attack on June 18 south of Ireland. Most likely Guggenberger as I.W.O. carried out this attack himself since traditionally nighttime and submerged attacks remained the skipper's prerogative. At any rate, this time U-28 did ascertain and report its victim by name. Over the next three days U-28 struck two more blows against the enemy in those very same waters: on June 19 a dusk attack against the old Greek steamer *Adamandios Georgiandis* (3,443 tons), and an early morning strike two days later against the *Prunella* (4,443 tons) then sailing in charter for the Royal Navy. By July 6, U-28 was back home in Wilhelmshaven. While Kuhnke's U-28 had not been quite as successful as others, like Engelbert Endrass' U-46, Victor Oehrn's U-37, Heinrich Liebe's U-38 or Hans Rösing's U-48, all of which were then stationed in the same general vicinity, it at least had made a solid contribution of its own.[7]

Kuhnke as commanding officer and Guggenberger as his First Watch Officer would undertake two more patrols together. The first lasted from August 11 to September 17, and the second from October 10 to November 15, 1940, each averaging some five to six weeks in length. This meant two weeks en route to and from their operational areas and about a month on actual patrol in their assigned positions. The latter shifted now to the Northern Approaches, i.e. the waters to the west of Scotland and northwest of Ireland, where convoy traffic to and from North America was picking up in intensity. In fact, on his third patrol Guggenberger got his first taste of what it was like to attack entire convoys with concentrated U-boat wolfpacks.

U-28 drew first blood in the afternoon hours of August 27 when she sank the small Norwegian steamer *Eva* (1,599 tons). The steamer's cargo of timber kept her afloat, and U-28 was forced to utilize both torpedoes and her 8.8-cm deck gun to send her to the bottom. The ship belonged to Convoy SC.1, which had assembled in Sydney, Nova Scotia, before sailing for the United Kingdom. By the time U-28 made contact, Lieutenant Commander Victor Oehrn in U-37 had already taken two vessels out of this convoy and the *Eva* appears to have been a straggler without the benefit of an immediate escort. This would explain why Kuhnke was able to report his victim by name and safely surface to use his deck gun. It is again likely that Guggenberger as I.W.O. was in charge of both the boat's artillery and torpedoes in this encounter. U-28 also took proper care of the freighter's survivors until Allied air attacks forced the submarine to dive. The very next evening, still in the North Channel, U-28 picked the British steamer *Kyno* (3,946 tons) out of another convoy, HX.66, which had originated in Halifax, Nova Scotia.[8]

Before heading for its new base in Lorient, France, U-28 ran into two more convoys in those crowded waters west of the British Isles. Early on September 9, in a coordinated action with Lieutenant Commander Günther Prien's U-47 of Scapa Flow fame, Kuhnke attacked SC.2 and destroyed the British vessel *Mardinian* (2,434 tons). Two nights later U-28 sent a spread of torpedoes into Convoy OA.210, outbound from the North Channel to the New World. She managed to sink the 20-year-old Dutch steamship *Maas* (1,966 tons) and damage the British vessel *Harpenden* (4,678 tons). While all previous victims of U-28 appear to have carried a full cargo, these last two were likely sailing in ballast. At any rate, this third of Kuhnke's and Guggenberger's missions in U-28 was their most successful to date, even though once again reported sinkings and tonnages ran somewhat higher than actual totals.

U-28's last patrol as a frontline boat turned out to be a disappointment. The flotilla's transfer from Wilhelmshaven to Lorient appeared poorly organized, one result being that shipment of the crews' personal belongings was delayed so that the men had to wear captured British uniforms before their regular ones arrived. Ship repair facilities in Lorient were still so limited that U-28 had to put into St. Nazaire to be fully prepared and equipped for her next mission. Apparently U-28 was the first German submarine to take advantage of St. Nazaire's excellent facilities.[9]

U-Boat Command again assigned Kuhnke and his crew to the patrol lines of U-boats guarding the Northwest Approaches, a promising area since virtually all inbound and outbound convoys had to pass through those waters on their way to or from Britain. Indeed, during the second half of October Germany's emerging U-boat aces, Otto Kretschmer (U-99), Günther Prien (U-47), Joachim Schepke (U-100), Engelbert Endrass (U-46) and Georg Schulz (U-124) among them, did frightful damage to Allied shipping, disposing of no fewer than fourteen ships on October 19 alone, with only slightly lower totals on the days before and after. These were indeed the "Happy Times" German submariners would later recall with sweet nostalgia. U-28 managed to torpedo only a single vessel—the relatively large and modern British steamship *Matina* (5,389 tons) in a dawn attack on October 26. Yet, despite U-28's efforts to send the *Matina* to the bottom, the vessel refused to go down. Three days later the hulk was still afloat before a coup-de-grace torpedo from U-32 finally sealed her fate.[10]

Part of U-28's poor luck on this patrol was the result of her involuntary role as a decoy. While enemy aircraft and surface escorts kept locating the boat, forcing her again and again below water and minimizing or eliminating any chances of scoring hits against the convoys, the other German boats could pounce on the enemy without significant interference. Fierce autumn storms and ferocious seas followed, making meaningful contact with the enemy nearly impossible. Indeed these storms crippled U-28 so much that it was decided to recall her to Germany and use her up as a training boat in the calmer and safer waters of the Baltic Sea. Still, while crossing the North Sea on her way home to Wilhelmshaven, U-28 survived a surprise attack by an enemy submarine whose torpedoes fortunately missed thanks to emergency turns and Kuhnke's expert handling of his boat. After a quick stay and repairs in Wilhelmshaven U-28 transferred through the Kiel Canal to Stettin on the Baltic for further repair work and eventual incorporation into the 24th Flotilla of the U-Boat Training Division.

With Kuhnke leaving his boat for a shore command, Guggenberger officially took over as U-28's commanding officer on November 10, 1940, and retained that position for three months until February 11, 1941. With U-28 in the dock and the Baltic badly iced over, there was little, however, to sweeten Guggenberger's first taste of being in charge of a boat of his own. During these weeks he took a well-deserved vacation in Ludwigsburg near Stuttgart where his family now lived, and completed the mandatory introductory course for new U-boat skippers.[11]

During these winter months of relative idleness Guggenberger had a good opportunity to reflect on the turns his career had taken in recent times. He had at last achieved what he could only dream about in all those years on the *Emden*, namely, becoming part of Germany's U-boat branch. Moreover, as his decoration with the Iron Cross (First Class) bore witness, his apprenticeship as First Watch Officer under Kuhnke in U-28 had been both instructive, successful and duly rewarded. In the meantime, the submarine campaign against Britain appeared to proceed well without losses and glitches that could not somehow be made good in the future. Guggenberger had proved that he could handle a boat under routine conditions as well as in combat situations, that he was a fine and respected leader of men, and that the time had come for U-Boat Command to entrust him with a frontline boat of his own. It was thus more with a sense of excitement and satisfaction than surprise that Guggenberger received orders to report to the Vulkan Shipyard in

Bremen-Vegesack, where a brand-new boat, U-81, awaited completion and commissioning.

As a Type VIIC boat, U-81 was a slightly larger and in several ways more sophisticated version of the older U-28. Its chief improvements over the VIIA design were its operational range of up to 6,500 nautical miles and two stronger diesel engines that could produce a top surface speed of 17 knots. Armament, crew size, pressure hull, diving characteristics as well as underwater speed and endurance remained unchanged. Guggenberger presided over the boat's festive commissioning ceremony on April 26, 1941, before taking U-81 through the Kiel Canal into the Baltic for shake-down exercises and the painstaking training of his officers and crew. He was very fortunate in receiving high-quality subordinates in First Lieutenants Claus von Trotha (Crew 36) and later Johann-Otto Krieg (Crew X/37), who would become his First Watch Officers, along with Second Lieutenant Horst Renner as chief engineer. Von Trotha would eventually move on to become the skipper of U-306, while Krieg took over U-81 when Guggenberger left in December 1942 to command U-513.[12]

Administratively U-81 was attached to Germany's 1st U-Boat Flotilla, formerly based in Kiel but lately transferred to Brest, still today France's major naval base on the Atlantic coast. Appropriately enough, the unique emblem on U-81's conning tower was a sword or dagger thrust through a ring-like opening, somewhat reminiscent of a torpedo hitting its target.[13]

After a two-week vacation in late May and early June at his parents' home in Ludwigsburg, Guggenberger, now 26 years old and a seven-year veteran, completed U-81's final training exercises and proceeded to the Baltic base at Kiel for the outfitting of his boat for its maiden mission in the North Atlantic. Guggenberger's first patrol as a commanding officer stood very much in the shadow of Operation Barbarossa, Hitler's attack on the Soviet Union. U-81 received orders to proceed north from Kiel through the Danish Straits and Norwegian coastal waters to Trondheim, about halfway up German-occupied Norway's Atlantic coast. From there on July 17, 1941, some four weeks after Germany and the Soviet Union had commenced hostilities, Guggenberger departed to be among the first German boats to threaten Russia's northern flank. Specifically he was instructed to look for enemy ship traffic bound for Murmansk and Archangel along the Kola Peninsula in the Arctic Sea.

Unfortunately for Guggenberger and his men, the long days of an Arctic summer were not ideal for U-boat operations and the Russians failed to cooperate. On August 7, U-81 ended its first patrol by entering Kirkenes near the North Cape in northernmost Norway. While they yielded no measurable accomplishments, the three weeks at sea gave Guggenberger and his crew valuable experience. Two days later U-81 moved on to Trondheim, where she arrived for a two-week layover on August 13.

If this first mission had lacked excitement, U-81's second operation, beginning in Trondheim on August 27 and ending in Brest, France, on September 19, was hardly routine. Once again Guggenberger became involved in a transformation of German strategy at sea. During this phase in the Battle of the Atlantic, England tightened her defenses around the British Isles considerably and the United States became more directly involved in the conflict by occupying Iceland as both a forward base and as a precaution against a German landing there. U-Boat Command consequently decided to shift its boats farther west. This change brought with it at least two advantages and two disadvantages from the German perspective. While the boats had less to fear from land-based aerial surveillance and gained additional time and space to attack Allied convoys, they took longer to reach their operational areas and also ran an increasing risk of a confrontation with the United States Navy. Indeed long before Pearl Harbor German U-boats and American naval units in the central and western Atlantic played a deliberate and dangerous game of cat-and-mouse with many close calls and at least one major tragedy. On Halloween 1941, Erich Topp's U-552 sank the U.S. destroyer *Reuben James* with a great loss of life while the latter was escorting a British convoy in violation of President Roosevelt's ostensible neutrality.

Guggenberger's U-81 was one of these boats ordered far out into the Atlantic. In a position just east of Cape Farewell, Greenland's southernmost tip, Guggenberger picked up the scent of convoy SC.42. Over the next week, from the 9th of September through the 16th, an epic battle ranged over 30 degrees of longitude from Greenland to the Irish Sea, as U-boat wolfpacks clung to the convoy and decimated it. No fewer than 18 Allied ships went down and two others were damaged as ten different U-boats scored hits on the enemy, while others assisted by keeping the overworked and desperate Allied escorts occupied. In the process two U-boats were destroyed. One was U-207, commanded by Guggenberger's Crew 34 comrade Fritz Meyer, who is credited with sinking three Allied ships before his own boat went down.

Guggenberger's U-81 inflicted the first kill in this veritable orgy of destruction. Before dawn on September 9, the Bavarian commander sighted the British freighter *Empire Springbuck* (5,591 tons) which during the night had lost contact with the convoy's main body and become a straggler. Two torpedo hits exploded the vessel and she disappeared beneath the waves. The battle had opened. Over the next 24 hours Guggenberger twice managed to maneuver his boat into favorable attack positions and fired two separate torpedo spreads into the convoy. In the din of battle—with other boats making simultaneous attacks, Allied escorts dropping depth charges that could only too easily be mistaken for torpedo hits, and vessels breaking up noisily as they went down—Guggenberger and his men became convinced they had sunk at the least two additional ships and damaged two more. Careful post-war analysis has since revealed that in reality only the British *Sally Maersk* (3,252 tons) fell victim to U-81's exertions. Guggenberger's example and experience show how innocently and easily submarine commanders could exaggerate their claims of enemy tonnage sunk and thus mislead U-Boat Command into assuming that England's situation looked much grimmer than was actually the case. At any rate, these attacks on the night of September 10 exhausted Guggenberger's torpedo supply and he was recalled to Brest, where he arrived nine days later. Docking in western Brittany, Guggenberger and his men were in a much more jubilant mood than after their abortive foray into Arctic waters. Good news followed his safe arrival in port when he learned that he had been promoted to the rank of lieutenant commander, effective September 1, 1941.

The battle for SC.42 gave Guggenberger and his crew not only a dramatic baptism of fire but the kind of shared teamwork experience without which no submarine can successfully function in the long run. Those tough days out in the Atlantic instilled pride in the men's accomplishments and confidence in their ability to go out and face the enemy again in similar situations. As their commanding officer, Guggenberger gained something even more crucial but ultimately intangible—his men's respect and affection. They knew now that their skipper was not only experienced, bright, capable, successful, and a leader who genuinely cared for his men, but also someone who could weigh risks and, above all, bring his men home again. This heartfelt dedication and respect made Guggenberger's leadership easier and more rewarding with every mission he and his men subsequently undertook. These same qualities also gained him an honored place among fellow U-boat commanders and garnered the attention of Admiral Dönitz. That, as a transplanted Bavarian, he always retained his native humor, joviality, and precious unpretentiousness at a time when so many others around him could not resist a certain ego inflation, must have seemed to his friends like icing on the cake.

When they reached Brest on September 19, Guggenberger and his crew had not the slightest inkling that their next mission would earn them a permanent place in the history books. With the war in Russia proceeding more or less according to expectations, with German forces in control of the entire Balkan Peninsula, and in the face of recurring Italian setbacks on land as well as at sea, Hitler and his advisers decided in August 1941 to force a speedier resolution of the Mediterranean situation. An important part of this new Axis strategy was to dispatch a number of German submarines from the Atlantic through the Strait of Gibraltar. The infusion of additional submarines was designed to help isolate Malta, protect Axis convoys on their way from Italy and Greece to North Africa, and generally reduce British naval strength in the Mediterranean. Hitler insisted on this decision, even though both Dönitz and Grand Admiral Erich Raeder, the Navy's Commander-in-Chief, repeatedly argued that U-boats as a strategic weapon represented a much more valuable asset in the Atlantic than in the restricted and peripheral waters of the Mediterranean. This was especially true at a time when the Atlantic convoy battles were going so well that Britain might be brought to her knees before the United States entered the war. Raeder lost the argument (and eventually his job), and Guggenberger and U-81 ended up heading for the Mediterranean.[14]

Raeder and Dönitz were right in their assessment of the strategic situation. Hitler made essentially the same mistake Churchill committed in both World Wars by believing that the war could be decided in the Mediterranean theater. In the end this miscalculation created a tragedy for Germany's U-boat force inasmuch as over the next three years no fewer than 64 precious boats, all of them of the Type VIIC design, moved into the Mediterranean. Not a single one of them would ever ply Atlantic waters again. As skippers like Guggenberger soon found out, the Mediterranean was very different from the Atlantic and far less suited for submarine warfare. From their bases in Gibraltar, Malta and Egypt, British aircraft flew deadly aerial surveillance. Unlike the Atlantic, the Mediterranean did not offer the maneuvering room to concentrate large wolfpacks. The nature of the region also posed other significant problems. The weather was for the most part subtropical and the waters more transparent, thus allowing for easier detection of U-boats on the surface or running shallow at periscope depth. Cooperation with the Italians turned out to be more difficult than anyone anticipated, with recurrent problems of friend-foe identification. Logistical considerations also dogged the Axis boats. The German bases at La Spezia (near Genoa), Pola (on Croatia's Adriatic coast), Salamis (near Athens) and later Toulon (near Marseille) were few, under-equipped, understaffed and relatively remote from the scene of action. The narrows at Gibraltar, after November 1941 tightly patrolled by the British, could normally only be negotiated on moonless nights and with the greatest skill, courage and patience on part of the U-boat skippers. In fact, over the course of the war no fewer than 21 German boats had to abandon their attempts to break through the strait, while nine others were sunk in the process. No wonder that by December 1941 even U-Boat Command in its war diary would characterize the Mediterranean as a "mouse-trap." Moreover, mine-fields covered wide stretches of the Mediterranean and rendered navigation hazardous. But most important of all was the fact that there were few targets to attack, since enemy ship traffic was restricted to heavily guarded supply convoys along the African shoreline and to Malta. Post-war statistics reveal that over the entire span of the war, submarines in the Mediterranean on average sank only 7,300 tons of enemy shipping before they themselves went down, while the corresponding figure for Atlantic boats was 28,700 tons, four times higher. In short, the U-boat was clearly the wrong kind of weapon to dispatch to the Mediterranean.[15]

But orders were orders. Guggenberger and his crew prepared themselves to be among the first German boats to break through the Strait of Gibraltar as part of "Group Arnauld," named after Lothar von Arnauld de la Perière, Germany's top U-boat ace of World War I. Arnauld had achieved most of his spectacular triumphs in the Mediterranean, albeit under far more favorable conditions than could be expected in the 1940s. On Wednesday, October 29, 1941, after a layover of some six weeks, U-81 sailed from Brest and headed on southwesterly courses into the Bay of Biscay. These waters were close enough to England to be constantly threatened by enemy aircraft, and on the next day, despite having placed his lookouts on heightened alert, Guggenberger was caught on the surface by a long-range flying boat. The plane managed to drop several bombs before U-81 could dive, and although none hit directly, near-misses caused enough damage for Guggenberger to break off his mission and return to Brest for repairs. After four days of refitting U-81 was ready to sail again on November 4. This time she passed through the Bay of Biscay without incident and one week later stood before Gibraltar, the eighth German submarine to attempt the passage.[16]

The African coastline rose over the horizon as U-81 slowly moved along toward Tangier and Tarifa. Guggenberger had to be careful not to betray his presence to a Spanish freighter and several fishing boats in the vicinity as he angled silently toward the strait. The weather was partly cloudy with light westerly winds and occasional rain showers. By nightfall navigational lights along both the Spanish and African coast were clearly visible. Still on the surface, even though the moon peeked through the clouds from time to time, Guggenberger reached Cape Tarifa, Europe's southernmost tip, at 0150. Forty-five minutes later U-81 passed Gibraltar itself. As his war diary bears out, Guggenberger was both surprised and delighted over the absence of British patrol vessels, although he found the abundance of small fishing boats with their nets attached to lighted buoys an annoyance he had to sidestep as he carefully proceeded eastward. Shortly after 0600 on November 12, with U-81 safely through the danger zone, Guggenberger received a radio message ordering him and Reschke's U-205 to occupy a patrol position east of Gibraltar. The boats were to observe radio silence except to warn other boats of unexpected dangers or to report enemy vessels. Early the next morning, a Friday, having spent most of the intervening hours submerged, U-81 picked up a follow-up message advising that Italian reconnaissance planes had located a British task force of a battleship, an aircraft carrier and cruisers and destroyers heading in his direction from Malta. "Force K" was composed of the aircraft carriers *Ark Royal* and *Argus*, the battleship *Malaya*, the light cruiser *Hermione* and seven destroyers. They had delivered urgently needed aircraft to the British island bastion of Malta and were now homebound for Gibraltar.

Shortly after Guggenberger received notice of the approaching naval vessels, U-205 reported contact with the enemy force, which was steering west at an estimated 16 knots.[17]

Guggenberger saw to it that U-81 got ready for what now seemed an inevitable encounter. He deliberately closed to within 25 miles of Gibraltar "to improve our chances of scoring hits," since the restricted waters would require the enemy to steer predictable courses. He also ordered a test dive to ascertain that the boat functioned properly in every respect. A minor problem with the diesel engines and their exhaust systems restricted his surface speed somewhat but not enough to cause concern. During the afternoon a destroyer and several distant aircraft forced Guggenberger to submerge, but U-81 remained undetected by the enemy. At 1530 "Force K" itself steamed in sight in good visibility. Maneuvering carefully at periscope depth and estimating enemy speed at 16 knots, Guggenberger prepared to launch a spread of four torpedoes running 150 meters apart and set to hit their targets five meters below the waterline. At 1636, when the enemy had closed to within 4,000 yards, he gave the order to fire. The sudden weight loss of four torpedoes almost forced the boat to the surface, but by sending all hands into the forward compartment and by quickly adjusting the ballast tanks, Guggenberger and his chief engineer managed to keep the submarine's bow beneath the waves. With the torpedoes on their way, Guggenberger took U-81 down to 120 feet to await developments.

For a long time nothing happened. Then, six minutes and six seconds after launching the torpedoes, a loud detonation echoed through the boat. Guggenberger, who had taken aim at the battleship, thought the explosion signified a hit against her. A second explosion followed some 90 seconds later. The delay between the explosions caused Guggenberger and his crew to assume that they had scored a hit on a large destroyer or even an aircraft carrier farther off to starboard. At any rate, there was little time for speculation. Acting quickly, enemy destroyers moved out and caught U-81 in their sonar and counterattacked. Over the next five hours, from 1725 to 2220, while Guggenberger slowly moved off to the northeast and frequently changed speed, course and diving depth to throw off his pursuers, the British destroyers dropped some 160 depth charges around U-81. Fortunately for the boat's occupants, none of them detonated too closely. Shortly before midnight, after the enemy had given up the chase, Guggenberger brought his boat to the surface and ventilated U-81 with the clear air of a peaceful Mediterranean night. After recharging his boat's batteries, he moved U-81 closer to the African continent and spent most of November 14 resting on the sea floor four miles off the coast. Not until 0553 on Sunday morning, November 15, did he go on the air to report to Admiral Dönitz at U-Boat Command: "13 Nov 1636. Spread of 4 torpedoes against battleship, *Ark Royal, Furious.* First hit against battleship, second target uncertain. Square CH 7645." Later that day, after listening to Wehrmacht reports and other news, Guggenberger noted in his war diary that the first torpedo apparently had left the *Malaya* afloat but dead in the water, while with the second he had hit and sunk the *Ark Royal.*[18]

In actually Guggenberger had missed the *Malaya* altogether. At 1541 (1641 German time) one of his torpedoes had exploded under the bottom of the *Ark Royal* (22,600 tons) between her keel and starboard side. The detonation opened the carrier's starboard boiler room to the sea, and within a quarter hour the massive warship was listing 18 degrees. Over the next fourteen hours rescue efforts to save the carrier continued and an attempt was made to tow her to Gibraltar. While

U-81's hit on the *Ark Royal* on November 13, 1941. The British fleet carrier remained afloat for fourteen hours before finally sinking 25 miles from Gibraltar. *U-Boot-Archiv*

Crewmen from Guggenberger's U-81 celebrate the sinking of the *Ark Royal* during a stop-over in Messina, Sicily. *U-Boot-Archiv*

some initial progress was made and power and steam restored temporarily, the ship continued to take on water and the listing increased. Uncontrollable fires and explosions in her engine rooms signaled the death knell for the British carrier. Gradually those members of her crew who had remained aboard were taken off, and at 0613 on November 14, her list now at 45 degrees, the *Ark Royal* rolled over and sank just a few miles east of Gibraltar. Incredibly and fortunately, only one man lost his life in the disaster. In the words of an English chronicler, Guggenberger and his crew had "destroyed the very core of the Royal Navy's striking power in the Mediterranean" and were entitled to a special sense of satisfaction inasmuch as the *Ark Royal* had played a key role in the destruction of the German battleship *Bismarck* earlier that year.[19]

Nor was this the only bad news for the British from the Mediterranean Theater in late 1941. Ten days after the *Ark Royal* went down, Guggenberger's friend and Crew 34 comrade Hans-Diedrich Freiherr von Tiesenhausen in U-331 sank the battleship *Barham* (31,100 tons) south of Crete with heavy loss of life. Before the year was out, a third major warship fell victim to German torpedoes. On December 15,

1941, U-557, commanded by still another member of Crew 34, Ottokar Paulssen, destroyed the cruiser *Galatea* (5,220 tons) in the eastern Mediterranean. As German U-Boats scored these stunning successes at sea, Italian commandos made their way into the Royal Navy's anchorage at Alexandria on December 19 and disabled the battleships *Queen Elizabeth* and *Valiant* in a daring underwater raid. Indeed, by year's end Hitler must have felt vindicated in his insistence to transfer those boats from the Atlantic into the Mediterranean. Unfortunately for the Germans, however, these early successes were flukes, lucky strikes that could not be maintained and repeated in the long run. The British redoubled their efforts to protect their shipping in the Mediterranean and in particular to ensure that the bottle-neck at Gibraltar acted as the kind of "mouse-trap" U-Boat Command had long feared it might become.[20]

After a brief visit to Messina in Sicily, Guggenberger and U-81 moved on into the eastern Mediterranean. There, during the night from December 5-6 off the North African coast, they encountered and attacked a small British supply convoy. None of the torpedoes found their targets even though Guggenberger seemed convinced the observed detonations had damaged a destroyer, a tanker and a freighter. Most likely he mistook his torpedoes exploding at the end of their run, together with enemy depth charges, for the hits he reported. After this disappointing episode U-81 turned around and stood for her new base of La Spezia in Italy on the Tyrrhenian Sea, where she arrived on December 10 after one of the war's most remarkable U-boat missions. The Bavarian's success was not lost on U-Boat Command, and the same day Guggenberger steamed into La Spezia he was awarded the Knight's Cross for his distinguished service. Early the following year in March 1942, the Duke of Aosta decorated both Guggenberger and Tiesenhausen with the Italian Silver Medal for Bravery to show the appreciation of Germany's Axis partner.

U-81 now belonged to the 29th U-Boat Flotilla, which comprised all German boats operating in the Mediterranean. The flotilla's strength would vary as the enemy took a steady toll and new boats were fed in from the Atlantic to replace those lost. In the end 64 U-boats made the perilous passage through Gibraltar, but rarely were more than 20 of them present and active in the Mediterranean at any given moment. Fifty-nine boats were sunk on patrol, while others fell victim to air attacks against their bases. The last boat, U-596, was destroyed in Salamis on September 24, 1944, before she could fall into enemy hands.

Guggenberger undertook six more missions in U-81 in the Mediterranean and through them all his luck held, at least in the sense of bringing his men safely home after each patrol. Between January 27 and March 4, 1942, he undertook another foray into the eastern Mediterranean to help Field Marshall Erwin Rommel's efforts by frustrating British ship and troop movements along the Egyptian and Libyan coasts. Although U-81 encountered a British cruiser on the night of February 15, Guggenberger was unable to duplicate his earlier success against the *Ark Royal*. After obtaining a firing position, he loosed a spread of torpedoes at the warship which were heard to explode after a run of a little over 4 minutes, but no damage resulted. His failure was not unique, for throughout the entire month of February not a single Allied vessel was destroyed or damaged by Axis submarines in the Mediterranean—even though seven boats, including U-81, claimed to have inflicted injury upon the enemy.[21]

A three-week mission to the coast off Lebanon and Palestine in April was considerably more eventful for Guggenberger and his men. In the evening hours of April 16, U-81 managed to sink two vessels out of a small Allied convoy some ten miles south of Beirut, the French armed steam trawler *Viking* (1,150 tons) and the larger and more valuable British tanker *Caspia* (6,018 tons). Not content with these successes, Guggenberger spent the next ten days playing havoc among coastal sailing vessels in the area, destroying or severely damaging eight of them in succession either by artillery fire or ramming. Most of these vessels displaced around 100 tons and were not worth the expenditure of a precious torpedo. On April 25 Guggenberger returned to base, this time to historic Salamis near Athens, where the Greeks had defeated a much larger Persian force under King Xerxes in 480 B.C. and saved their independence in one of history's epic naval encounters. The famous island served as Germany's principal base for surface and U-boat operations in the eastern Mediterranean.

His next two patrols in May and June 1942 must have been especially frustrating for Guggenberger. Despite weeks of patrolling the dangerous Mediterranean waters, the net result was but a single unsuccessful attack against a tanker off the North African coast on the 11th of June. Even though Guggenberger later claimed he "observed a

large flash" and that the "tanker was left burning," Allied records do not
confirm the German skipper's claim. Again one must suspect that
wishful thinking and poor opportunities to observe actual success rather
than deliberate exaggeration came into play in this instance. While he
enjoyed little success against the enemy during these patrols, Guggenberger managed to save a number of valuable German lives when, on
June 2, he rescued and brought home to Salamis the entire crew of the
scuttled U-652. Georg-Werner Fraatz's boat had been caught on the
surface and fatally bombed by Allied aircraft. Fortunately for all involved, U-81 was near enough to render prompt assistance.[22]

From June 24 until October 5, 1942, U-81 and her men enjoyed a
prolonged break from the action as the boat underwent long scheduled
repairs and standard maintenance at La Spezia. In July and August
Guggenberger traveled north for a well-deserved five-week vacation in
Passau on the Danube, and in Ludwigsburg with his parents. When
Guggenberger returned to La Spezia and readied his boat for further
missions, the overall situation in the Mediterranean had begun to dete-
riorate rapidly for the Axis powers. In Egypt Rommel, the legendary
"Desert Fox," finally met his match in Field Marshal Sir Bernard
Montgomery, who defeated him at El Alamein and pushed him west.
Not long afterwards the Allies initiated "Operation Torch," the American landings in Morocco and Algeria designed to occupy formerly
French-held areas and put pressure on Rommel from the opposite direction. The Italians and Germans threw everything they had into the
region to hold their positions. For U-81, this meant operations against
the Allied invasion fleet off the Algerian coast.

Already underway since October 5 and on stand-by in the western
Mediterranean, Guggenberger received orders on November 7 to close
in on enemy units reported off the coast between Oran and Algiers. In
the early morning hours of November 10, U-81 sent a spread of torpedoes into an Allied formation before diving away to safety. Guggenberger later claimed to have damaged a freighter and a patrol vessel in this
encounter. In reality he sank the British vessel *Garlinge* (2,012 tons)
while his friend Wilhelm Dommes in U-431 sent a British destroyer to
the bottom in the same general vicinity. Three days later, in a rare
daylight attack on the afternoon of November 13—precisely one year
after hitting the *Ark Royal*—U-81 destroyed the escorted British motor
vessel *Maron* (6,487 tons) again immediately under the Algerian coast.

With these successes in hand, Guggenberger returned to La Spezia on November 16 to refuel and rearm. Just eight days later he was at sea again, heading for the U.S. invasion fleet. This time U-81's luck ran empty. After three frustrating weeks trying to break through the Allied defenses, Guggenberger received orders to return to a different base, Pola, located on the Istrian Peninsula in the Adriatic Sea, which once had been Austria's main stronghold in World War I.

Although he did not know it at the time, Guggenberger had made his last patrol in U-81. Orders awaited him in Pola to turn his command over to his I.W.O. Johann-Otto-Krieg and to report to BdU for further instructions. Leaving U-81 was not easy for Guggenberger. After all, this had been his first command, and he and his men had cobbled together a remarkable record in the Arctic Sea, the Atlantic, and all over the Mediterranean. One consolation was that he left the boat in experienced hands. U-81 continued to excel under Krieg, who likewise earned a Knight's Cross for his courage and leadership. U-81's luck continued to hold until an American air attack on Pola in January 1944 destroyed the boat in its base. Two crew members perished in the attack.

If Guggenberger had hoped his seafaring days were over, he was mistaken. But at least he got a temporary break from frontline duty and a further recognition of his outstanding performance. On January 8, 1943, at Führer Headquarters, Adolf Hitler himself bestowed upon Guggenberger the Oak Leaves cluster in addition to his Knight's Cross. The Bavarian commander was only the 18th U-boat officer to be so honored, the third in his Crew 34 after Engelbert Endrass and Erich Topp, and the first among U-boat commanders who had served in the Mediterranean. The ceremony lasted about ten minutes and included a brief address by Hitler, which Guggenberger later remembered as hesitant and lifeless to the point of incoherence. Afterwards Hitler invited Guggenberger and three fellow honorees for a more relaxed fireside chat. Hitler seemed profoundly shaken by the Stalingrad catastrophe, then in its last phase, and placed bitter blame on the Luftwaffe for having failed to keep Paulus' 6th Army supplied. He actually asked for Guggenberger's advice as to what to do: to continue to rely on conventional weapons or to hope that new technology might make the difference. Not surprisingly, the visit to Führer Headquarters left Guggenberger disappointed and depressed.[23]

The Oak Leaves cluster. Adolf Hitler bestowed the highly-coveted award upon Guggenberger and other holders of the Knight's Cross on January 8, 1943. They are (from left to right): Karl-Friedrich Merten, Wolfgang Lüth, Guggenberger and Werner Töniges (the latter an S-boat squadron commander). To Hitler's immediate right are his naval ADC Captain von Puttkamer and Grand Admiral Karl Dönitz. *U-Boot-Archiv*

The decorated U-boat ace was recalled soon after the awarding of the Oak Leaves and given command of a new, larger boat, U-847, which was then being completed at the Deschimag shipyard in Bremen. At close to 2,000 tons displacement and with a maximum range of 23,000 miles, this Type IX D2 boat was designed for long distance patrols as far away as the Indian and Pacific Oceans, where lucrative hunting grounds remained well away from the dangerous convoy routes of the North Atlantic. Guggenberger oversaw the completion and commissioning of U-847, but he would never take her into combat. On February 5 he was instructed to turn the boat over to Jost Metzler, a seasoned flotilla commander who wished to return to frontline duty.

Edged out in this manner, Guggenberger instead became an operational staff officer at BdU Headquarters in Paris (and later, Berlin). The Battle of the Atlantic was reaching its crucial phase, and Grand Admiral Dönitz, who recently had become Commander-in-Chief of the entire Kriegsmarine, wanted to create a small, intimate "anti-staff" of successful U-boat commanders who might share their valuable expertise and first-hand experience at a time when the larger regular staff appeared short on new ideas to invigorate Germany's effort at sea. Between February and May 1943, despite the fiercest convoy battles to date, U-boats began succumbing in frightfully large numbers to Allied superiority in materiel, manpower, technology, air power and—never fully realized by the Germans—cryptanalysis and intelligence. Even Guggenberger's advice could not prevent the terrible bloodletting of "Black May" 1943, when no fewer than 41 boats failed to return to their bases.

Despite the general anxiety pervading those months, or perhaps because of it, Guggenberger obtained leave from March 19 to April 13 for a very special occasion—his honeymoon. His bride was Brigitte Jenisch, née Steffan, who, according to personnel records, had either been divorced from her first husband or become widowed. Very likely there was a Navy connection, since at least two officers named Jenisch (Crews 29 and 33) had been skippers of U-boats early in the war, in U-22 and U-32, respectively. The former went down with his boat in 1940, while the latter had ended up in Allied captivity. At any rate, the wedding took place on March 21, 1943, in Saxony, where Guggenberger's future wife then resided.[24]

By mid-May 1943 Dönitz decided to return some of his experienced staff officers, among them Fritz Guggenberger, back to the front "to find out the cause of our heavy losses." The admiral also intended to shift the boats' operational areas to waters where Allied anti-submarine measures appeared less threatening than in the North Atlantic and Mediterranean.[25] Guggenberger's new boat was U-513, a Type IXC attached to the 10th U-Boat Flotilla in Lorient, France. Like U-847, U-513 was designed for long-distance operations, but

The decorated U-boat ace: Fritz Guggenberger wearing his Knight's Cross with Oak Leaves. *U-Boot-Archiv*

her effective range of 11,000 miles limited her to Atlantic waters. With 1,200 tons displacement, she was almost twice as large as U-81 and could carry 22 torpedoes instead of 14. She also mounted a 10.5-cm deck gun in addition to 3.7-cm and 2-cm anti-aircraft weaponry, and could run almost 19 knots when surfaced. U-513's complement of 53 officers and men was also larger than that of a Type VII boat.

Unlike U-847, U-513 was not a new boat. Her record was one of solid but not stellar success, accumulated the previous fall and in the recent spring offensives under her first skipper, Commander Rolf Rügge-berg of Crew 26. In operations off Newfoundland, in the Caribbean and in the central Atlantic, U-513 managed to sink two ships and damage a third. On her most recent return to Lorient in April 1943, U-513 barely missed being blown up by a mine but an hour away from her base. Now Guggenberger was to take her even farther afield into the South Atlantic to test Allied defenses along the coast of South America.[26]

On May 18, U-513 departed Lorient, negotiated the ever-dangerous Bay of Biscay unharmed, and made her way southwest into the Atlantic. Guggenberger placed special emphasis on diving drills, trying to reduce the interval from the first alarm to the time the boat ran safely below the surface. This precaution was all the more crucial since by mid-1943 Allied aircraft seemed to lurk everywhere, and a single second could make the difference between life and death for boat and crew.

By mid-June U-513 had reached its operational area off the Brazilian coast accompanied by U-199, commanded by Guggenberger's friend and Crew 34 comrade Hans-Werner Kraus. Kraus was also a veteran of the Mediterranean theater of operations, where he had been in charge of U-83. The fellow Crew member had likewise earned a Knight's Cross for his successes in that arena. It did not take long for the German boats to begin scoring successes. On June 21 Guggenberger drew first blood when he sank the small Swedish vessel *Venezia* (1,673 tons) in the shipping lanes southeast of Rio de Janeiro. In the same waters four nights later U-513's torpedoes damaged the larger and more valuable American tanker *Eagle* (6,003 tons), which managed to limp into port on her own power. These were indeed good hunting grounds for the Axis boats, and enemy defenses both at sea and in the air were much less alert than in the North Atlantic. In the first three days of July Guggenberger added two more victims to his tonnage score, the Brazilian steamer *Tutolia* (1,125 tons) and the modern American freighter

Guggenberger's last command, U-513, was a large Type IXC boat. This photo shows a sister boat, U-516, on patrol. Note the 10.5-cm deck gun and the 3.7-cm. anti-aircraft gun mounted forward and aft, respectively, of the conning tower. *U-Boot-Archiv*

Elihu B. Washburne (7,176 tons). Cruising slowly down the coast, U-513 bagged yet another Liberty ship off Florianopolis on July 16, the *Richard Caswell* (7,177 tons), which was en route from Buenos Aires to New York. With two torpedoes left, Guggenberger reversed course and moved back up toward Rio, possibly with the intention of sinking the old Brazilian guard destroyer patrolling offshore. He also went on the air with a long message home reporting his latest successes and the ease with which he was able to prey on the largely unescorted ship traffic along the South American coast. Guggenberger suggested that Dönitz dispatch additional boats as soon as possible.[27]

The events that followed must be reconstructed from Allied records and Guggenberger's personal recollections, because U-513's war diary went down with the boat and Guggenberger sent no further recorded radio messages. To all appearances his lengthy radio signals enabled Allied interceptors to obtain a fix on his exact position. On July 19, a two-engine U.S. PBM Mariner attached to the nearby seaplane tender *Barnegat* (AVP-10) and piloted by Lieutenant (j.g.) R. S. Whitcomb took off to look for the reported submarine. Whitcomb located the unsuspecting U-513 on the surface 40 miles off the coast and immediately closed in for a bombing run from an altitude of about 300 feet. Blinded by the sun peeking through the cumulus clouds, the lookouts on the bridge had barely enough time to alert Guggenberger, who was resting below, to the rapidly approaching danger. Before U-513 could even open fire with her automatic weapons or change course and speed, let alone dive, four bombs bracketed the doomed boat. One of the charges detonated directly on her bow section, and this single hit sealed the U-boat's fate. As sea water rushed into the perforated forward compartment, U-513 dropped like a rock toward the ocean floor. Only the bridge personnel and gun crews, a dozen men, had an opportunity to jump into the water. Everyone else perished as U-513 took her final plunge.[28]

The twelve survivors, many of them wounded, found themselves scattered over a radius of about 1000 feet when the American flying boat dropped a life raft and life vests among them. In the end only seven men had the strength to drag themselves onto the raft. Among the lucky survivors was the severely wounded and barely conscious Fritz Guggenberger, whom his fellow survivors managed to pull into the tiny raft by his hair. Sharks attacked and killed at least two of the others, who disappeared beneath the surface and were not seen again.

The luck of the seven survivors continued to hold when, five hours after U-513 had gone down, the *Barnegat* arrived on the scene to pick them up and take them to Rio de Janeiro. Guggenberger was the most critically injured of the bunch, having partially broken three vertebrae, several ribs and one of his ankles—among other problems, including blood loss and shock. After receiving initial medical attention he was flown from a Brazilian military base near Rio to Miami, Florida, and from there to Washington, D.C. At the Bethesda Naval Hospital American surgeons gradually restored his health so that by October he could be transferred to a regular POW camp in Crossville, Tennessee. In January 1944, following routine interrogations by U.S. intelligence personnel at Fort Hunt, Virginia, Guggenberger was transferred to a camp at Papago Park in Phoenix, Arizona.

At Papago Park Guggenberger met up with several fellow U-boat commanders, including three of his own Crew 34. Hans Werner Kraus' U-199 had experienced an almost identical fate as U-513 when she succumbed to an air attack off Rio de Janeiro on July 31, just twelve days after Guggenberger's debacle. Camp resident U-595's Jürgen Quaet-Faslem was, like Kraus and Guggenberger, a veteran of the Mediterranean campaign. August Maus of U-185, the fourth member of Crew 34, had been captured in August 1943 in the central Atlantic after many distinguished combat missions. The Allied authorities did not realize the danger inherent in throwing together men of such resilience and ability. Unwilling to sit out the remainder of the war behind barbed wire, the U-boat veterans and old friends developed a brilliant scheme to escape from the camp with the hope of crossing into nearby Mexico, which they mistakenly supposed to be still neutral. The ultimate goal was to make it home to Germany. The result was the largest POW breakout from an American camp during the entire war, entertainingly retold by John Hammond Moore in his book, *The Faustball Tunnel*.[29]

Actually there were two attempts. In the first one on Saturday, February 12, 1944, Maus and Guggenberger—the latter playing the role of a stranded Greek sailor because of his poor English as well as his dark hair and complexion—were smuggled out of the compound by fellow prisoners in a truck on a work detail. The pair managed to make it by train to Tucson, where they learned that no buses or trains ran into Nogales, Mexico, until the following Monday. Unsure what to do next, they decided to wait at the bus depot, where an alert police officer ended their excursion and returned them to Papago Park. Paradoxically, no one in the camp had missed the escapees, even though they were gone some thirty-six hours. While Maus and Guggenberger were quickly recaptured, a second group of German officers, including Quaet-Faslem, actually made it 40 miles into Mexico, sleeping by day and walking at night. Two weeks into their adventure they were finally recognized, arrested and returned to their camp without any great formality—despite efforts to remain in Mexican custody and prolong their outing.

From this earlier experience plans emerged for a more ambitious mass escape. Virtually unmolested, the prisoners used much of the fall of 1944 to dig a 178-foot tunnel underneath the outer fences of their compound to a drainage canal beyond the wire. On a dark and rainy December 23, 1944, with a weekend approaching and their guards' minds diverted by Christmas preparations (as well as deliberate distractions staged by other prisoners), 25 officers and enlisted men slipped out of camp in small groups, among them Guggenberger and Quaet-Faslem. Their idea was to reach the Gila River, since maps indicated that one might be able to raft on it or just follow it practically all the way to Mexico. Unbeknownst to the prisoners, who had no firsthand experience with the Arizona countryside, the river is actually dry for most of the year. Incredibly, the camp authorities did not learn of the break-out for some twenty-four hours, although a massive manhunt was ordered once the prisoners were found missing. Eventually all escapees were recaptured. Guggenberger and Quaet-Faslem managed to get within ten miles of the Mexican border and enjoyed two weeks of freedom before a search group caught up with them on January 6, 1945. Thus ended Fritz Guggenberger's last wartime adventure.

In May 1946, the 31-year-old Guggenberger returned to Germany to pick up the pieces of his life. For a time he worked as a bricklayer and later as a civilian employee for the U.S. occupation forces in southern Germany. Although he would have preferred to enter medical school, the lengthy course requirements caused him to consider other avenues of study. He eventually settled on architecture, since the curriculum could be completed relatively quickly in eight semesters. But the sea was not done with Guggenberger. By late 1955, shortly after he had opened his own architectural firm, the newly-created West German Navy offered him reactivation at the initial rank of Commander.

Without much hesitation Guggenberger accepted this opportunity to resume his former career. Rising in rank to full Captain by 1961 and Rear Admiral by 1968, he held over the years a number of challenging appointments both ashore and with the fleet. They included a year at the U.S. Naval War College in Newport, Rhode Island, and two years as Chief of Staff to the German representative of the NATO Military Committee in Washington, D.C., at the time of the 1961 Berlin Crisis. His last position before retirement to Garmisch in December 1972 was that of Deputy Chief-of-Staff for Planning and Operations at the NATO Command AFNORTH in Oslo, Norway. Guggenberger's post-war career closely paralleled that of his good friend and Crew 34 comrade Erich Topp. Topp, who had also studied architecture after the war, was reactivated in 1958 and served both in Washington, D.C., and in desk jobs in Bonn. The former enterprising commander of the Red Devil Boat also rose to the rank of Rear Admiral, and had been slated for the same NATO position in Oslo that eventually went to Guggenberger.[30]

On a more personal note, Guggenberger's first marriage did not survive the long separation occasioned by his three years in captivity. In 1949 he married his second wife, Liselotte, with whom he had five children, including a pair of twins. By all appearances it was a happy and successful union despite the many relocations that necessarily accompany a military officer's career. One can imagine how much the two later enjoyed their retirement years in the Bavarian Alps.

In November 1987 the Guggenbergers moved to a nursing home in the town of Erlenbach on the Main River. By this time Guggenberger was suffering severely from Alzheimer's disease. On May 13, 1988, he told his wife he was going out for an extended walk. He never returned. Despite an immediate search he remained missing for more than two years until his badly decomposed body was accidentally discovered not far from Erlenbach. Positive identification was only possible thanks to his wedding band. His date of death at the age of 73 was fixed as the day on which he had wandered away from his home. His wife died on January 21, 1991, apparently still uncertain about her husband's fate.[31]

Fritz Guggenberger's tragic end was indeed a sad conclusion to a remarkable human odyssey.

*   *   *

Victor Oehrn of U-37, returning from his first, and most successful, patrol. In only 85 days at sea, Oehrn sank 24 ships totaling just over 100,000 GRT, possibly the most economical use of time by a U-boat commander in World War II. *Courtesy of Victor Oehrn*

Jordan Vause

Victor Otto Oehrn

The Ace With No Name

easured by the number of ships he sank, the awards he won or the days he spent on patrol, Victor Otto Oehrn does not favorably compare with many other World War II U-boat aces. Oehrn is never placed in the same category as U-Bootwaffe superstars Otto Kretschmer or Günther Prien, for example, nor in the company of the "gray wolves" as a group. Strictly speaking, Oehrn was a staff officer, a member of a much-derided class of shore-bound U-boat officers. He commanded a U-boat in combat for less than six months, and as he admitted, he was for most of the war "a man with no name," who labored behind a desk for the greater glory of his superiors. Thus he has little if any reputation outside either the historical community or the parochial confines of the U-Bootwaffe. Many people have never heard of him at all.[1]

Oehrn always displayed the virtues that marked the real German military—the organization behind the facade of National Socialism. He represents the lineage of the Prussian military system and the naval tradition that Kriegsmarine commander-in-chief Erich Raeder always wanted for Germany. He is a dignified man, self-effacing, loyal to his country and to his military superiors—but aware of their shortcomings. Oehrn makes no effort to defend the system he fought for, but he will defend Germany—a distinction that escapes many of his peers. He listens to criticism of his service without rancor, and responds politely. He is a gentleman and a professional. He is, perhaps, the ideal U-boat officer, eagerly sought after by apologists of the service—and the one so often ignored in favor of the meteoric Prien or the tenacious Kretschmer.

And yet Oehrn is a remarkable man who deserves recognition for his stellar—and unique—service. He was anything but a common desk lackey and in fact was Karl Dönitz's A1—his Deputy Chief of Staff for Operations—for most of the war. In this role Oehrn was responsible for planning many of the special operations and most of the (relatively) routine patrol activity that made the U-Bootwaffe such a terrible weapon in its time and such a captivating entity in the public imagination then and today. Günther Prien's sinking of the *Royal Oak* in 1939 and the U-boat offensive of 1940 are two conspicuous examples of Oehrn's influence. During the brief time he was a commander at sea, Oehrn sank enough tonnage during his three patrols to win the Knight's Cross. In addition, he is given considerable credit for restoring U-Bootwaffe morale after the disastrous torpedo failures of the spring of 1940. Finally, he achieved a personal victory during the war unique in his branch of service: he was gravely wounded in a land battle, captured by the enemy, imprisoned, repatriated and restored to his position—all within eighteen months.

*   *   *

Victor Otto Oehrn was born in Kedabeg in the southern part of Russia on October 21, 1907. His place of birth set him apart, along with a very small percentage of his fellow commanders, as an Auslandsdeutscher, a German national born and raised outside Germany. His father, a director in the Siemens Corporation, was stationed in the Caucasus, and the young Victor grew up comfortably in a country that was at once foreign and intimately familiar to him. "Many nationalities, races, and religions lived together peaceably in my parents' house," he wrote. "My first teacher. . .was a Frenchwoman: Mlle. Glere. Our servant and our cook were Armenians, the driver and many of the female help were Russian, and so was the washerwoman. The gardener, the grounds keepers, and the guards were Tartars."[2] As a result of this mix his life was forever colored by the images of devout Muslims, fierce Tartars and sturdy Slavs, for all of whom he harbors lasting affection. Oehrn speaks perfect Russian, and his philosophy of life reflects both the fatalism of

Islam and the resilience of Christianity. His love of the old Russia, however, did not translate into an equal love for the new Soviet Union. In 1921, the Bolsheviks drove his family out of the country under threat of death, and he developed an intense hatred of Communism and a strong nationalism that is the mark of the Auslandsdeutscher. The concept of a Greater Germany, in whose borders all ethnic Germans might safely live, appealed to many people in Oehrn's situation. It was something that Adolf Hitler would later find easy to manipulate.

Oehrn finished his education in the more conventional setting of Berlin before joining the Reichsmarine at the age of nineteen. He became a member of Crew 27, one of the small band of officer candidates who survived the rigorous selection process conducted annually to ensure the "suitability" of officers in a postwar navy. His basic training was conducted in April 1927 on the Dänholm, a desolate island on the Baltic coast.

Oehrn's reason for joining the Reichsmarine was less common than most. When asked why they joined the naval service, many U-boat veterans will give adventure, prestige, travel or perhaps family history as their first motivation.[3] For Oehrn, it was a desire to correct the wrongs he believed had been inflicted upon Germany by her former enemies. "One often reads in modern history that the decisive point in our development was the Treaty of Versailles," he explained. "Germany considered this 'treaty,' which had the effect of strangling her, to be stupid, short-sighted, unjust, and discriminatory. This is the reason I decided to enter the German military." Even his place of birth played a role in his decision. "I am an Auslandsdeutscher. I knew from experience what it was like to be unprotected and I wanted to do what I could to change that."[4]

U-boats could not have affected his decision to join the navy, for there weren't any in the Reichsmarine when he joined the service. Submarines had been banned by the Treaty of Versailles, and although a great deal of secret research in submarines and submarine warfare was being carried out with a view toward eventual return of the U-boats, Oehrn had no reasonable knowledge of it. In any case he had become rather comfortable in the surface fleet. After basic training and the Marineschule Mürwik (the German Naval Academy) had come his first junior officer assignment in the light cruiser Königsberg, followed by shore duty as a company officer on the Dänholm and the light cruiser

Karlsruhe. The last billet was a prestigious position in the woefully small Reichsmarine. The *Karlsruhe*, Germany's showcase warship, often circled the globe as a training platform for new officer candidates. At that time U-boats must have seemed very small and damp to Oehrn—relics of the old navy and a futile pursuit for the ambitious officer of the New Order.

Oehrn was initially approached about possible assignment to the U-boat service in 1934 while serving on the *Karlsruhe*. "My old Seekadett training officer Fritz Bonte, who [in 1940] commanded the German destroyers at Narvik, was Chief of Personnel for Naval Station East at that time," recalled Oehrn. "When I left for the 1934 world cruise in *Karlsruhe* as a training officer he asked me what I would like to do when I returned. 'If there are U-boats,' he said, "would you like to be assigned to them?' I said no. 'If I did that. . .I would have to spend my life looking through a periscope.'"[5]

Despite his firm initial refusal, Oehrn joined the U-Bootwaffe just one year later. He never explained why. It is difficult to believe his earlier ambivalence vanished so quickly. The young officer had never set foot on a U-boat, nor had he yet met the charismatic Kapitän zur See Karl Dönitz, commander of the first new U-boat flotilla "Weddigen." When the two finally did meet, however, Oehrn found a man he respected and admired, an officer he wanted to follow for the rest of his life. From that day forward he took to the U-Bootwaffe as a fish to water.

When Karl Dönitz took command of Flotilla Weddigen, he had already conceived a mission, a strategy, an order of battle, a set of tactics and a support organization for a future U-boat fleet of 300 boats. Such a comprehensive vision as Dönitz's also required a large and efficient officer corps, which had to be built from scratch. Veterans from the first war were not a part of Dönitz's plan: they had their own ideas and might be reluctant to conform to the new tactics he envisioned employing. He preferred men he could train himself and upon whose loyalty he could always rely. As a result, Flotilla Weddigen's first twelve commanders were surface fleet officers, men relatively young and unfamiliar with submarine warfare but eager to learn and willing to follow Dönitz into hell if that was what it took to please him. Although few of these "apostles" of the new fleet would go on to become successful in war,

Admiral Karl Dönitz. Dönitz recognized Oehrn's organizational abilities early on and began to groom him as a staff officer. *National Archives*

they laid the groundwork and set the standards for those who would follow.

One of the twelve apostles in January 1936 was Victor Oehrn, who was given command of U-14, a small 250-ton Type II boat known within the service as an Einbaum, or "canoe." He led his crew for almost two years in a grinding schedule of drills in Mecklenburg Bight and extended exercises at sea. The U-Bootwaffe grew steadily during this period. Another flotilla was added in 1936, and Dönitz was bumped up to become Führer der U-Boote (Commander, U-Boats, or FdU). Despite his high rank Dönitz never forgot a face, lost touch with one of his officers, or flagged in his efforts to forge his men into the best submariners in the world. When they went to war, he told his crews, it would never be as bad as it was at home in Mecklenburg Bight. Along with the basic tools and tactics of submarine warfare, many of which had not been used for almost twenty years, Dönitz ran his boats through newer and more sophisticated exercises. His crews, for example, were trained to operate at night on the surface, with both air and surface support. More significantly, his U-boats learned to operate in groups controlled from a central point by means of radio communications. This last development, which was to become Dönitz's most potent tactic of the war, was called Rudeltaktik, later known as "wolfpack." Victor Oehrn spent months absorbing these new principles in a rigorous and stressful training program which was to prove very useful to him in ways that he could not have imagined.

While Oehrn enjoyed U-boat command and was very good in that role, other talents also began to display themselves. One of these was in the thankless domain of staff work. Dönitz recognized Oehrn's organizational abilities early on and began to groom him as a staff officer. After he left U-14, Oehrn was sent back to the Marineschule for a tour as a company commander, attended formal U-boat school in Neustadt, and completed a course and subsequent training cruise as an admiralty staff officer. In August 1939 he was assigned to the staff of Kapitän zur See Oskar Schomburg, who would soon direct U-boat operations in the Baltic during the Polish Campaign. When the war began Oehrn was reassigned to FdU as first admiralty staff officer (First Asto, or simply A1). Stationed at Dönitz's headquarters in Sengwarden, Oehrn suddenly found himself responsible for planning U-boat operations. He would hold that important position, in one capacity or another and with only two interruptions, from that day until the end of the war. He was standing at Karl Dönitz's side on September 3, 1939, the day Great Britain declared war on Germany, and he would be there on May 5, 1945, the day Dönitz sent a final signal to his boats calling them back from six exhausting years of combat. And it was in this position that he would make his first major contribution to the war effort.

The best known U-boat operation of the war was the penetration of the Royal Navy anchorage at Scapa Flow by Günther Prien in October 1939, and his subsequent sinking of the battleship *Royal Oak*. The Scapa Flow operation returned the threatening image of the U-boat to the public mind, and allowed Dönitz to solidify his rather tenuous grasp on the resources and prestige he felt his service needed to survive and prosper. The attack also made a hero out of Prien, who primarily because of that exploit is today perhaps the most renowned U-boat ace of World War II. Victor Oehrn, who was laboring in the bowels of the wooden huts at Sengwarden before, during and after the operation, is rarely mentioned in connection with Scapa Flow. Yet, it was Oehrn who recognized that a penetration of the British anchorage was possible, and he planned the operation from start to finish.

Scapa Flow was a heavily-guarded body of water surrounded by seven large clumps of windswept Scottish dirt that make up most of the Orkney Islands. During the First World War U-boats had twice attempted to enter Scapa Flow; both boats were lost. In 1919, the Imperial German Navy had suffered the additional ignominy of having to scuttle its own ships in Scapa Flow to prevent them from being distributed between the winners of the war. The thought of slipping a U-boat into the sacred naval anchorage was therefore doubly appealing to Dönitz, who realized that a successful penetration was an almost impossible proposition. Reconnaissance by both submarines and aircraft revealed that two of the entrances to Scapa Flow were open in 1939 but heavily patrolled, while the rest were obstructed by sunken ships held in place with large chains or cables anchored on land. Carefully sifting through the evidence, Oehrn discerned that despite its obstructions, Kirk Sound—one of a half-dozen entrances into Scapa Flow—might be accessible on the surface at high tide. His excruciatingly detailed planning managed to convince first Dönitz and then Prien, a daredevil by nature, that the operation was indeed possible.

The hazardous undertaking was a major success. Following Oehrn's operational plan, Prien guided U-47 into Scapa Flow on the evening of October 13, 1939, and after some amount of agitated searching in an almost empty anchorage, found and attacked *Royal Oak*. After two salvoes the aging battleship turned turtle and sank, taking with her to the cold bottom of Scapa Flow almost 900 men. Prien escaped and returned to a hero's welcome in Germany, where he was greeted in Wilhelmshaven by Dönitz and Erich Raeder. Prien and his entire crew were flown to Berlin and trooped through the streets and into the Chancellery, where U-47's commander was personally decorated by Adolf Hitler with one of the first Knight's Crosses. For Prien, Scapa Flow was the beginning of a new career as a media star. For Dönitz, who now held the title of Befehlshaber der U-Boote (Commander-in-Chief, U-Boats, or BdU), Scapa Flow meant a promotion to flag rank and a much-needed infusion of money and resources for the tiny U-Boot-waffe. Oehrn, however, was never publicly recognized for Prien's success, and to this day has not sought the recognition he deserves for the operation. "The staff officer," he wrote, quoting the nineteenth-century German field marshal von Moltke, "has no name."[6]

While Oehrn was an excellent staff officer, he was keenly aware of the distinction between officers like him, who did most of their work in the relatively safe confines of an office, and the commanders at sea, who risked their lives in frontline boats. He also knew that everyone else drew the same distinction. As a result, the desk-bound Oehrn envied his fellow officers in the boats. This was especially so when he found himself in close contact with them, such as when he delivered his pier-side briefings to departing commanders and handed them their orders. (This ritual was called the "last rites," for reasons that became increasingly obvious as the war went on.) He refused to wear the Iron Cross (Second Class) that Dönitz awarded him for his role in Scapa Flow, believing that staff officers had no right to wear what he regarded to be an award for valor. Despite his discomfort with his situation, Oehrn continued to perform his duties well and never openly complained. But the perceptive Dönitz could not have missed Oehrn's desire for service on the amorphous and ever changing line in the sea that U-boat sailors simply called "the front."

Oehrn's role in the expanding war changed dramatically shortly after the Norwegian campaign, which in spite of Oehrn's usual planning genius, was a debacle for the U-boats. The disaster was largely due to the failure of the new electric torpedo systems. Morale among the U-boat crews plunged, and commanders were openly upset at having to fight with torpedoes that routinely failed to detonate. The situation was so desperate that Dönitz had little choice but to recall his boats into port to address the matter and reassure his crews. After this dismal state of affairs had dragged on for several weeks, Dönitz called Oehrn into his office. How long, the admiral wanted to know, would it take a veteran commander to prepare an unfamiliar boat for sea? Five days, Oehrn replied. To the staff officer's utter shock, Dönitz informed him that he had five days to prepare U-37, a 750-ton Type IX boat, for patrol. Oehrn, Dönitz continued, was U-37's new commander, and would be the first man to go back to sea on a new offensive. The date was May 10, 1940, the day Germany invaded the low countries. A grateful Oehrn left BdU at once for his new command and somehow managed to take his new boat out of Wilhelmshaven in just under his own prescribed time.[7]

If there was any point in Victor Oehrn's career when he shed his cloak of anonymity and became, at least temporarily, a well-known figure in Germany, it was upon his return from his first war patrol as commander of U-37. Traditionally, this is because Oehrn—by being the first commander to complete a patrol after the resounding collapse of U-Bootwaffe morale in April—helped redeem the German torpedo and thus restored the spirit of the service. His patrol also initiated the highly successful U-boat campaign of late 1940 that would come to be known as the "happy times" of the U-Bootwaffe. But in this case tradition is not entirely correct. Oehrn was not the first commander out after the Norwegian debacle; that distinction belongs to Wolfgang Lüth, commander of the tiny Type II *einbaum* U-9. Lüth, working in the North Sea and the English Channel, sank four ships in two patrols with the same torpedos Oehrn used, and he returned from his second outing before Oehrn returned from his first. As for the torpedos, Oehrn seems to have had no fewer problems than anyone else, and had to resort in many cases to sinking his targets with his deck gun. It is difficult to picture an entire officer corps hoisting itself back on its feet because one of their number enjoyed a successful patrol. U-boat morale was boosted less by Victor Oehrn than by the triumph of the Wehrmacht in Europe, the occupation of France, and by the fact that the men who crewed the boats were an incredibly resilient bunch to start with.[8]

Nonetheless Oehrn deserves recognition for conducting an extremely successful maiden combat patrol. Though it lasted just 26 days, he sank ten ships for a total of 41,000 gross registered tons (GRT).[9] Like all commanders he made some mistakes, was lucky enough to survive them, and went on to learn from them. As Dönitz' A1, for example, he had routinely told commanders to use the Fair Island Gap when exiting the North Sea into the Atlantic. After being attacked from the air while following his own advice, however, he realized that the route was ill-advised. He also had no idea how to act with survivors, which led to at least one awkward situation after a sinking in which he attempted to engage enemy crewmen in lifeboats with cheerful conversation. Despite these troubles, however, the patrol was a superb undertaking—especially when one considers that it was launched on just five days notice by a man who had not commanded a U-boat in three years and never in wartime. Oehrn had every reason to be pleased when he sailed into Wilhelmshaven on June 9 with the aplomb of a well-fed schoolmaster amidst a crowd of small boys.

Hungry for heroes, the German media was waiting to pounce on U-37. Oehrn's exploits were celebrated with front page stories and pictures of him and his crew. Dönitz, whose gamble in choosing Oehrn had obviously paid off, basked in the glory as well. "The spell had been broken," the admiral wrote in his memoirs. "The fighting powers of the U-boat had once again been proved. My convictions had not played me false. It will be readily appreciated that I was particularly grateful to the commander of U-37 for what he had achieved," Dönitz wrote, "for he, too, understood how much depended upon the success or otherwise of his patrol. Now, however, the other U-boats put to sea convinced that what U-37 had done, they, too, could do." For the time being Oehrn was a bona fide U-boat hero, much as Prien had been when he returned from Scapa Flow. Given the difficult circumstances under which Oehrn operated and the success he achieved, the award of a mere Iron Cross (First Class) the day after his return seems rather unimaginative.[10]

But fame is usually fleeting, and Oehrn's case was no exception. His second war patrol, which began August 1 in Wilhelmshaven, Germany, and ended 29 days later in Lorient, France, drew almost no notice from the German propaganda machine. The oversight is difficult to understand, especially since Oehrn was able to sink eight ships for about 33,000 GRT. The lack of attention was probably for the best, for although the cruise was almost as successful as his first patrol, Oehrn and his crew came within a hair's breadth of returning as war criminals instead of U-boat heroes. The fast pace of the war at sea often made the distinction between hero and criminal a thin one, as postwar trials would prove, and the events that played out during Oehrn's second combat patrol demonstrated how easy—and quickly—it was to swing from one extreme to the other.[11]

On August 23, three weeks into his second patrol, Oehrn sighted the British steamer *Severn Leigh* and sank her with gunfire. During the barrage a wayward shell struck the side of the ship and a lifeboat that had been lowered took the full force of the blast and much of the resulting shrapnel. The boat tumbled down the hull of the sinking ship, dumping its human contents into the sea. Even from a distance Oehrn could see that the damage to the boat and its occupants was serious. The incident so unnerved Oehrn that he considered sinking the remaining lifeboats with gunfire so no survivors would be left to tell the tale. He went so far as to order his guns trained on the boats—but could not give the command to fire. As he describes the tense moment in his memoirs, the standoff lasted for several breathless minutes before common sense prevailed and he guided his boat into the field of flotsam to offer assistance to the survivors instead of death.

Anyone who knows Victor Oehrn finds such an incident hard to believe, but there are at least three reasons that account for his balancing act on the thin line between successful commander and war criminal. First, as A1 Oehrn was well aware of the adverse consequences of any act that could conceivably inflame the enemy and its media outlets. He knew of the *Athenia* incident, for example, in which a British passenger liner was sunk without warning in September 1939, and Dönitz's subsequent attempts to cover it up. Second, Oehrn knew also that Adolf Hitler had declared unrestricted submarine warfare around the British Isles just days before he sank the *Severn Leigh*. With his blunder coming so soon afterward, there was little doubt the enemy press would magnify and distort the account to suit their needs. Lastly, Oehrn's reaction was in part based on instinct—the tendency to hide one's errors is human nature. It is to Oehrn's everlasting credit that he overcame this tendency.[12]

Oehrn completed his third and final war patrol on October 22, 1940, after four weeks at sea. Like his previous pair of patrols, his third outing was also successful, netting him six ships for approximately 30,000 GRT. His total for three patrols was 24 ships for 104,000 GRT.[13] His numbers were impressive and compared favorably to many of the aces—especially since it had only taken him three patrols to eclipse the 100,000 GRT mark, which qualified a commander for the Knight's Cross. Despite passing the 100,000 ton plateau, Oehrn did not do as well on his third patrol as many of the boats then at sea. Several circumstances contributed to Germany's significant victories in the North Atlantic in October 1940, including Dönitz's wolfpack tactics, the forward basing of U-boats in France and the critical lack of resources on the part of the enemy. Two running engagements in which German wolfpacks tore up Allied convoys SC 7 and HX 79, for example—the "Night of the Long Knives"—are legends in naval warfare and often used to describe both the ferocity of the U-boat in general and the performance of the great aces (Otto Kretschmer, Günther Prien, Heinrich Liebe, Heinrich Bleichrodt, Joachim Schepke, Fritz Frauenheim, and Herbert Schütze, to name but a few), in particular. Oehrn was not considered on the same level as these men, and whether he had the luck—or the innate ferocity—to survive for long in the unforgiving arena of the North Atlantic is an open question. For reasons known only to Dönitz, the admiral made an unexpected decision at the end of October and relieved Oehrn of command, turning over U-37 to her first watch officer, Nicolai Clausen. The blow was softened by the award of the Knight's Cross, and with a promise that he would be given a second boat at a later date. But Victor Oehrn never get another boat, and as a result never enjoyed the opportunity to achieve the heights of a Prien or a Kretschmer.[14]

In assessing Oehrn's performance as a U-boat commander, three accomplishments mark him as an officer of special merit. First, the fact that a staff officer with no wartime experience could take command of a boat, and with but five days notice succeed as he did, is in itself extraordinary. BdU and OKM staff officers occasionally received U-boat commands, but their performances were usually unexceptional and sometimes tragic. Second, his ratio of GRT to days at sea was very high: i.e., he managed to find and sink ships quickly. Oehrn claims to have won his Knight's Cross after fewer days on patrol (85) than any other commander. Although his claim is difficult to verify, it seems to be contradicted in any case by Günther Prien's award in 1939. Third, Oehrn played a role and deserves some credit—however qualified—for initiating the highly successful U-boat offensive of 1940.[15]

Though there may have been other reasons that contributed to Oehrn's reassignment, the primary motive behind Dönitz's decision seems to have been his own lack of a good staff. With the Battle of the Atlantic heating up, Dönitz badly needed Oehrn back at his old desk directing operational planning. With combat experience beneath his belt Oehrn was even more valuable to Dönitz than before. In addition, Oehrn had jettisoned some dangerous preconceptions about U-boat warfare (and Dönitz may have privately hoped that Oehrn's constant yearning for sea duty was behind him). On October 27, 1940, he reported to Dönitz's new headquarters at Kerneval, a large villa built by a sardine merchant on the outskirts of Lorient, France. He held the post of A1 for thirteen months, during which time the fortunes of the U-Bootwaffe would take a rather drastic turn for the worse.

The U-Bootwaffe lost three of its best and high profile commanders the following March when Günther Prien and Joachim Schepke were killed at sea, and Otto Kretschmer was captured and sent to Britain (and eventually Canada) as a prisoner of war. Two months later the battleship *Bismarck* was lost, having failed in her bid to draw her pursuers across a line of U-boats that Oehrn had set up as a trap in the North Atlantic. Two significant events transpired in June: one was of epic proportions but of little immediate import for the U-boats, while the other held greater significance for U-boat operations but was unappreciated (because it was unknown to the Germans) at the time. On June 22, 1941, Germany invaded the Soviet Union. Six weeks earlier on May 10, U-110, commanded by Fritz-Julius Lemp (who had torpedoed the *Athenia* earlier in the war), was sunk and Lemp was killed under mysterious circumstances. More importantly for the Germans, the boat was not properly scuttled. British sailors were able to board the submarine and recover an enigma machine and other valuable code books and intelligence information that would soon enable them to decipher U-boat radio signals. Another stunning command lapse followed two months later when the commander of U-570, Hans-Joachim Rahmlow, surrendered his U-boat at sea. Rahmlow allowed the Royal Navy to capture and tow his boat back to Britain, where she was thoroughly tested before being put into service as the *HMS Graph.* And all during that fateful summer the warships of the United States Navy had begun to make their presence felt in the convoy lanes. Although not officially at war with Germany, the actions of the American ships were becoming increasingly provocative as the end of the year approached.[16]

Neither Oehrn nor anyone at BdU had any idea of the loss they had suffered with U-110. While the Germans occasionally raised suspicions about the security of their communications, the U-boat high command never realized that U-boat radio traffic was being intercepted and read on a daily basis. Rahmlow's decision to blithely deliver his boat to the enemy made him an outcast in the U-Bootwaffe community, but according to Oehrn, Dönitz did not leap to any conclusions and made no judgment of him until after the war. The invasion of the Soviet Union Oehrn greeted with mixed feelings. After all, he had been raised in Russia and knew the people well. It was not long before he realized that Germany was mishandling the offensive. In the early months, he wrote, the German forces were welcomed in many parts of the Soviet Union as saviors. Had they accepted this role, instead of instituting a regime that was in many ways worse than Stalin's, they would have succeeded and kept the moral advantage as well. As for the Americans, Oehrn was as frustrated as anyone at BdU by Hitler's decision to avoid confrontation for as long as possible. He knew it was only a matter of time before formal hostilities would begin and BdU would be able to plan offensive operations against the United States. What he did not know was that he would not be available to assist the U-Bootwaffe when that time arrived.[17]

In October 1941, Hitler ordered several U-boats out of the North Atlantic and sent them into the Mediterranean Sea to support Erwin Rommel's embattled land forces in North Africa. Dönitz, who voiced disagreement over this strategic shift of U-boats, realized that the posting of German submarines to the Mediterranean required a competent staff in the theater to oversee their operational direction. In November the new post of Führer der U-Boote—Italien (Commander of U-boats, Italy, or FdU–Italy) was created in Rome. This position would ordinarily have been filled by an officer with prior flotilla command experience and a rank of Kapitän zur See. Dönitz, with typical disregard for the rules and niceties of the Kriegsmarine, assigned his A1, Victor Oehrn, to fill the position. A delighted Oehrn packed his bags and left immediately.[18]

It was a dream assignment. Rome during the war was still Rome, and Oehrn quickly warmed to the haunting scenery and swirling social life of the city, a life he was expected, as a representative of his country, to take part in. U-boat operations in the Mediterranean were going reasonably well, although the work was less than he expected. It was during this time that he met his future wife, Renate von Winterfeld, secretary to the senior Kriegsmarine officer in Rome, Eberhard Weichhold. But Oehrn's dream turned to dust just weeks after his arrival. In February 1942, Erich Raeder, displeased that the new position had been given to an officer of Oehrn's rank (he was a KorvettenKapitän at the time), overruled Dönitz and directed him to replace Oehrn with a more senior officer. Oehrn was to become the A1 for FdU–Italy, a position lower than the one he had left in Kerneval. The blow was devastating. Bitterly disappointed, Oehrn decided to request sea duty again—after all, he had been promised another boat and the U-boat offensive against the United States was reaching a crescendo. Before he could request a transfer to a frontline boat, however, Dönitz called him to apologize and asked him to stay in Rome until his replacement arrived. Always the courteous subordinate, Oehrn agreed, not knowing that his decision would have fateful consequences.[19]

In May 1942, after chasing the British Army back and forth across the North African desert for over a year, Erwin Rommel was preparing to attack the fortified city of Tobruk. Still in charge at FdU–Italy and with no replacement in sight, Oehrn decided to transfer his small staff operation across the Mediterranean Sea to Libya, where he could better supervise U-boat attacks against the expected Allied evacuation convoys. He expected to be back in Rome within days, and the night before he was due to leave, over dinner at the Casino Valadier, he asked Renate von Winterfeld to marry him. She accepted his proposal and they agreed to announce their engagement as soon as he returned from Africa. Oehrn arrived in Derna the following morning and watched with awe the collapse of Tobruk over the next few days. The fall of the city, however, had been expected. What Oehrn did not anticipate was an order from his titular commander in Rome, Weichhold, naming him Kriegsmarine liaison officer to the staff of Field Marshal Albert Kesselring, who was responsible for all land operations in the Mediterranean Theater. The order was effective immediately. His planned ten-day stay in Libya had been extended indefinitely. Any connection he had with

FdU–Italy (or, for that matter, with BdU) was severed by his assignment to Kesselring's staff, and his engagement to Renate was placed on an indefinite hold.[20]

Under the circumstances Oehrn handled the transfer well. He soon became fond of Kesselring, whose staff meetings he attended and with whom he dined periodically. He also began to develop an admiration for Rommel that matched his devotion to Dönitz. Much like Dönitz, Rommel was a charismatic and dynamic leader, and Oehrn's association with the head of the Afrika Korps filled a void in his life that had been empty since his transfer to Rome.

After the capture of Tobruk Rommel began his advance across the desert towards El Alamein so quickly that Kesselring, ostensibly in charge, could only follow in his wake. As the Germans drove east, Oehrn, in a small truck with a couple of radio operators, had all he could do to keep up with Kesselring. Oehrn became swept up in the excitement that swirled in Rommel's wake (quite the opposite of Kesselring, who regularly predicted that the lightening advance would falter) and began to send optimistic reports of his progress back to Berlin. When Rommel's exhausted forces stalled just short of El Alamein in July 1942, many Germans believed that it was only a matter of time before the "Desert Fox" would regroup his men and push into Egypt and across the Nile. The British forces in Cairo believed it as well and began to burn their classified papers. Weichhold, in an attempt to bolster Rommel's chances for success, detached Oehrn from Kesselring's staff and ordered him to report to Rommel and offer the resources of the Kriegsmarine to assist in his final attack. In retrospect it was a ridiculous mission, for the only assistance Oehrn had to offer Rommel was a single Schnellboot squadron, and there was no reason for him to see him in person to make such an offer. But, Oehrn's enthusiasm for the man made the assignment rather appealing, and he looked forward to joining Rommel.[21]

Oehrn set out for the "Desert Fox's" headquarters on the morning of July 13, 1942. He was dressed in his best uniform, desert khaki modified to look something like what a naval officer would wear, his medals, including his Knight's Cross and the U-boat badge, topped with a blue garrison cap. He was able to locate a kübelwagen and a driver, since any officer of importance had both, and a last photograph was taken before they set off into the desert. Oehrn had only the vaguest notion where they were going and even less of an idea where Rommel actually was, and within a very short time they were lost. Oehrn brought the kübelwagen to a stop at the top of a sand dune to survey the area, and they were spotted by an Australian scouting unit, a forward element of the British Eighth Army. The Australians opened fire on the fleeing Oehrn and five bullets ripped into his shoulder, hip and leg. The force of the blows knocked him to the ground, where he soon lost consciousness. When he awoke several hours later, it was dark and the Australians were standing over him. "Are we good soldiers?" they asked.[22]

Victor Oehrn was a most unlikely prisoner of war, and his captors must have realized it, for they immediately tossed him into a field ambulance and rushed him over several hundred miles of bone-clattering roads to a temporary hospital in Egypt. After surgery he drifted in and out of consciousness for several weeks, and recalls gaining the full use of his senses only on August 28, 1942. The first thing he remembers was the realization that he was in a full plaster body cast. The bullets had broken his shoulder, hip and leg, and caused a host of serious internal injuries. The hospital, he learned, was deep in Allied territory and the prospect of his being rescued or making it back to Germany by any means was dim. His injuries and plaster body armor made it impossible for him to move even as far as the hospital door. For Oehrn, it appeared the war was over.

The extent of his injuries, his sense that he had been forgotten by the Kriegsmarine and by his country, and his wholly unexpected separation from Renate—which for all he knew might last for years—cast Oehrn into despair. The former U-boat commander grew listless and did not care whether he lived or died. His mental state concerned the British doctors, for Oehrn's apathy was affecting his physical recovery. It was, in fact, his doctors who began to drag him out of this despair. Several of them struck up a friendship with Oehrn, one a Jew who had emigrated from Germany before the war. They talked freely about the war and Germany's role in it—even about the tenets of National Socialism. Oehrn's willingness to debate soon became common knowledge, and his room became a gathering point for anyone who wanted to visit a real German officer. Oehrn was able to hold his own in these conversations while remaining gregarious and unfailingly polite. "Really, we have no quarrel," he liked to tell anyone who would listen to him, "it is the Bolsheviks who are our common enemy. It's foolish for us to fight among ourselves when we should be fighting together against them."[23]

Did Oehrn believe this? Probably he did, for the experiences of his youth had instilled a loathing for the Soviet Union and communism that went far beyond the official party line. The real enemies were not the British or the Americans, with whom he seems to have got on well, but the Soviets. This is not to say that Oehrn did not agree with the general war aims of the Third Reich, including revenge for past injustices and the need for a Greater Germany. But as with so many others, the war Hitler started as a calculated grab for power had become for Oehrn a crusade to save Europe from Bolshevism. It is difficult to judge his enthusiasm for Hitler, who Oehrn seems to believe was necessary to correct the inequities of the Versailles Treaty. It is equally hard to measure his acceptance of National Socialism; he seems to have held many of its less pleasant aspects (those he knew about) in complete disdain. But to Oehrn these issues were not as important as the fact that his country was fighting a just war. The Fatherland was under attack and it was his duty to defend her regardless of its government, its leaders or its noxious behavior at home. If his defense of Germany could only be made in the form of words from a hospital bed, so be it.[24]

Oehrn proved to be such a persuasive debater that his room was finally declared off-limits to all but medical personnel. The visits stopped and so did much of the therapeutic conversation. Despair began to creep back into his sedentary life. He still had no idea of his fate. He had heard disturbing stories about German POWs being sent to Australia for the duration of the war, and about an Allied interrogation center up the road in Mahdi at which torture was practiced. He was especially worried about Renate and tried to contact her by mail, initially to let her know he was alive and safe—and to break off their engagement. He knew it was unfair to make her wait years for him to return to her. His attempts to reach her were unsuccessful. In the end it was Renate who found him. One day as he was lying in bed, a Catholic priest walked in and asked him if he was Victor Oehrn. Yes, he replied warily, not knowing who the man was or what he wanted. Oehrn was not a Catholic himself, but a Lutheran, and he had been raised to distrust Catholics. The priest handed him a letter. "This is from Renate von Winterfeld," he said. "If you wish to reply by letter, I will wait. Otherwise you may dictate a reply to me now."

Oehrn was shocked. After all this, it had not been the German Government who had tracked him down, nor the Kriegsmarine—nor even Dönitz. It had been the Roman Catholic Church, an organization for which he had little interest and no love. The fact that the Church would take the time during a world war to do this for two people who were, as he later described it, "as two grains of sand in the desert," impressed him. The love Renate demonstrated in initiating the search impressed him even more. Clearly she was not interested in breaking off the engagement.[24] As soon as the mysterious priest had left his room with a letter for Renate, he resolved, somehow, to return to her. He began to pray regularly. His appetite returned and he exercised his shattered limbs as best he could. By the spring of 1943 he was walking again.

The priest's visit seems to have been a turning point in Oehrn's life. Before then, though no longer in danger of death, he was in a state of despair and had given up on almost everything that was dear to him. He had resigned himself to losing Renate, to remaining a prisoner for the duration of the war, to being a cripple for the rest of his life. Further U-boat service seemed as far away as the stars. After he heard from Renate, however, and realized that she still loved him—even to the point of sending someone to find him in such a remote location—his despair began to evaporate, his limbs to heal and his resolve to strengthen. The old Oehrn, the one who had stood so proudly in front of his kübelwagen for a photograph, could not have summoned the inner resources to overcome these difficulties. It had been necessary to him to suffer and heal, to be lost and then found.

Soon after he began hobbling around the camp, Oehrn made a decision. He was, after all, still a German officer, and one responsibility of an officer in captivity was to make every effort to escape. Buoyed by his new determination and in apparent contradiction to his location and physical state, he resolved to do so. Oddly enough, an opportunity for escape soon presented itself, though not in a way Oehrn might have expected.

One day he heard through the hospital grapevine that a committee from the International Red Cross planning a visit for the purpose of determining candidates for repatriation. He knew that their standards were very strict, and he also knew—doubtless with some sense of irony—that he had recovered from his physical wounds to the point that he would probably not qualify. He determined there was only one solution to the problem, and immediately began to starve himself. It was a dangerous move, and something which, under the circumstances, demonstrates an astonishing measure of self-discipline—especially after what he had already been made to endure. After a couple of weeks his weight began to drop precipitously, and by the time the Red Cross committee arrived, he was little more than a walking skeleton. He had not expected the strategy to work, but after his medical examination the committee recommended him for repatriation without much debate. The odds of his being able to make it back to Germany before the war ended had been infinitesimal, but with courage and self-discipline (and a bit of luck) it looked as though he was going to make it. It appeared that he would be able to fulfill the promise he made to himself after Renate had found him.

Oehrn's elation ended suddenly when he was told he would have to go through the dreaded interrogation center at Mahdi on his way home. He was terrified of Mahdi, and not without reason. The desire of his captors to send him there in the fall of 1943 suggests that they finally realized who he was and what he might have to offer in the way of useful information. Since the beginning of the war, captured U-boat crewmen, especially commanders, had been taken directly to London for extensive interrogation. These sessions were not physically painful, but they were rigorous, and new prisoners were often sent to their camps having given up more information than they would have liked. The British knew Victor Oehrn by name and were aware of his professional relationship to Admiral Dönitz. The fact that he was left alone for months while recovering in Egypt seems to indicate that they did not know for some time that he was in their captivity; otherwise, he would have been sent to London as soon as he was able to walk. He would certainly not have been allowed to return to Germany, which by this time was losing the Battle of the Atlantic. Yet, it was not until the paperwork was completed and Oehrn's name appeared on the repatriation list that someone finally seems to have noticed who was occupying one of their hospital beds. By that time, however, the best anyone could do was detour him through the nearest local interrogation facility. Obviously the British lost a major opportunity to obtain valuable intelligence information.[25]

Oehrn's fears proved unfounded. His sojourn at Mahdi turned out to be far less unpleasant than he was led to believe, and not once was he questioned by experts from London. His principal interrogator was a commander in the United States Navy, and the questioning seems to have been relatively low-key and courteous. From Oehrn's description of the questioning, one may surmise that it was geared less towards information-gathering and more towards lowering his morale. By late 1943 the U-boat was less of a threat than it had been when he was captured. Since Oehrn was going back to Germany, however, he might as well be returned with a defeatist attitude. Unhappily for Oehrn and his country, this was best accomplished by telling him the truth (which he steadfastly refused to accept): the war at sea was over. In addition, German forces were being driven out of the Soviet Union, the Allies controlled Europe's skies and Germany's cities were desolate ruins. It is doubtful whether this patent attempt to demoralize Oehrn succeeded—especially since the overall military situation as presented was so at odds with what he knew it to be at the time of his capture. In any case he told his interrogator that it didn't matter at all. Germany was his country, and she needed him. The process ended with little accomplished on either side, but Oehrn believes that he and his interrogator parted as friends.

Victor Oehrn was released from the camp at Mahdi in October 1943 and began his tortuous journey back home, first by sea from Egypt to Marseille via Barcelona, and then by land from Marseille to Germany. He arrived in Berlin in November, a physical wreck in a city of wreckage—the American's information had been correct after all. A photograph of Oehrn was taken shortly after his return which shows the ravages of his injuries and the effects of months in captivity. Earlier in the war he had been a stocky man, full in the face and cheerful-looking. After his return from Egypt, he was thin and gaunt, with deep lines in his face. His cheerful visage had been replaced with a wistful, almost sad, expression, as though his entire outlook on life had changed. This photograph calls to mind Erich Topp's description of Wolfgang Lüth: "I can see him during a last conversation shortly before his death, 'with hollow cheeks and sunken eyes,' like one of the figures in Rodin's 'Burgesses of Calais,' exhausted after years of siege, a rope already at his neck, delivered unconditionally into the hands of a merciless victor."[26]

Some semblance of stability once again entered Victor Oehrn's life. On November 15, 1943, Oehrn limped back into the service of Karl

This formal portrait of Victor Oehrn was taken in January 1944, after his return from British captivity in North Africa. The effects of his injuries, his imprisonment and the psychological trauma he endured are all obvious—especially when compared to the photograph on page 108. *Courtesy of Victor Oehrn*

Dönitz, who was now based outside Berlin at Lager Koralle as the Commander-in-Chief of the entire Kriegsmarine.[27] The following month he married Renate von Winterfeld in Berlin. Although over the next several months he was assigned to various "special duties" at BdU and its surrounding commands, the truth is that he spent most of his time in painful rehabilitation. For several weeks he was so frail that a worried Dönitz arranged for the two of them to have breakfast together every day to make sure that he was eating properly. Finally, in August 1944, Oehrn assumed his old position as Dönitz's A1—this time with a larger staff and with the responsibility for larger and more complex operations. Despite his capture, severe injuries, the loss of any real prospect for another U-boat command (a condition of his repatriation was that he stay within the borders of prewar Germany), and the clear fact that Germany was losing the war, Victor Oehrn was probably as happy as he had ever been. He was in love and together again with Renate, and he was working side by side with Karl Dönitz.[28]

Oehrn's talents as an operational planner were needed less and less as the final year of the war dragged on. He was now responsible for operations within the German surface fleet as well as the U-Bootwaffe, but the fleet was shattered and could no longer function effectively, and the Battle of the Atlantic was, for all practical purposes, at an end. Allied control of the skies and the effective use of radar had brought about the end of Rudeltaktik, and U-boats had been operating alone since January 1944. The last opportunity to perform as an organization came during the first days of the Allied invasion of Normandy (before Oehrn resumed his duties), but the German response was ill-planned and ineffective. In the following months U-boat strategy became a simple exercise of sending boats out to sea, hoping that they would come back, and praying that the long-promised "miracle boats" would arrive. The predictable result was a bloodbath of enormous dimensions, and nothing Oehrn did could change that.

Happily, though, Oehrn was able to contribute a service of a different kind. In the closing months of the war he witnessed firsthand the increasing isolation of Dönitz from his men. The transfer of U-boat headquarters, first to Paris and later to Berlin, meant that the admiral no longer visited returning boats at the docks in France. Instead, commanders traveled to Dönitz in Berlin—if possible. In addition, his once trusted staff of U-boat officers, who formerly offered comment and criticism, was now composed of sycophantic OKM staff officers, self-absorbed service chiefs and sundry party hangers-on. When Oehrn arrived at Dönitz's new headquarters at Lager Koralle, he could not help but notice that his predecessor was anxious to get away. He soon realized why: the place was rapidly drifting from reality, and Dönitz's former A1 seemed to be one of the few reasonable voices left to counsel the admiral. He resolved to use it as often as he could.[29]

Two examples of this are especially striking. In the autumn of 1944 Dönitz and his senior staff gathered to discuss the fate of the giant battleship *Tirpitz*. The sister ship to the tragic *Bismarck* had never ventured far to sea, and had in fact spent most of her time in a Norwegian fjord. Her potential to escape and raid enemy shipping lanes posed a constant threat to the enemy until September 1943, when Allied bombing and mines made it all but impossible to effectively utilize her. Dönitz, however, judged that it was time to bring her home. The question being debated was the mechanics of the move itself. Despite his relative influence, Oehrn was the junior officer in the room. He sat quietly as ideas were discussed, and for one reason or another, rejected. As he continued to listen, the ideas became increasingly unrealistic, even delusional. Oehrn finally spoke up and declared that any attempt to return *Tirpitz* to Germany was a bad idea. Why do the enemies' work for them by bringing her out into the open sea? Oehrn's declaration was the last thing Dönitz wanted to hear, and the Grand Admiral flew into such a towering rage that Oehrn was forced to leave the gathering. Later that evening Dönitz phoned and thanked Oehrn for his candor, asking that he always give his honest opinion—whatever the reaction.

The second incident happened much later. At OKM it was Dönitz's practice to issue "orders of the day" to the fleet. These were often sprinkled with stale Party slogans, National Socialist buzzwords, and rather hollow (by that late date) exhortations to final victory. Oehrn did not approve of Dönitz's methods, but said nothing until Dönitz, in March or April of 1945, handed him a draft of his last order and asked him for his comments. Oehrn reviewed it and told Dönitz that neither statements of National Socialism nor unrealistic promises were appropriate for men who knew the war was over. Rather, he said, Dönitz should appeal to their love of country, their love of God and their sense of family. After all, Oehrn concluded, those were the things that mattered now. The war was lost; they must look to the future. Dönitz thought about this and later told Oehrn he had been correct in his assessment. Although the order went out unchanged—which baffled Oehrn—it is worth noting that Dönitz's final radio transmission to his boats on May 5, 1945, was much closer to what Oehrn had considered appropriate. Perhaps Oehrn's opinion was remembered and taken into account after all.[30]

So closely, it seems, did Karl Dönitz value Victor Oehrn as a confidant and friend that just before the admiral was captured, the two men shared a conversation that was remarkable in its intimacy. Oehrn was in the hospital, flat on his back after still another operation to relieve the pain of his injuries, and Dönitz, perched on a steel chair, had come to visit. The obvious topic of discussion was the end of the war and their own fates, and Dönitz was sure he would not survive the armistice for long. Oehrn found this impossible to comprehend, but Dönitz went on to say that he would be the victim of a political process, and that he would ultimately be tried as a war criminal and put to death. His only wish, he told Oehrn, was that his U-boat men would stand by him. Oehrn assured him that such a trial would never come to pass, but that if anything was to happen, the men of the U-Bootwaffe would support him to the end. Shortly afterwards Dönitz was arrested and carted off to prison to await the convening of the War Crimes Tribunal in Nuremberg. Oehrn, who may have avoided postwar detention because he had already been imprisoned and repatriated—and because his cell was a hospital bed—was left to pick up the pieces of his career.[31]

*   *   *

Victor Oehrn's postwar life followed a path typical for men in his position. For several months he served in the minesweeping service set up by Allied occupation authorities to clear German and international waterways. Afterward, he found work where he could get it, as a driver, an interpreter, a farmhand, and finally a businessman in the booming postwar German recovery. Throughout the hard years following the end of the war he remained close to his former commander-in-chief and mentor, Karl Dönitz. He was one of the first to see Dönitz after his release from Spandau Prison in 1956, and he was present at the Grand Admiral's funeral in 1981.

The relationship between Oehrn and Dönitz helps to define Oehrn himself. His accomplishments, while genuine, could not have been made without Dönitz's support and intercession. It was Dönitz who trusted Oehrn enough to originally make him his A1, and who allowed him to formulate operational plans and make decisions at a level normally beyond that of a lowly Kapitänleutnant. It was Dönitz who sent him to sea in U-37 and later to Rome as FdU–Italy. It naturally follows that Oehrn's virtues of loyalty and obedience shone brightest when directed towards Dönitz, who gave him all he had and called him his friend as well. Dönitz was and had been a large part of his own life. When Oehrn wrote his memoirs long after the war (two volumes that will not be published until the end of the century), he could have written about his own life on his own terms; instead, his writings are centered as much on Dönitz—his commander, mentor and comrade—as himself.[32]

For these reasons it is understandable that Oehrn defends Dönitz's record, perhaps more than Dönitz objectively deserves. When asked for his opinion, Oehrn praises Dönitz as a man, a leader and a human being. When offered criticism of Dönitz, he is politely silent. Unlike some in the U-Bootwaffe community for whom any slight of their beloved Grand Admiral is an invitation to every form of slander, abuse, and eventual ostracization, Oehrn realizes that there are valid arguments for and against the officer and his actions. He is most concerned that the truth about Dönitz prevail, whatever that truth may be: "At my age," he wrote in 1992, "it is my aim to do what I can to transfer into public opinion the reality concerning that exceptional man, who is even in Germany very often not seen as he really was. . . .Lots of people think that they know D[onitz] very well, but really they know [very little]! Nobody in this world is perfect. . . .From my point of view it is much more important to know *where* a man is perfect. . ."[33]

In spite of his encounter with the mysterious priest in Egypt, Victor Oehrn never made a formal move towards Catholicism, but he still has a high regard for the Church and enjoys attending Mass with his grandchildren. Today, three years after their golden wedding anniversary, Victor Oehrn and his wife Renate live quietly outside Bonn.

Although its ranks are thinning with the passing years, the U-boat community is still riven by dissent and discord. Oehrn, however, seems to have remained above the fray and is respected on all sides as a man of integrity and competence. "According to my opinion," wrote Jürgen Oesten, commander of three boats during the war, "[Oehrn] was decent, intelligent, quiet and matter-of-fact. . .equally qualified as a commander of submarines as for staff work." Otto Kretschmer, a man of many different views than Oesten, recently described Oehrn as "not only the man with the highest IQ at BdU, but probably also the one officer who used it effectively." In this observation Kretschmer presumably meant to include not only Karl Dönitz (whose IQ as measured after the war approached the genius level), but also several capable members of Dönitz's staff, including Eberhard Godt, Günther Hessler, and Adalbert Schnee.[34]

The significance of Oehrn's career can be considered on several levels. He was without question a talented planner at both the operational and tactical levels (the Scapa Flow operation comes immediately to mind), and it was he who provided much of the work behind U-Boot-waffe operations for the first two years of the war. When he returned from captivity in 1944 he could no longer contribute as much in that capacity, but he was nonetheless a valuable stabilizing force in Dönitz's staff and a voice of reason in an increasingly irrational world. He served as a U-boat commander for only six months, but in that brief span he accomplished what many were unable to do throughout their careers, and is widely credited with sparking the fierce and sustained campaign of mid-to-late 1940 known as the U-boat's "happy times." Given Oehrn's remarkable career, the little attention thrown in his direction is curious—particularly when one considers the numerous books and articles written about lesser feats and less able commanders.

Ultimately, Oehrn overcame the substantial hardships and physical pain that accompanied wartime capture and serious injury and emerged a better man for it. For Oehrn, at least, this personal victory is the most significant of all.

*   *   *

Heinz-Wilhelm Eck, while a cadet member of Crew 34. *National Archives*

Dwight R. Messimer

Heinz-Wilhelm Eck
Siegerjustiz and the *Peleus* Affair

Kapitänleutnant Heinz Eck of U-852 holds the distinction of being the only U-boat captain tried, convicted and executed for war crimes at the end of World War II. But was he really a war criminal?

Both World Wars were fought against a backdrop of good versus evil. It did not matter which side you were on—yours was good and the enemy was evil; your soldiers heroes, enemy soldiers criminals.

But the reality of both wars differed considerably from the rhetoric. After World War II, the Allies—still under the influence of their wartime rhetoric—conducted a series of showcase war crimes trials. Many of the Axis leaders convicted during those trials deserved to be punished. But others, notably soldiers whose conduct was no different than that of their Allied equivalents, were treated much more harshly than they deserved. Heinz Eck was one of them.

*   *   *

Heinz-Wilhelm Eck was born in Hamburg on March 27, 1916, and was raised in Berlin. He joined the Reichmarine on April 8, 1934, as a member of Crew 34, passed through a series of training programs and specialty schools, and was commissioned Lieutenant z.S. on April 1,

U-852 being put into commission, June 15, 1943. Her first and last patrol would start six months later. *National Archives*

1937. He spent the next five years aboard mine sweepers, commanding one from 1939 to 1942.[1]

In February 1942, Eck volunteered for U-boat assignment, was quickly accepted and reported for training at Pillau on June 8, 1942. From October 28, 1942 until February 21, 1943, he was the captain-in-training aboard the U-124, commanded by a fellow Crew 34 classmate, Kapitänleutnant Joachim Mohr. A few months later on June 15, Eck assumed command and commissioned the newly-constructed U-852. Early the following year, January 18, 1944, her sea trials completed and fully provisioned, Eck took U-852 out of Kiel en route to the German U-boat base at Penang in Malaya. Before he departed, the young kapitänleutnant was briefed by a Crew 34 classmate, Korvettenkapitän Adalbert Schnee. Schnee, a veteran U-boat commander and holder of the Knight's Cross with Oak leaves, ranked number 22 among Germany's most successful U-boat captains. Eck listened very carefully to what his friend told him about the dangers that lay ahead.[2]

Schnee reminded Eck that U-852 was among the largest, slowest and most easily hit U-boats then in service. He particularly warned him about the strong air cover in the Atlantic Narrows, especially between Freetown and Ascension Island. "Be very careful in this region," the veteran classmate cautioned him, pointing out that traces of wreckage from a torpedoed ship could be recognized from the air for "the next few days." Schnee underscored his warning with the ominous news that all four type IXD2 boats that had preceded U-852 had been lost, either in the South Atlantic or near Ascension Island. The South Atlantic zone was, in Schnee's understated words, "very difficult for us." That Eck took Schnee's warnings seriously was evidenced by what happened fifty-four days later.

Eck was also briefed by FKpt. Günter Hessler, who like Schnee was a Knight's Cross holder and a U-boat ace. Hessler, who was Admiral Dönitz's son-in-law, was also the chief-of-staff to Konteradmiral Eberhardt Godt, who directed the day-to-day conduct of the U-boat war. Hessler underscored the warnings Eck had received from Schnee, emphasizing that Eck should avoid anything that would attract the enemy's attention.

Back in Kiel, Eck received another briefing from FKpt. Karl-Heinz Moehle. Moehle discussed the *Laconia* incident with Eck, reminding him of what had happened to KKpt. Werner Hartenstein. Whether or not Moehle also talked with Eck about the so-called *Laconia* order is not known. But the September 17, 1942 order had been read by all U-boat captains and was included in U-852's standing orders. (The *Laconia* incident and its ramifications are discussed later in this essay when the issues surfaced during Eck's trial.)[3]

Eck's operational orders were direct. He was to take U-852 south, pass through the Atlantic by way of the Cape of Good Hope and operate in the Indian Ocean. He was then to join *Gruppe Monsun* at Penang. U-852 sailed from Kiel on January 18, 1844, taking the "north-about" route around Scotland and into the North Atlantic. Eck ran down the globe toward the African west coast, running on the surface only at night to recharge his batteries. Clearly, he heeded the warnings about staying out of sight as much as possible. It took nearly two months before U-852 reached the Equator, in the middle of the most dangerous area about which he had been warned.

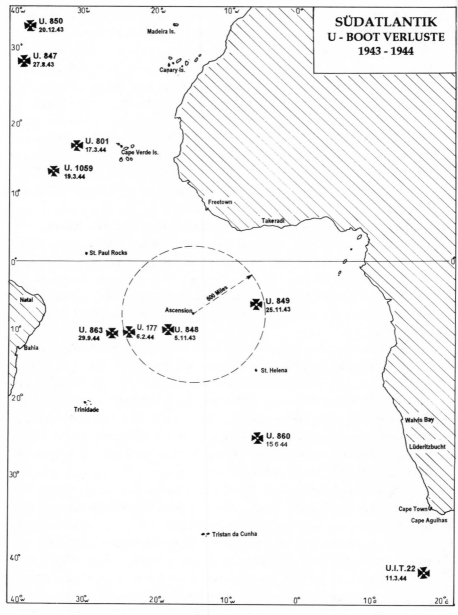

The South Atlantic was a dangerous area for U-boats, as shown by this chart of U-boat losses between August 28, 1943 and September 29, 1944. The circle around Ascension Island was the most dangerous area, and it was within the northern part of this circle that Eck sank the *Peleus*. *Map prepared by Ilona Hoffmann, Berlin, Germany*

On the afternoon of March 13, 1944, U-852 was patrolling about 300 miles east of the Freetown-Ascension Island line, approximately 500 miles north of Ascension Island and 700 miles south of Freetown. The U-boat was cruising on the surface when at 5:00 p.m. a lookout spotted a freighter ahead and off the starboard bow. The ship in the distance turned out to be the *SS Peleus,* a Greek-registered freighter of 6,659 BRT built by William Gray & Company in 1928. Under charter to the British War Transportation Ministry, *Peleus* had left Freetown in ballast five days earlier bound for South America and the River Plate. She carried a crew of thirty-five.[4]

Eck ordered U-852 to full speed and laid a course to put the U-boat ahead of the target. The chase lasted two and a half hours, and it was dark by the time U-852 was in position to attack. At 1940 Eck made a night surface attack, firing two torpedoes from the bow tubes. The torpedoes slammed into the freighter just moments apart, the first exploding in the number two hold, the second just aft in the number three hold. From U-852's bridge, Kapitänleutnant Eck observed that the "detonation was very impressive." The doomed *Peleus* went down like a rock.[5]

It is impossible to know how many of the thirty-five man crew got off the ship before she was swallowed by the sea, but there could not have been many. Chief Officer Antonios Liossis was knocked unconscious and blown off the bridge into the water. Rocco Said, an off-watch greaser, was on deck when the torpedoes struck. To Said, who had been at sea since his youth, "it was clear the ship would sink immediately." He and other crewmen who were on deck at the time determined to take their chances in the ocean.[6] The freighter went down so quickly that almost none of the survivors had time to don life vests or life belts. Those who jumped overboard clung to hatch covers, timbers, and any other piece of wreckage that floated. Rafts that had been stowed on deck bobbed clear as the freighter went down, and some of the survivors made for them. Chief Officer Liossis and a seaman, Dimitrios Konstantinides, swam toward a raft. While they were still in the water U-852 moved slowly among the flotsam. After the U-boat passed, Liossis and Konstantinides climbed aboard the raft.[7]

The only officers on U-852's bridge at this time were Kapitänleutnant Eck and his first watch officer, Oberleutnant z.S. George Colditz. The other occupants consisted of two enlisted lookouts. As the U-boat cruised slowly among the debris, Eck and his crewmen on the bridge could hear whistles and shouting. They also saw lights on some of the rafts. At about this time the ship's doctor, Oberstabsarzt Walter Weisspfennig, came on the bridge. His sole purpose for going topside was to see what was transpiring, and he stood behind a periscope about fifteen feet away from Eck and Colditz.[8]

Whenever possible, U-boat captains were supposed to question survivors about the ship, its cargo and destination. Eck called down and ordered his chief engineer, Kapitänleutnant (Ing.) Hans Lenz, on deck. Because Lenz spoke English, he sent the engineer forward to the bow to question a survivor. Lenz was joined in the trek forward by the second watch officer, Lieutnant z.S. August Hoffmann.[9] Hoffmann had come off watch at 4:00 p.m., an hour before the *Peleus* was sighted. He had been below deck during the attack and was not scheduled to go back on watch until midnight. Hoffmann also spoke some English, but he had not been specifically ordered to accompany Lenz to the bow. Apparently he, like Weisspfennig, was there to see what was going on.

As the two officers reached the bow, Eck maneuvered U-852 along-side one of the life rafts. The raft he picked was occupied by the *Peleus'* third officer, Agis Kephalas, a greaser named Stavros Sogias, a Russian seaman named Pierre Neuman, and a Chinese fireman whose name no one recalled. Kapitänleutnant Lenz beckoned the third officer to come aboard the U-boat. Lenz and Hoffmann questioned the man about the ship. They learned that she was in ballast and that she was sailing from Freetown and bound for the River Plate. Third officer Kephalas also told them that another, slower ship was following them to the same destination. With the questioning concluded, Hoffmann told the Greek officer that he and the other survivors would be picked up the next day by the British. He helped the man back onto his raft and both officers started back toward the conning tower to report what they had learned.

After the Greek sailor returned to his raft, Eck ordered U-852 to proceed slowly while he listened to Lenz's report. When Lenz told him about the Greek officer's account of the approaching, slow moving freighter, Eck discounted the claim as "too much of a good thing."[10]

At this point there were five officers on the bridge: Eck, his first officer (Colditz), the second officer (Hoffmann), the chief engineer (Lenz), and the doctor (Weisspfennig). The doctor was still standing away from the others and did not participate in the conversation that followed. Apparently Hoffmann also remained far enough away from the group that he could not clearly understand what the other three men were discussing.[11]

The conversion had taken an ominous turn. Eck told Colditz and Lenz that he was concerned about the amount and size of the wreckage. He believed that the morning air patrols out of Freetown or Ascension Island would spot the wreckage and recognize it as the result of a U-boat attack. The discovery would trigger an immediate search for the U-boat, and given the number of U-boats lost during the previous six months, Eck felt his boat did not stand a chance if discovered by enemy aircraft.[12] His choices, however, were limited. He could leave the area and run on the surface at maximum speed until dawn, but by the time the sun rose, U-852 would still be less than 200 miles from the scene of the sinking—well within range of aircraft. In the time it took U-852 to travel about a half mile from the scene of the sinking, Eck decided that in order to protect his boat and his crew, he had to destroy all traces of the *Peleus*.[13]

Eck ordered two machine guns brought up on the bridge. While the weapons were being retrieved from below, both Colditz and Lenz protested the captain's decision. Eck listened to both officers but dismissed their objections. According to Eck, it was necessary to destroy all traces of the sinking, and he justified the destruction of the wreckage as an operational necessity to protect his boat from discovery and destruction.[14]

As the U-boat turned back toward the rafts Lenz went below, leaving four officers on the bridge: Eck, Colditz, Hoffmann and Weisspfennig. Both machine guns were brought up and mounted on the railing on the after part of the conning tower—one to port and one to starboard. Exactly what was said and happened next is not entirely clear. Apparently Eck made it known to the officers on the bridge that he wanted the rafts sunk. He made no mention of shooting at anyone in the water, nor did he ever give an order to kill any of the survivors. It was accepted, however, that by sinking the rafts the survivors would lose any hope for survival. Eck had chosen to use machine guns because he believed the rafts were mounted on hollow floats, and thus piercing the floats with bullets would cause the the the rafts would sink. In fact, the rafts' floats were filled with buoyant material.

It was now about 8:00 p.m., and the night was very dark and moonless. The rafts appeared as dark shapes on the water, their lights having been extinguished by the occupants when the U-boat first approached. Eck apparently turned to Weisspfennig, who was standing near the starboard machine gun, and ordered him to fire at the wreckage. The doctor complied with the order, directing his fire at a raft he estimated was about 200 yards away.[15] Weisspfennig's gun jammed after he had fired just a few bursts, and he could not make it operate again. Hoffmann, still off watch, went to Weisspfennig and cleared the jam. The second officer then took over on the gun and opened fire on the raft that had been Weisspfennig's target. The doctor took no further part in the attempt to destroy the rafts, although he remained on the bridge.

Despite the machine gun fire directed at it, the raft refused to sink. Eck ordered the signal light turned on in order to examine the craft to determine why it was still afloat. The examination, conducted at considerable distance and in poor light, proved inconclusive. The U-boat continued to move slowly through the wreckage, firing intermittently at the rafts. Apparently all the firing was being done from the starboard side, and at this point only Hoffmann was shooting. Weisspfennig did not shoot again, and neither Eck nor Colditz ever fired.

Nor was the firing continuous. In fact there were long periods when there was no firing at all. In part the pauses were the result of poor visibility due to the dark, moonless night. The other reason for the interruptions was the ineffectiveness of the machine gun fire on the rafts. They were not sinking, despite the rounds being pumped into them. Eck's goal of eliminating surface wreckage was not being achieved.

At about this time Hoffmann suggested using the 37mm gun, reasoning that its explosive rounds would destroy the rafts. Some consideration was also given to using the 105mm deck gun, but Eck rejected both suggestions because he did not think the guns could be brought to bear at such close range. He did, however, tell Hoffmann to try the twin 20mm anti-aircraft guns.[16] The attempt to sink the rafts with the 20mm guns was also a failure, prompting someone to suggest placing demolition charges aboard the rafts. Eck rejected that idea because he did not want any of his crew to leave the U-boat. Instead, he ordered hand grenades brought up, and maneuvered U-852 within thirty yards of a raft.[17]

The only person who can be identified as having thrown any grenades is Hoffmann. How many he threw at the raft, or if he threw grenades at more than one raft, is not known. It appears that two or three grenades were thrown, and that perhaps two of the rafts were targets. The grenades also proved to be useless in sinking the rafts. Throughout the grisly operation it was not Eck's intent to kill any of the survivors. That they might be hit by gunfire, and would certainly die if their rafts were destroyed, was obvious to him. But he assumed that whoever was on the rafts had jumped into the water when the shooting started. His assumption was incorrect.

Instead of diving into the sea, Chief Officer Antonios Liossis threw himself down on the floorboards of the raft and squirmed head first under a bench when the machine gun opened fire. Behind him he heard Dimitrios Kostantinidis cry out in pain as he was hit several times. The seaman collapsed on the floor of the raft and died. Later, when the U-boat made another pass and grenades were thrown, Liossis was wounded in the back and shoulder by shrapnel.[18] Aboard another raft were the third officer, Agis Kephalas, and two seamen. Both of the latter were killed and Kephalas was badly injured in the arm. It is unclear whether these men were killed or wounded by grenade fragments or machine gun fire. Despite his wound, Kephalas managed to roll off the raft and swim toward the boat occupied by Liossis.[19]

Seaman Rocco Said dived over the side when the firing started and was in the water near his raft when the shooting was turned in his direction. Around him other swimmers "threw their hands up" as they were machine-gunned, and sank below the surface.[20]

Below decks in U-852 the crew was unaware of exactly what was happening topside. Some of the men heard the firing and everyone was aware that the boat was maneuvering slowly. Obviously they were still in the area of the sinking and many wondered why. Some of the men knew that two machine guns had been taken up to the bridge and that hand grenades had also been requested. They could only guess at what it all meant.

Chief Engineer Lenz, who had vacated the bridge and had spent the last four hours writing the report of his conversation with the Greek officer, supervised the reloading of the forward torpedo tubes and passed the time checking on the boat's trim. He had to see that the boat was, as he later put it, "ready to submerge at any time." Lenz heard the intermittent firing and the explosions of the hand grenades. He was the only man below deck during that time who knew for a certainty what the sounds meant.

By this time it was midnight and the watch was changed. Colditz was relieved by Hoffmann and went below. The enlisted lookouts were also relieved, one of the reliefs being Matrosenobergefreiter Wolfgang Schwender. As soon as Schwender took his place on the bridge, Eck ordered him to man the port side machine gun and fire at the large pieces of wreckage. Schwender complied with the order and opened fire on a raft that was about thirty-five yards away.[21] After firing one burst Schwender's gun jammed. He was clearing the jam when Lenz came up on the bridge. Schwender had just cleared the jam and was preparing to fire again when Lenz shoved him roughly aside, took control of the gun, and opened fire on the raft. Schwender assumed his duties as a lookout and did not fire again.[22]

How long Kapitänleutnant Lenz manned the port side machine gun is not clear. But it appears that he fired only at one raft and then quit firing. The question that bears asking is why was he firing at all? The captain had given the assignment to Schwender, not Lenz. The answer to that question is hard for many people to comprehend. According to Lenz, he took the gun from Schwender because he thought the Greek officer he had questioned might be on that raft. He didn't want him "hit and killed by bullets which had been fired by a soldier who in my view was bad." To Lenz it was a matter of honor, consideration and duty to insure that if anyone was killed, he was killed by a bullet fired by an honorable man.[23]

By 1:00 a.m. on March 14, 1944, Eck had tried to sink the rafts with machine guns, 20mm anti-aircraft guns, hand grenades and ramming. His attempts to destroy all traces of the sinking had failed utterly. Worse, U-852 had spent nearly five hours on the scene and dawn was only six hours away. It was long past time to go. Realizing the precariousness of his situation, Eck took U-852 out of the area at maximum speed shortly thereafter, leaving behind four survivors on two rafts. Three lived to be rescued thirty-five days later.

While U-852 was steaming through the night, news of the attack on the wreckage spread through the boat and seriously affected morale.

"I was under the impression that the mood on board was rather a depressing one," Eck later said. "I myself was in the same mood." In view of the crew's sullen attitude, Eck felt obligated to explain why he had made the decision to destroy the wreckage.[24] He addressed his men over the boat's loudspeaker system, telling them that he had made the decision "with a heavy heart," and that he regretted that some of the survivors may have been killed during the attempt to sink the rafts. He acknowledged that, in any event, without the rafts the survivors would surely die. He warned his crew about being "influenced too much by sympathy," citing that "we must also think of our wives and children who at home die as victims of air attack."[25] The explanation failed to ameliorate the crew's sinking morale or dispel their distaste for what had transpired. In addition, Eck had failed to explain to them the circumstances that caused him to see the destruction of the rafts as an operational necessity.[26]

Despite having lingered for so long at the scene of the *Peleus'* destruction, U-852 managed to avoid the enemy and slip away to the south. The two and a half weeks following the sinking were uneventful. U-852 moved steadily south along the west coast of Africa toward the Cape of Good Hope. Although Eck was being very careful, the British knew he was there. Eck had sent a radio message on March 15 regarding the *Peleus'* sinking, and the transmission had been picked up by radio direction finders.[27]

According to U-boat Headquarters (BdU) records, U-852 maintained radio silence until April 4. On March 30, however, British anti-submarine warfare forces in Capetown were warned that radio traffic from a U-boat had been picked up, indicating a submarine was northwest of Capetown.[28] Two days later, on April 1, Eck torpedoed the 5,277 ton freighter *SS Dahomian* ten miles west-south-west from Cape Point. This time he made no attempt to identify the vessel, and the forty-nine survivors were rescued by two South African mine sweepers the next day. Crew members described this successful attack as being "in order." Morale on U-852 improved.[29]

The *Dahomian* was the first U-boat success in South African waters since August 1, 1943. In response, the British dispatched a strong anti-submarine warfare group to hunt down the U-boat responsible for the sinking. The search, which lasted through April 3, did not find so much as a trace of the offending submarine. On the following day Eck broadcast his success in a lengthy transmission to BdU that was intercepted by the British. They finally found their U-boat, its position fixed only 150 miles east-south-east of Point Agulhas.[30]

U-852 remained in the Capetown area until mid-April, vainly looking for targets. Eck fired a spread of three torpedoes at what he thought was a troopship, but all missed. The area around Capetown offered too many risks and too few vessels to warrant staying there any longer, and Eck started north toward Penang.[31]

Eck's luck, however, was slowly running out. On April 20, 1944, only a few days after Eck headed north, survivors from the *Peleus* were rescued by the Portuguese steamer *SS Alexandre Silva*. Three men, chief officer Antonios Liossis, greaser Rocco Said, and seaman Dimitrios Argiros, were still alive. The third officer had died twenty-five days after the attack from gangrene and yellow fever.[32] When the *Alexandre Silva* docked in Lobito, Angola, one week later, the British learned for the first time of the events that occurred on the night of March 13-14. At the time there was little they could do since they did not know which U-boat had sunk the *Peleus*. After caring for the survivors, they filed their reports and passed the information on to the Admiralty.

While the three *Peleus* survivors were being questioned by British intelligence officers, Eck was moving into very dangerous waters. The defenses in the area had been beefed up with the addition of a hunter-killer group composed of nine frigates and sloops, plus the escort carriers *HMS Begum* and *HMS Shah*. The shipping zones were heavily patrolled by aircraft, and air bases were located on both Addu Atoll and Diego Garcia.[33] On the last day of April, British radio intelligence placed U-852 approaching Cape Guardafui on the southern tip of the Gulf of Aden. RAF Wellingtons were sent out from Aden to hunt the U-boat. On May 2, they found her.[34]

It was just after dawn. U-852 was cruising on the surface and Leutnant Hoffmann was the watch officer when the British bombers caught the U-boat completely by surprise. Coming out of the sun, the British planes strafed and bombed the doomed boat. Six depth charges straddled her, one of them damaging the 37mm antiaircraft gun on platform II. As tons of water crashed down on U-852, Hoffmann frantically ordered the U-boat to dive.[35]

U-852 managed to submerge before the Wellingtons could make a second run, but the situation was serious. In addition to flooding,

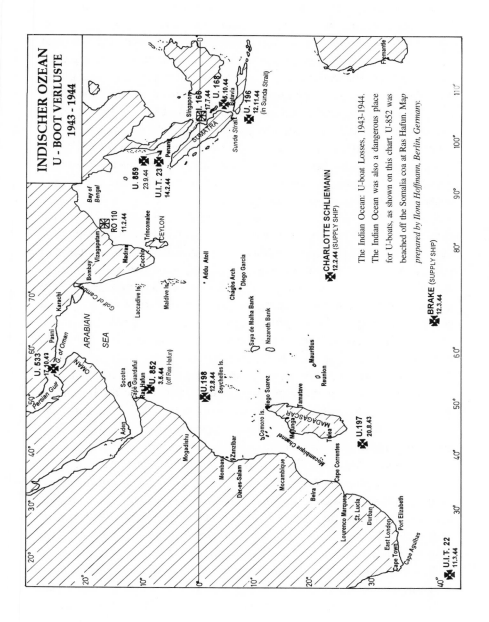

INDISCHER OZEAN
U - BOOT VERLUSTE
1943 - 1944

The Indian Ocean: U-boat Losses, 1943-1944. The Indian Ocean was also a dangerous place for U-boats, as shown on this chart. U-852 was beached off the Somalia coa at Ras Hafun. Map prepared by Ilona Hoffmann, Berlin, Germany.

deadly chlorine gas, caused by burst battery cells, was filling the boat. Fifteen minutes after she went under, U-852 shot to the surface at a 60° angle. The steep slant caused the batteries to spill even more acid, increasing the levels of chlorine gas inside the boat.[36]

As U-852 broke the surface her gun crews swarmed out and manned the antiaircraft guns. Even as the crewmen were reaching their battle stations, the Wellingtons were starting their second strafing run. The planes roared overhead and smothered the boat with fire. Oberleutnant Georg Colditz and Matrosenobergefreiter Josef Hofer both died on the bridge.[37] U-852 was down by the stern, unable to dive and under attack. By this time it was clear to Eck that his boat was finished. While he could not save his boat, he was determined to save his crew, and his only hope of accomplishing that was to beach U-852 on the Somaliland coast before the British sank her.[38]

Although doomed the U-boat managed to hold off the British throughout much of the day, her gunners beating off each aerial attack. Several of the crewmen were killed or wounded during the repeated strafing runs, but casualties were surprising light given the circumstances. That afternoon, while still under attack, Eck managed to save the bulk of his crew by beaching his battered boat off the Somaliland coast at Ras Hafun.[39] After grinding to a halt, Eck ordered the crew to abandon ship and set about to destroy U-852. Exactly what happened next is not clear, but two things are certain. First, Eck's attempt to destroy his boat with demolition charges was only partially successful, and one crewman was killed in the process. Second and more important to the events that would follow, Eck somehow failed to destroy the boat's war diary—the Kriegstagebuch. The oversight would cost him and two of his officers their lives.

Beached, listing heavily to port, her bow a twisted mass of junk, U-852 was obviously finished. But the British aircraft continued to attack, shifting their attention to U-852's crewmen who were coming out of the hatches and leaping into the water. Many were already swimming toward shore, and a few were clinging to rubber rafts filled with wounded that bobbed near the hulk. August Hoffmann was helping a badly wounded sailor into a raft when the Wellington's made their pass. Machine gun bullets frothed the sea around him, hitting men in the water and puncturing the raft. Hoffmann was hit in the leg by one of the rounds. Despite his wound, the young officer continued to help the wounded sailor toward shore. British aircraft continued to strafe the Germans who were struggling through the surf toward the beach.[40]

Exhausted and with several crewmen wounded and some dying, U-852's crew lay on the beach and waited for whatever was going to happen next. It was not long in coming. The following day, a British naval landing party, supported by a unit of the Somaliland Camel Corps, took the surviving members of U-852's crew prisoner.[41] The British boarding party that entered U-852 found more than just a battered hulk. She yielded a wealth of information which, coupled with the capture of the entire crew, proved to be enormously important. But the most significant discovery was the intact Kriegstagebuch (KTB), U-852's war log. The KTB would eventually link Eck and U-852 to the *Peleus* sinking and the harrowing events described by the three survivors. But that relationship, which was not immediately apparent, would only come about through the joint efforts of two navy intelligence officers, Lieutenant Burnett, RNVR and Lt. J.T. Rugh, USNR. Both officers were assigned to the Naval Section, Combined Special Detachment, Intelligence Collection (CSDIC).[42]

On May 17, two weeks after their capture, thirty-four of U-852's crew arrived on Cairo from Aden, where they had been screened by Lieutenant Burnett. Burnett, who was in charge of the Naval Section, CSDIC, sent orders that twelve of the men, among them the medical officer, Weisspfennig, were to be separated and sent to another camp.[43] Lieutenant Rugh, apparently unaware of why Burnett wanted the twelve separated from the others, "spent two hours with the medical officer as a courtesy to a non-combatant, protected person whose early repatriation was to be expected."[44]

During the two hours Rugh spent with Weisspfennig, all the prisoners were processed in Cairo before the twelve special prisoners were taken away. As soon as the twelve were gone, Rugh started questioning each of the remaining twenty-two Germans. He spent two weeks, working until after midnight each night, questioning the prisoners and writing his interrogation reports. It was during those interrogations that stories about the machine-gunning of the *Peleus* survivors began to leak out.[45]

On May 20, Rugh went to Heliopolis to pick up nine more men from U-852, including Heinz Eck. Rugh escorted Eck back to Cairo, but

British soldiers and navy intelligence officers aboard the wreck of U-852, May 5, 1944. The British were astounded to find her log still aboard. *National Archives*

did not question him. Within two days, Eck and four unnamed crewmen were aboard an airplane bound for England.[46]

Rugh sent a telegram on May 23 to the Admiralty reporting that
U-852 was the U-boat that had sunk the *Peleus*. The information was
required in London to assist intelligence officers at the Admiralty who
were about to question Eck on routine intelligence matters. Rugh did
not mention the alleged shootings because at that time he lacked confirmation of the story.[47]

In the meantime, Burnett visited the wreck of U-852 and returned
to Cairo with the U-boat's KTB. After conferring with Rugh and com-
paring notes, Burnett confronted the chief engineer, Hans Lenz, with
the incriminating evidence. According to Burnett, his "accusation of
murder on the high seas to the engineer officer produced confirmation
of that story." Not only did Lenz confirm the sordid tale, he signed an
affidavit detailing the event.[48]

Rugh and Burnett next visited Matrosenobergefreiter Johann
Coirniak and Obersteuermann Wilhelm Schmidtz. Both men had been
lookouts on the bridge during the torpedo attack and during most of the
time Eck was trying to destroy the wreckage. Both men signed affidavits
as to what had transpired.[49] Based on the veracity of the information
the two intelligence officers gathered from U-852's crewmen, the Admiralty flew the three *Peleus* survivors to Capetown. There, on June 7,
1944, the three men signed sworn affidavits describing the events. As
the Greek sailors were preparing their accounts, Rugh was detailed to
escort Dr. Weisspfennig, Coirniak and Schmidtz to London. His task
was to prevent Weisspfennig from suspecting why he was being sent to
England, and to "prevent the medical officer from knowing that the
witnesses were also going to the United Kingdom."[50]

Eck, Lenz, Hoffmann, Weisspfennig and Schwender arrived in England by June 8. By that time they must have suspected that the British
were planing to try them as war criminals, though they had not yet
been charged with any crimes. The trial, however, was postponed until
Germany's defeat, which by June 1944 was a virtual certainty. Until
then, the British classified the Eck-*Peleus* affair as Top Secret.[51]

Five months after the war in Europe ended, Heinz Eck, August
Hoffmann, Dr. Walter Weisspfennig, Hans Lenz and Wolfgang Schwender were moved to the Altona prison in Hamburg. On October 6, 1945,
they were formally charged with war crimes. There were two charges

against Eck and his four crewmen. The first count illustrates that the British, even by this late date, had still not accepted the reality of unrestricted submarine warfare. The defendants were accused of sinking the *Peleus* "in the violation of the laws and usages of war." The phrase "violations of the laws and usages of war," refers to the Prize Rules that were still in effect during the First World War (1914-1918). Under the Prize Rules, torpedoing a merchant vessel without warning was a crime. By 1939, however, the Prize Rules no longer applied, for the usages of war with respect to unrestricted submarine warfare had changed.[52]

The second count accused the Germans of being "concerned in the killing of members of the crew. . .by firing and throwing grenades at them." This charge, of course, was the underlying issue in the whole trial. The defense against this count, at least in Eck's case, hinged on two legalistic arguments. First, there was no specific intent to kill the crew; and second, the usages of war with respect to killing survivors had changed from absolute prohibition to acceptance under conditions of operational necessity. The basic defense for the other four defendants was that they were following Eck's orders.[53]

Judge Helmut Sieber, the only active German navy judge in Hamburg after the war, organized the defense. He selected Fregattenkapitän Hans Meckel to be the special advisor to the defense, and Dr. Harold Todsen, a fifty-one year old Hamburg attorney, to represent Heinz Eck. Two other German attorneys, Dr. Max Pabst, age seventy-four, and Dr. Gerd-Otto Wulf, age forty-six, represented Hoffmann jointly, while Dr. Pabst alone represented Schwender. Lenz selected his own attorney, Major Lermon, Barrister at Law, Headquarters 8th Corps District. Dr. Albrecht Wegner, a sixty-two year old expert on international law, was retained on behalf of all the accused.[54]

Dr. Pabst got his look at the case on October 9, but could not make any preparation because he was sitting as a judge in Cuxhaven. He would not be available to start preparing a defense until after October 12. The other attorneys were not notified of the case until October 13.[55]

Day One

The trial opened four days later on Wednesday, October 17, 1945, in Hamburg, Germany, under the authority of a Royal Warrant issued on June 14, 1945. The Warrant empowered British military courts to try cases of "violations of the laws and usages of war committed during any war in which we have been or may have been engaged at any time after 2 September 1939."[56]

The Judge Advocate presiding over the trial was Maj. A. Melford Stevenson, K.C.; the prosecutor was Colonel Halse of the Advocate General's Office. The members of the court, essentially the jury, were three British army officers, two Royal Navy officers and two officers of the Royal Hellenic Navy. The outcome of the trial was evident from the moment it opened.

There were several features about the case that made defending Eck and his men a daunting task. First, there was the deep seated British resentment toward the Germans' use of unrestricted submarine warfare in two back-to-back wars. In addition British dissatisfaction still lingered over the sentences handed down by the German Supreme Court in the *Llandovery Castle* case in 1921. More immediate than the quarter-century old trial was the Allies' reaction to the brutal excesses of the Nazis, which caused them to tar all Germans with the same brush.

On its face, the *Peleus* Affair seemed to justify the popular opinion that Nazi excesses were common to all Germans. The killing of shipwrecked sailors, whether deliberately or as the result of some other intended act, is atrocious. Heinous acts, however, were regularly committed by all the belligerents of World War II. In fact, war itself is atrocious. But the fact that a medical officer took part in the killing made the act even more odious.

As the course of the trial demonstrated, Judge Advocate Stevenson believed the defendants were guilty before the trial even started. That opinion was probably also shared by the seven members of the court who acted as the jury. The predisposition of the court toward a speedy conviction and sentencing was made clear from the beginning of the proceedings when Major Lermon, on behalf of all the defendants, requested a one week postponement so that the lawyers might have time to prepare an adequate defense. Lermon pointed out that none of the defense lawyers, including himself, had had more than three days to view documents and prepare their respective case strategies. He also noted that witnesses who were vital to the defense had not yet arrived, and there had been no time to order documents needed for the defense. Lermon also made it clear that the defense lawyers needed additional time to study legal references on military and international law, which were not yet available for such study. In fact, Dr. Pabst had received just one book on international law the night before the day the trial was set to begin. Compounding the problems of the defense, explained Lermon, none of the German attorneys were familiar with British court procedures and practices, and thus they would need time to learn them.[57]

Despite these compelling arguments, Judge Advocate Stevenson refused the request for adjournment. Instead, he ordered the prosecutor to present his case, at the end of which the matter of witnesses for the defense could be reexamined if they had not yet arrived. The question of the documents needed by the defense was not even addressed. It was to be a speedy trial.[58]

The charges drawn up against Eck and the others were flawed. In the charge sheet, the defendants were alleged to have ". . .sunk the steamship "Peleus" in violation of the laws and usages of war. . . ." According to that wording, they were being charged with a violation of international law as it was understood during World War I. That is, they sank the *Peleus* without warning in violation of the Prize Rules.

No such interpretation of the law existed during World War II, and thus as charged, the defendants were clearly innocent. The mistake might have been exploited by the defendants' lawyers. On the other hand, given the attitude of the court, letting the charge stand probably would not have helped the defense.

When the charges were read and the defendants asked to plead guilty or not guilty, Major Lermon objected, pointing out that if it was the contention that the *Peleus* was sunk in contravention of the laws and usages of war, it was a bad charge. The Judge Advocate and the prosecutor agreed, and the charge sheet was amended to show only one charge and not two. It was a small victory for the defense, and the only victory.

The case for the prosecution was presented in less than three hours. Colonel Halse began by introducing three affidavits signed by the three *Peleus* survivors, after which he called five former U-852 crewmen to the stand. Thereafter Halse introduced admiralty documents showing that the *Peleus* was under charter to the British, and that the men who had signed the affidavits were in fact crew members. The defense strenuously objected to admitting the affidavits because there was no opportunity for cross-examination regarding the truth of their content.

The defense also strongly objected to admitting hearsay evidence contained in one of the affidavits, arguing to the court that all three Greek seamen were within the reach of the Admiralty and could be produced in court. The objection was overruled.[59]

The Judge Advocate's ruling was a major setback, which was compounded by a lackluster cross-examination of the five German witnesses. But even the indifferent questioning produced the fact that none of the German witnesses supported the prosecution's contention that the *Peleus* survivors had been intentionally fired upon. At the close of the prosecution's case, the defense reopened the request for a one week adjournment. They needed witnesses, documents and time to prepare. As the discussion continued it became evident that the Judge Advocate was not interested in delaying the proceedings. Nor was he interested in having witnesses called. In fact, one witness he rejected was Konteradmiral Karl Schmidt, who had been in command of the destroyer *Erich Giese* on April 13, 1940.[60] Admiral Schmidt's testimony was vital to Dr. Todsen's argument that the usages of war had changed with respect to attacks on survivors. Todsen's defense of Eck was based on "operational necessity," and thus it was critical that he demonstrate that throughout World War II, all of the belligerents had justified attacks on shipwrecked survivors on that basis.

The case of the German destroyer, *Erich Giese*, sunk near Narvik on April 13, 1940, is but one well-documented example. After the *Erich Giese* had been sunk, British destroyers fired on the 200 German survivors who were flailing about in the water and clinging to life rafts. The British had claimed the killing was an "operational necessity" to prevent the German sailors from reaching shore and joining the German troops in Narvik.[61]

Killing shipwrecked survivors to prevent them from joining their own forces was not unique to the British. Dr. Todsen, however, was probably unaware of two other similar incidents that had occurred in the South Pacific during World War II. On January 26, 1943, the USS *Wahoo*, on her third war patrol, sank a Japanese troopship off the New Guinea coast. The *Wahoo*'s skipper, LCdr. Dudley W. "Mush" Morton, surfaced to charge his batteries and, according to his own operational report, "destroy the estimated twenty troop boats now in the water." "We surfaced in a sea of Japanese," Lt. George W. Grider wrote. "They were on every piece of flotsam, every broken stick, in lifeboats everywhere." According to Lt. Richard O'Kane, the *Wahoo's* executive officer, the captain said to him, "I will prevent these soldiers from getting ashore. . ." O'Kane, however, was careful to avoid the accusation that the *Wahoo's* fire, which was "methodical. . .sweeping abeam forward like fire hoses sweeping a street," was specifically aimed at the Japanese. According to O'Kane, "Some Japanese troops were undoubtedly hit in this action. But no individual was deliberately shot in the boats or in the sea."[62]

The second incident occurred during and after the Battle of the Bismarck Sea, March 2-5, 1943. According to Capt. Robert R. Buckley, Jr, USNR (Ret.), "thousands of Japanese troops from sunken transports were adrift in collapsible boats." On March 4, those survivors became the targets of repeated air attack, and for several days American PT boats hunted down and sank the rafts. The justification was to prevent the survivors from reaching the New Guinea coast. The explanation was so plausible that the attacks were widely reported in *Newsweek* and *Life*. The Americans, at least, made no secret that the usages of war, with regard to shipwrecked survivors, had drastically changed.[63]

The defense attorneys continued to ask for a one week adjournment. They still needed time to prepare, and there was much to do. Bending slightly, the Judge Advocate granted them an adjournment until 2:15 p.m. the following day.

Day Two

Heinz Eck's attorney, Dr. Todsen, opened the case for the defense on the afternoon of Thursday, October 18, by admitting that the basic facts of the case were not in dispute—his client confirmed everything the five prosecution witnesses had said. But the destruction of the large rafts, argued Todsen, was an "operational necessity" created by the presence of efficient anti-submarine units—especially aircraft—in the South Atlantic. The fact that the *Peleus* survivors would certainly die as a result of the rafts' destruction was an unavoidable cost. He argued that there was no intent to specifically attack the survivors.

Professor Wegner, the international law expert retained on behalf of all of the defendants, stepped forward to address specific issues in his area of expertise. Wegner's presentation, similar in style to a classroom lecture, was essentially an outline of legal issues that would be fully addressed later. He began by noting that the charges against the accused were for a breach of the "customary" laws of war, not any article of any specific Convention. He stated that since 1914 there had been continued and progressive changes in the usages of war, although he did not provide any examples. He did, however, hint that the "modern conception of war crimes" was at odds with those changes.[64] Wegner also raised five other points without arguing any of them. Two of the points were clearly intended as the basis for an aggressive defense. First, he cited the Latin phrase *Nullum crimen sine lega, Nulla poena sine lege* (no crime without the preceding law, no punishment for an act committed before the law was enacted), an unambiguous reference to the vague nature of the charges against Eck and his crew. The charge of war crimes, Wegner concluded, presumes a guilty knowledge or intent. Unfortunately, the court was not going to listen to arguments based on fine legalistic grounds, and the defense was simply not aggressive or adept enough to convince it otherwise.

After Wegner concluded his lecture-style defense, Dr. Todsen again took the floor. During World War I, he argued, "both sides were, under certain conditions, allowed to attack lifeboats, even survivors." Although his reference was vaguely stated, he may have been referring to the *Baralong* Affair and the so-called *Baralong II* Affair.[65] The HMS *Baralong*, a Q-ship commanded by LCdr. Godfrey Herbert, sank U-27 and shot the survivors in the water. Some of the Germans, including U-27's captain, Kaptlt. Bernhard Wegner, sought refuge aboard the SS *Nicosian*, which had been abandoned by its crew and was still afloat. Herbert sent marines aboard the *Nicosian* who hunted down and killed the remaining German survivors. The deed would have gone unreported except that among the *Nicosian's* crew were several Americans who told the story to the American press when they got home. The British response was to claim "operational necessity" based on the possibility that the Germans might have armed themselves and escaped aboard the *Nicosian*.[66]

The other event to which Dr. Todsen was probably referring was the destruction of U-41 by the same British Q-ship on September 24, 1915. In that case the *Baralong*, renamed *Wiarda*, lured U-41 into range and sank the U-boat with gunfire. After the *Wiarda* left the area the only two survivors, Oberleutnant z.S. Crompton and U-Steuermann Godau, climbed aboard an abandoned lifeboat. About three hours later the

Wiarda returned and deliberately ran down the lifeboat. Miraculously both men survived the ramming and, in a turn of events, were subsequently rescued up by their former attacker.[67]

Whatever Todsen was referring to, the argument received an immediate and clever response from the prosecutor, Colonel Halse. Halse informed the court that if Todsen was going to introduce evidence to support his claim, the prosecution would have to ask for an adjournment to prepare a rebuttal. The Judge Advocate indicated that if needed, he would grant the adjournment.[68] At this point it became evident that Todsen was not prepared to follow-up on his claim with actual evidence. Instead, he told the court he assumed the fact was common knowledge and that the court would take judicial notice thereof. When the Judge Advocate refused to do so, Todsen let the matter drop.

Why did Eck's attorney back down so quickly? Certainly he had no way of knowing what the Americans had done in the Pacific during World War II, but he was on solid ground with several other examples from both world wars, about which there was ample information. Had he pressed the matter the court would have adjourned to give the prosecutor time to prepare. That same adjournment could have been used by the defense to obtain the documentary evidence it needed. Todsen crumbled in the face of Halse's thinly-veiled bluff, and an important opportunity to bolster his client's defense slipped past.

In Todsen's defense, he probably recognized that the court had already made its decision about the defendants' guilt, and thus further effort in obtaining such evidence was useless. It is also possible that he believed he would antagonize the court by introducing examples of similar British acts for which his client now faced execution. But by that time it was obvious which direction the court was leaning, and antagonizing the court would not have made things any worse than they already were.

Heinz Eck took the stand that afternoon. If Todsen was hoping the ex-U-boat commander's testimony would bolster the sagging defense, he was sadly mistaken, for Eck did nothing to help his case. His answers, short and often abrupt, failed to explain why he had been so concerned about the threat from aircraft. Todsen also turned in another weak effort by failing to provide Eck with the opportunity to expand on his answers. It was a poor performance by both men.

Eck did establish, however, that his sole intent was to destroy the rafts because he believed they would have been easily spotted by aircraft the following morning. He also told the court he had been concerned about the possibility that the rafts might have been equipped with emergency radio transmitters. But he insisted that though he knew, and accepted, that the survivors would die as a result of his action, it was never his intent to kill them. Eck also explained that he thought the rafts were built on hollow floats and would sink if the floats were punctured by machine gun fire. When that did not happen, he had the signal light turned on so that they could examine the rafts and determine why they would not sink. The decision to use hand grenades to blow up the life rafts came about only because the machine guns had failed to do the job. Nevertheless, he continued to fire at the rafts with machine guns because there did not seem to be any other way to accomplish his goal.

Eck insisted he never saw any signs that the rafts were occupied during the attack because it was too dark to see clearly. The rafts, he testified, were simply large, dark forms on the water, and he assumed the occupants had jumped off at the first machine gun burst. He admitted, however, that he realized there might be people on the rafts even after the firing started. Regardless of whether or not he knew there were survivors in the water, he was forbidden by orders from rescuing them or offering any assistance. Eck concluded with an explanation of why he felt it had been necessary to explain the action to his crew. He said that he had "made the decision with a heavy heart." At this point the Judge Advocate interrupted the questioning.[69]

Judge Advocate: "What decision?"

Eck's answered the court in German, which was translated by a court interpreter. "To destroy the remainder of the sunken ship." A problem arose at this point from the English translation of the German word, "Überreste."

Dr. Todsen, who spoke English, quickly objected to "the remainder of the sunken ship" being the translation for "Überreste." "That is not quite a translation," he told the Judge Advocate. "It could be wreckage or it could be rafts."

"In French it would be debris—wreckage?" queried the Judge.

Todsen, still speaking in English, handed the Judge Advocate an opening to exploit. "Literally it means all that has been left by the sunken ship."

Judge Advocate, exploiting the opening, addressed his question to Eck, "That would include survivors, did it not?"

Eck answered in German which was translated, "I cannot remember the verbal message any more."

"That is not what I am asking," said the Judge Advocate. "Did you say just now that you had made your decision with a heavy heart?"

Eck answered, "yes."

"That was the decision to destroy what you call the Überreste?"

Eck, "Yes."

"The Überreste included survivors, did it not?" pressed the Judge Advocate.

Eck's answer in German translated as, "I do not know exactly the words I did use at that time." Eck's answer sounds evasive, but it may not have been. He certainly used the word "Überreste" in court. But on the night of March 13, he may have used the term "Schiffstrümmer," a nautical expression for wreckage. In any event, he should have stated clearly that "Überreste" meant the wreckage, and had nothing to do with human survivors.[70]

In a stunning legal lapse, Dr. Todsen, whose command of English was excellent, failed to intervene on his client's behalf and blunt what was clearly a prejudicial attack from the bench. Todsen could easily have made it clear that the German word for survivors is "Schiffsbrüchige." By failing to act forcefully on behalf of his client, Todsen allowed the court to equivocate an act in which the intent was limited to the destruction of wreckage, with an act that included the intent to kill the survivors.

Todsen tried to recover some of the lost ground. What, he inquired, would "your enemy have done in a similar position?"

He knew the direction he wanted to go with the question. He was trying to open the issue of the *Laconia* Affair to support his claim that the usages of war had changed and the Allies also were willing to justify killing shipwreck survivors as an operational necessity. The *Laconia* Affair seemed to be safe ground because it involved American servicemen instead of British personnel. Thus, bringing it up might not antagonize the court.

The *Laconia*, a 19,700 ton former Cunard liner, was torpedoed and sunk by Kkpt. Werner Hartenstein in U-156 on September 12, 1942. Unbeknownst to Hartenstein, the *Laconia* carried some 3,250 people, among them eighty British women and children, 160 Polish ex-POWs, 188 British service personnel and 1,800 Italian POWs. After he sank the liner, Hartenstein surfaced and discovered to his astonishment over 2,000 people struggling in the water, many of them Italian POWs. Hartenstein immediately began rescue operations and notified BdU. Admiral Dönitz ordered two other submarines, U-506 and U-507, to the area to assist in the rescue. The Italian submarine *Cappellini* also raced toward the scene. Even the Vichy French were asked to assist. In clear English Hartenstein broadcast that if he was not attacked, he would not interfere with any ship aiding in the rescue.

The recovery of survivors was still in progress on the morning of September 16. By this time Hartenstein's U-156 was crowded above deck and below with 110 British and Italian survivors, including five women. The U-boat also had four lifeboats in tow filled with additional victims. She was cruising on the surface for a rendezvous position with a French ship when an American B-24 from Ascension Island came into view at 9:30 a.m. The other U-boats (U-506 and 507) were similarly loaded with survivors. Hartenstein ordered a Red Cross flag draped across the forward deck gun and sent light signals to the bomber asking for assistance. The B-24, piloted by Lt. James D. Harden turned away and radioed Ascension Island for orders. It should have been clear to him that a rescue operation was underway.

The officer called upon to make a decision that day was Capt. Robert C. Richardson III. As he saw the situation, he had two choices. He could recall the B-24, which would mean that the U-boats would later be able to attack Allied shipping. Or, he could order an attack, accepting the fact that many of the survivors would certainly be killed. The signal sent to the B-24 was short and direct: "Sink sub."

Harden turned his B-24 back toward the scene and dropped down to make a low-level attack with bombs and depth charges. One bomb fell among the four lifeboats being towed behind the U-156, while the others exploded around the U-boat. Under attack, Hartenstein was left with no choice. He ordered the survivors huddled on deck back into the water, and sought the safety of the deep. Captain Richardson justified his decision as an "operational necessity" based on the need to protect

Allied shipping from future attacks. The fact that shipwrecked survivors—including women and children—would probably be killed was an unfortunate reality that had to be accepted.[71]

Eck told the court what he knew of the *Laconia* Affair, and concluded with about the strongest statement he made in his own defense. "This case showed me that the enemy's military reasons go before human reasons, before saving the lives of survivors. For that reason, I thought my measures justified."[72]

Todsen completed his direct examination of his client, and Colonel Halse rose to cross-examine Eck. His opening questions were intended to reestablish the facts of the case in Eck's own words, an easily obtained goal. Over time the tone of the questions subtly changed as Halse laid the groundwork to snare Eck. By precisely choosing the right words in his queries, and getting Eck to use specific words in response, Halse depicted Eck as a heartless brute. Certainly the manner in which Eck's answers were translated for the court was important in helping to develop the desired effect.

First, Halse compelled Eck to admit that U-852 had been on the surface during daylight despite the threat of being discovered by aircraft. He then concentrated on the attack on the rafts, which lasted for five hours. Picking his questions carefully, Halse secured from Eck an estimate as to the number of survivors in the water during the attack on the rafts. Eck estimated the number to be about twelve. Halse now had the information he wanted.

Having established that Eck had at least some idea about how many people were in the water, the colonel struck hard and fast.

"It was essential that the rafts should be destroyed?" asked Halse, knowing there was only one consistent answer Eck could provide.

"Yes," came Eck's reply.

"And at one o'clock the rafts were not destroyed?" Halse further inquired, once again knowing in advance the answer to the question.

"No."

"Why did you stop firing at the rafts at one o'clock?" Halse was carefully setting his verbal trap for the unsuspecting Eck.

"I saw no further possibility to destroy the rafts," explained Eck. "I had tried it with machine gun fire, hand grenades and ramming, but it was no good."

Halse sprung his trap. "Was it not because there were no more survivors left?"

"I did not concern myself with that," Eck responded. Given the line of questioning the answer was a good answer. It was not the best answer he could have given, however, and the damage was done.

Halse, however, was far from finished. Questions about the speech Eck made to the crew and the reason for the speech set up the ex-U-boat commander for the next body blow.

According to Eck, he had told his crew: "If we are influenced by too much sympathy, we must also think of our wives and children who at home die as the victims of air attack."

"Sympathy about wreckage?" Halse asked incredulously (and disingenuously).

"It was quite clear that the survivors would also die," Eck responded. Again, Eck had missed an opportunity to blunt Halse's pointed attack. He should have told the court he had sympathy for the survivors, and their inevitable death was a source of grave concern to him. That he was faced with an operational necessity, and the survivors' deaths were a tragic consequence of war. He said none of these things.

"You did not mind whether they died or not?" Halse continued.

There was a hint of irritation in Eck's answer. "In my remarks over the loudspeaker I had said that I did care about it." Either Eck was angry or the translation was particularly prejudicial.[73]

Dr. Todsen reexamined Eck in an attempt to plaster over some of the damage Colonel Halse had inflicted. Unfortunately for Eck, Todsen's questioning was once again unimaginative, and Eck's answers did little in the way of assisting his defense. With little or no new ground being covered by Todsen's line of questioning, the Judge Advocate again interrupted with his own line of inquiry.

"How many times have you seen a ship sunk?" was how he opened his examination. Clearly the Judge Advocate had been pondering Eck's claim that he was trying to eliminate all traces of the sinking.[74]

"Five times," Eck answered, referring to his training war patrol aboard Mohr's U-124.

"Have you ever seen a ship sunk that did not leave a large patch of oil on the surface?" The thrust of the question was clear, but either Eck missed the point or the question was incorrectly translated into German. In any event, his answer did not match the question.

"They were not all tankers," he answered.

"I am not talking about tankers. I am talking about traces of oil from ships of any kind."

"I tried twice to find any traces from ships," Eck replied, "but I was unable to find any."

This response provided Todsen an opening to exploit. Here was an opportunity to discuss the effect that weather and the speed with which a ship sank might have on whether a ship left oil behind, or how visible on the surface that substance might or might not be. Todsen failed to grasp the opportunity.

"Do you say that such a ship as the *Peleus* can be sunk without a trace of oil?" continued the Judge Advocate.

"If it is a coal burning ship, it is possible," came Eck's poorly-worded reply. Eck knew the *Peleus* was not a coal burner. At best the answer made him appear to be splitting hairs or, more likely, evading the question.

The Judge Advocate changed tack with a series of hard hitting questions that would have been better asked by the prosecutor. "Would it not have been much safer for you and your boat to clear out as soon as possible?" he asked, wanting to learn why Eck had not used his ability to cruise at high speed on the surface to leave the area, instead of lingering around the scene of the sinking for five hours.

He also asked if Eck had made any attempt to find out if the rafts were in fact equipped with radios. When Eck said he had not, the Judge Advocate asked, "You could have done so; could you not?"

The Judge Advocate also revealed for the first time that first watch officer Georg Colditz had objected to the decision to destroy the rafts. Then came a slanted—and loaded—question: "When you said that you regretted your decision, was that not a reference to a *decision to kill survivors*?" (emphasis added).

Eck's response, if it had been consistent with his previous testimony, would have been that he had never made a decision to kill survivors. Instead he simply said, "yes."

The Judge Advocate continued the attack, asking why Eck had chosen to use machine guns to destroy the rafts instead of the 105mm deck gun. The range, Eck replied, was too short to accurately aim the gun. Again, Eck left himself vulnerable and the Judge Advocate jumped at the opportunity. "Of course, if you only wanted to destroy survivors, a machine gun would be a better weapon; would it not?"[75]

Yet again Dr. Todsen tried to mend the damage wrought by the Judge Advocate's questions and Eck's poorly-worded replies, but his indifferent questioning led nowhere and Eck's answers were too brief.

The second day of the trial ended at 5:00 p.m. with Eck still on the stand. The other defense counsels would have an opportunity to cross-examine Eck when the court reconvened at 10:00 a.m. the next day.

While it had not been a good day for Heinz Eck, neither was it for the remaining defendants. Unlike Eck's situation, the defense of Weisspfennig, Hoffmann, Schwender and Lenz rested on the concept that they were following orders, a requirement essential to military order and discipline in all armies. The issue at hand, however, was not a matter of simply following an order. In this court there was a higher standard—the order had to be a *legal* order. Therefore, it was essential that Eck's "operational necessity" defense succeed. If Eck was found guilty, the others would likewise be convicted.

Day Three

Friday, October 19, was the first full day the court was in session. In cross-examining Eck, the defense of the remaining four defendants had to establish that in the German navy, disobeying an order was a capital offense. In fact, anyone disobeying an order could be shot on the spot by his superior officer. That point was clearly made by Major Lermon, who was defending Lenz.

"Is it a serious offense to disobey an order on active operations?" Lermon inquired of Eck.[76]

"For not carrying out an order in the face of an enemy," Eck flatly stated, "one is punished with death."

"Who can carry out that punishment?" Lermon asked.

"At sea the commander has the right of doing that," Eck told him.[77]

The cross-examination by Drs. Pabst and Wulf lacked vitality and developed no information to further support what Major Lermon had established. International law specialist Dr. Wegner questioned Eck about what he had said to the crew after the shooting. At issue was the translation of the German word "Schlagwort." The court interpreter had translated it as meaning "slogan," implying that Eck addressed the crew using propaganda terms. Wegner argued that "catch-word," though not exactly proper, would have been a better translation.

Speaking in English, he told the court, "Schlagwort means to put a thing as sharp as possible. Sometimes we also say, 'to speak in telegram style.'" Then he asked Eck what he had meant by the word "Schlag-wort."[78]

Eck answered that it had been his intention "to make everything clear to the crew in short sentences. . . . That is why I gave the example of the air attacks in order to make clear to the crew that also with the enemy military reasons could lead to disregarding women and children."[79]

British policy, which had initially refused to bomb targets in the Ruhr in 1940 for fear of damaging private property and killing women and children, evolved into the wholesale slaughter of civilians in area bombing of cities. Clearly such a policy shift constituted a major change in the usages of war. But even the British were careful not to admit that they were targeting civilians. In their words they were simply "dehousing Germans."[80]

His testimony at an end, Heinz Eck stepped down and Dr. Todsen recalled a prosecution witness, Mr. John C. Mossop, who had been involved in the interrogations of all the U-852 defendants. It was Todsen's hope that he could use Mossop to demonstrate that the threat of air attack on U-boats in the South Atlantic was substantial. He asked Mossop about aircraft coverage between Freetown and Ascension. Mossop told him that in a maximum effort, five or six aircraft could be kept airborne between Freetown and Ascension. He also said that aircraft carriers operated in that area from time to time.

Todsen also quizzed the witness about the "Hartenstein Affair," meaning the *Laconia* Affair. Mossop described the event with about the same detail Eck had used when he described it on the trial's second day. Eck's counsel, however, took a different direction than that which might have been expected. Instead of using the incident to show similar behavior by the Allies, and thus demonstrate a change in the usages of war, he asked if the BdU had issued any instructions following the incident. Mossop answered, correctly, that orders were issued that no attempt of any kind should be made to rescue survivors.

Todsen then called Adalbert Schnee, who was to be his star witness, to the stand. Korvettenkapitän Schnee, holder of the Knight's Cross with Oak Leaves, ranked twenty-second among the war's most successful U-boat commanders. He had commanded U-6, U-60, U-201 and an experimental Type XXI, U-2511. He had also served on the BdU staff for nearly two years. Schnee was one of the officers who had briefed Eck before U-852 went to sea.[81]

Under direct examination Schnee essentially repeated what he had told Eck in January 1944. Todsen asked him about the effect of debris left in the wake of a sinking. Debris, Schnee responded, could be recognized from the air for several days. Todsen then asked Schnee what could be done about the wreckage. "He could try to destroy and sink all the bigger pieces below the surface," came his answer.[82]

Todsen next turned his attention to reducing the damage done by the Judge Advocate's questions about oil left after a sinking. Schnee, an experienced U-boat captain, agreed that oil-fired steamers left large patches of oil on the surface. But, he added, "one can find on routes occasionally smaller patches of oil which do not necessarily suggest a sinking," he explained. "They also occur from the cleaning of bilges," he added.

"If you had been on Eck's boat," Todsen inquired, "and it was your intention to sink rafts, which weapons would you have chosen to destroy them?"

Schnee told the court he would have done what Eck did—used the machine guns to sink the rafts on the grounds that the rafts were probably supported by hollow bodies. He rejected, as had Eck, the use of the deck gun and demolition charges. Coming from an experienced, highly decorated U-boat captain with an unblemished record, Schnee's testimony weakened the prosecution's case.[83]

Colonel Halse's cross-examination started out mildly. He asked about Schnee's experience, how many ships he had sunk, and what were the differences between operations in the North and South Atlantic. Then the tone changed abruptly.

"What would you have done as an experienced U-boat commander, if you were in Eck's position?"[84]

Before Schnee could answer the hypothetical question Major Lermon interrupted. "In my submission the witness ought to be warned that he need not answer that particular question as it might incriminate him. I do not think Dr. Todsen realizes the position."

"I am not so sure that the witness does enjoy that privilege," the Judge Advocated answered Lermon. Then, speaking to Schnee and choosing the wording of his statement very carefully, the Judge Advocate made it clear just how thin the ice was upon which Schnee was treading.

"You can refuse to answer a question if you think it might expose you to prosecution for war crimes."

Schnee was in a tight spot. If for any reason he did not answer a question, the court would take it as an admission that he had committed some sort of war crime. Given the biased attitude of the Judge Advocate, that could lead to just one thing: Schnee's arrest.

Grasping immediately the box within which the witness was now in, Colonel Halse immediately re-asked the same question: "As an experienced U-boat commander, what would you have done if you were in Eck's position on the night of 13 March?"

Schnee gave an honest answer. "I do not know this case well enough to give an answer."

This, of course, was not what the Judge Advocate wanted to hear. "Come; you can do a little better than that. You know the circumstances of this case, do you not? You have been giving evidence about them."

Schnee said something in German that was not translated.

"You have dealt in great detail with the propriety of leaving the site of the sinking; have you not?" continued the Judge Advocate.

Again, Schnee's answer was not translated. Whatever he said, the Judge Advocate, who spoke enough German to understand the answers, was not happy with the wary officer's replies.

"You were asked what would you have done if you had been the commander of U-852 and had just sunk the *Peleus*."

Schnee doggedly stuck to his position. "It is very difficult for me to give an answer to that."

"Would you try?" the Judge Advocate insisted.

"Now that the war is over, I cannot possibly put myself in such a difficult position as Captain Eck was in at that time." Schnee was dancing in a minefield.

The Judge Advocate was not having any of that. He knew the answer he wanted and he was going to get it. "The fact that the war is over hasn't deprived you of your imagination, has it? Just answer yes or no."

Schnee could see what was happening, and there was nothing he could do to prevent it. "No," he answered.

Having made his point, the Judge Advocate re-asked the question. "What would you have done if you had been in Eck's position?"

Schnee knew that he was beaten. All he could do now was protect himself against the court's wrath and prevent his own indictment, while doing his best to limit the damage his testimony would do to Eck. "I would under all circumstances have tried my best to save lives, as that is a measure which was taken by all U-boat commanders, but when I hear of this case, then I can only explain it as this, that Captain Eck through the terrific experience he had been through lost his nerve."

He still had not answered the question directly, and the Judge Advocate was not going to let him off the hook. "Does that mean that you would not have done what Captain Eck did if you had kept your nerve?"

"I would not have done it," was how Schnee finally answered the question.

The Judge Advocate had beaten the witness into submission and had rehabilitated the prosecution's case at the same time. It was left to Colonel Halse to put the icing on the cake.

"Have you heard of any other U-boat commander who has done the same thing as Eck did in this case?" The question had far-reaching consequences.

"No, I have not."

"Did the BdU approve of the killing of survivors?"

"No, it did not approve, not at the time when I was a member of the BdU staff," Schnee responded.

"Were orders issued that survivors were not to be killed?"

"It was not necessary because this order had already been issued at the outbreak of war."

Dr. Todsen tried to soften the Judge Advocate's attack by asking Schnee the same question. "If you had been in Eck's position, would you have destroyed wreckage?" Schnee, who had just testified that he would not have done as Eck had, reversed himself and answered in the affirmative. "Yes."

The Judge Advocate quickly interrupted. "Have you ever seen a raft destroyed by machine gun fire?"

Schnee admitted he had not.

"Have you ever tried it yourself?"

Schnee answered the question with a denial.[85]

Dr. Pabst, Schwender's individual attorney, was mainly interested in reinforcing the fact that in the face of disobedience, a German officer had the right to "make use of arms." Schnee confirmed that fact. Whether the order was legal or not, refusal to obey could result in immediate execution, a powerful motive to obey one's superior. Pabst had made his point, and Schnee stepped down from the stand.[86]

The last witness to take the stand before the noon recess was August Hoffmann. Like Eck before him, Hoffmann's testimony did little to help his defense. Under direct examination by Pabst, Hoffmann simply restated what had already been said about the night of March 13.

When Dr. Wulf, who together with Pabst was jointly defending Hoffmann, questioned his client about his background and family, the Judge Advocate said, "This court is perfectly prepared to assume that this is a man of good character, *apart from the matter which the court is now investigating.*" (emphasis added). Dr. Wulf asked no further questions of Hoffmann.[87]

Colonel Halse cross-examined Hoffmann and almost immediately was able to get the young officer to contradict himself.

"You knew then that there were people on the rafts?" the prosecutor inquired.[88]

"We had to assume that," Hoffmann answered.

"You fired at the rafts?" It was as much a statement as a question.

"Yes."

"Knowing there were people on them?"

"No." Hoffmann said. When he realized he had been lulled into contradicting himself, Hoffmann attempted to backtrack and explain that he assumed the people had jumped into the water. But the damage was done.[89]

Hoffmann's fate was all but sealed when Halse established that he had not actually received a direct order from Eck to fire and that Hoffmann was the only one who threw the hand grenades.

Oberstabsarzt Weisspfennig followed Hoffmann to the stand. Of all the defendants, Weisspfennig's case was the hardest to defend. In fact, it was impossible to defend because he was a non-combatant, specifically prohibited from taking up arms except in self-defense. Still, he plead superior orders on the grounds that he had in fact received a direct order from Eck to fire at the wreckage.

Dr. Pabst's questioning was weak. Since the facts of the case were not in dispute, however, there was little Pabst could ask or Weisspfennig could answer that would mitigate his position. The role Weisspfennig played in the trial was that of a millstone around the necks of the other defendants, and in his cross-examination, Colonel Halse did an efficient job of insuring that the stone was very heavy.

Chief Engineer Lenz followed Weisspfennig. Questioning by Major Lermon established that Lenz had objected to Eck's plan "out of sympathy for the survivors," and that he was below deck during most of the shooting. Then Lermon asked Lenz to tell the court why, in view of his objection to Eck, he had taken the gun from Schwender.[90]

"I thought that if Schwender fired on those pieces of wreckage, a human being whom I had spoken to a short while ago might be hit and killed," Lenz tried to explain, "and I did not want that that man should be hit by bullets which a soldier, who in my eyes was considered bad, had fired." It was a difficult answer to fully understand.[91]

Under cross-examination by Colonel Halse, Lenz admitted that he had not received a direct order from Eck to fire. According to Lenz the order was "im Laufen," in the course of being carried out. He believed that though he had received no direct order, he was nonetheless bound by it since it was "im Laufen."

Lenz's justification for shoving Schwender aside, taking the gun and opening fire fit his concept of honor and chivalry. The court, however, found it absurd. As a result Lenz, too, became a millstone around the necks of his fellow crewmen.[92]

The last defendant to take the stand was Wolfgang Schwender. His defense was by far the easiest to articulate and rested on reasonably solid ground. He was an enlisted man, hardly in a position to question an order whether it was legal or not, and he had been given a direct order to fire. His participation in the firing, such that it was, was extremely limited. He had been below deck during most of the shooting, and Lenz had taken away the gun after Schwender had fired just one burst.

When Schwender stepped down, Professor Wegner spoke at length on international law. Dr. Wegner had a distinguished legal career before the war as an expert on international law. He was the author of two books on the subject, one of them, published in 1925, defended the decisions, but not the sentences, handed down in the 1921 Leipzig trials. He had spent the war in England and was a close personal friend of Dr. George Bell, Bishop of Chichester.[93]

But it was a thoroughly exhausted Wegner who rose to speak, asking the court for an adjournment. "I think the position is that the defending counsel would like an adjournment until ten o'clock in the morning from now," he stated. "I should like to start tomorrow morning. I must admit that I am dead tired now, because I have been working all night on it."

The Judge Advocate was in no mood to grant an adjournment. "The court wants to continue until five o'clock."[94]

Wegner opened his speech by citing the verdict handed down by the German Supreme Court in the *Llandovery Castle* Case. As previously alluded, the professor brought up the verdict in the 1921 case on the first day of the trial, and referred to it again on the second. If there was any hope for a defense victory, they had to defeat the opinions expressed by the German court—the very opinions that Dr. Wegner had defended in 1925.

The hospital ship *Llandovery Castle* was torpedoed by U-86 on June 27, 1918, 116 miles south-west of Fastnet. Fortunately the ship had no patients aboard when she was torpedoed, her compliment being eighty RAMC doctors, fourteen nurses and a crew of 164. After the hospital ship had gone down, U-86 surfaced and the U-boat's captain, Oberleutnant z.S. H. Patzig, two of his officers, Leutnants z.S. Ludwig Dithmar and John Boldt, and an enlisted gunner, Bootsmaat Meissner, opened fire on the life boats. Of the 258 people on board the *Llandovery Castle*, only twenty-four survived.

A trial over the incident was held in July 1921. Only two of the accused even showed up. The captain of U-86, Patzig, simply stayed away, while the enlisted gunner, Meissner had died by the time the trial started. That left just two officers in the dock, Ludwig Dithmar and John Boldt. They were found guilty as accessories to the crime of killing survivors in life boats and sentenced to four years imprisonment. Both men "escaped" from prison a short time later.[95]

The leniency of the sentences handed down by the German court in 1921 was one of the reasons that Eck and the others were being tried by a British military tribunal in 1945. The British were outraged by the light sentence and determined that it would not happen again.

But the real significance of the *Llandovery Castle* case was that it involved two elements common to the *Peleus* trial: the first was the ruling that "firing on the boats was an offense against the law of nations," and "the subordinate obeying an order is liable to punishment, if it was known to him that the order. . .involved the infringement of civil or international law."[96]

Dr. Wegner noted that he had defended the court's verdict of guilty against strident nationalist opposition. But he now argued that the usages of war had changed and the principles established in the 1921 trial no longer applied.

The professor was in a position to support his view that the usages of war had changed by citing specific cases. Certainly he had many from which to choose from both wars. Instead, he lapsed into gratuitous compliments on the conduct of the present court and started to recount a wartime experience he had with Dr. George Bell, Bishop of Chichester.

The Judge Advocate interrupted Wegner with an embarrassing scolding. "Professor, the court is most ready to receive any help you can give it on any question of international law, but it is not prepared to to listen to an account of your experiences with the Bishop of Chichester. Let us hear anything you have to say about international law, but please keep to that."[97]

Despite the reprimand from the bench to focus his argument, Wegner's speech continued in the form of a lengthy dissertation without clearly defined parameters. Occasionally, however, he showed signs that he might be developing an aggressive defense. The principles established in the Leipzig trials, he argued, could not apply because "our situation is that now our accused are not before a German court, and we do not exactly know what law we are going to apply to their case." He also made perhaps his most telling contention by maintaining that "we cannot call any man a war criminal without his doing wrong and being guilty according to a law enacted before his deed."

Wegner attempted to use a dispute that had occurred between the United States and Great Britain in 1837 to show that an individual acting under orders of his government is not answerable for crimes committed during the act. The *Caroline* Case involved a violation of U.S. territorial waters that resulted in the death of two American citizens. Although the effort was a good one, the legal precedent was not. Wegner may have used it simply because he had nothing else and there was too little time and insufficient reference material available for him to come up with something better.[98]

Despite these occasional flashes of sagacity, Wegner's speech was rambling and disjointed. The Judge Advocate thought so as well, for he once again interrupted the professor. "If you have found any authority which justifies the killing of survivors of a sunken ship when they are in the water, will you try to come to it quickly, because that is what we want, you know."

This second reprimand notwithstanding, Wegner—apparently very tired and perhaps a bit confused—continued to ramble on. Near the end of what had become little more than a classroom lecture, Wegner expressed his true feelings about the attitude of the court and the trial's inevitable outcome. "I have no doubt that the passions of today will pass and will be replaced by calmer and more peaceful judgment on war crimes and alleged German crimes. Then he who is now yielding to the feeling and mood of the moment, or even to the mob, will be ashamed." Wegner was all but conceding the ultimate conviction and execution of Heinz Eck.[99]

The court adjourned at 5:00 p.m., exactly on time.

Day Four

The trial reconvened on Saturday, October 20, at 10:00 a.m., for what would be the longest day of the trial—the closing arguments. Dr Todsen began his close in English, arguing that there had been no evidence to show that the survivors were intentionally killed. He also argued that Eck had no motive to kill the survivors, as had the officers of U-86 in the *Llandovery Castle* case. Therefore, the judgment in that case could not apply to this one. Todsen restated the "operational necessity" defense, citing the strength of Allied aircraft in the area and the fates of four previous Type IXD2 boats that had passed through that sector. Where did a U-boat captain's priority lay, Todsen asked the court rhetorically, with the boat and his crew, or with the survivors?

Dr. Todsen missed two chances to expand on the argument that the usages of war had changed by not arguing the belligerents' bombing raids against cities and the Allied killing of survivors in the *Laconia* Affair. He touched on both subjects, but did not elaborate. In the end he tried to hook up with Dr. Wegner's weak *Caroline* argument, but even then, he made only a passing reference to it.

Dr. Pabst addressed the court in German on behalf of Dr. Weisspfennig, August Hoffmann and Wolfgang Schwender. Pabst, who read quite clearly the grim writing on the wall, followed a new line of reasoning instead of merely rehashing what the court had already heard. If the court found the accused guilty, Pabst maintained, then the court must decide if the men were guilty of murder, manslaughter or involuntary manslaughter. In an obvious attempt to sway the court away from a murder finding and open at least the possibility of a conviction of manslaughter, Pabst asserted that the judgment of the defendants was clouded by excitement and strain on the night the *Peleus* was sunk.

Switching gears, Pabst devoted some time and hit hard on the defense that the crewmen were obeying orders, and thus on March 13, 1944, the accused were subject to German military law. And, he added, as POWs they were still subject to German military law. He then addressed the case of each man individually, beginning with Wolfgang Schwender.

None of the testimony established that Schwender had actually aimed at a human being. In fact, the evidence showed that he had fired only at wreckage, and for only a very short time. Schwender had, argued Pabst, not participated in the killing of human beings.

August Hoffmann and Dr. Walter Weisspfennig posed more difficult problems. Hoffmann had never been given a direct order to fire (and yet did so), while as a doctor, Weisspfennig was prohibited from taking any offensive action (although he too had used a machine gun). With little choice, Pabst fell back on the simple plea of superior orders, citing German regulations found in the Militärstrafgesetzbuch. Since they acted on a binding order, the order lifted responsibility from them. He, too, cited the *Caroline* case, reciting the observation that "the English government recognizes the fact that the order of a superior does not make the subordinate responsible." He followed that with reference to the 1921 German court decision in the *Dover Castle* case.[100]

The hospital ship *Dover Castle*, sunk on May 26, 1917, by UC-67 in the Mediterranean, was carrying wounded from Malta to Gibraltar. Six men were lost. UC-67's captain, Oberleutnant z.S. Karl Neumann, was never charged with a war crime, but at the direction of the German Attorney General, "an enquiry was held to decide the point whether the accused on 26 May 1917, intentionally killed six men. . . ." The proceedings ended in his acquittal. The court ruled that Neumann was following orders when he torpedoed the hospital ship.[101]

Seizing on this case as precedent, Dr. Pabst argued that because the British had never protested the decision, they accepted the principle of superior orders. In the *Llandovery Castle* case, the judgment against the two officers was based on the grounds that they knew the order they had received was illegal. In the case of Weisspfennig and Hoffmann, they did not know.

Engineer Hans Lenz's counsel, Major Lermon, opened his closing statement by restating a portion of Dr. Pabst's closing argument: no witness had testified that any of the survivors had actually been shot at. The only contrary evidence were the affidavits signed by the three *Peleus* survivors, and the major wondered aloud why the three crewmen had not been brought into court so they could be faced by the accused. He pointed out that the prosecution had fourteen months to arrange for their appearance in court.

Lermon lectured the court on the issue of "superior orders":

> If you hold that superior orders are no defense to an individual, then you are putting in an impossible situation any individual who is subject to military law and to military discipline, particularly any member of the German Wehrmacht. As you have already heard from Dr. Pabst, and as you have already heard in evidence, under German law, when on active service, if a person refuses to obey an order, his superior has the right to mete out a death penalty. If you decide that superior orders are no defense, you put the individual into this impossible position that if he disobeys the order he is liable to be shot immediately; but if he obeys the order he is liable to come before a court and be charged on a capital offense with a war crime.[102]

While his argument was cogent and focused, he still had to somehow explain why Lenz took the machine gun from Schwender and opened on the rafts. And, of course, there was little he could say except to restate that for Lenz, it was a matter of honor.

Colonel Halse wasted little time in getting to the heart of his argument against Eck and his crew members. Eck's orders on the night of March 13, argued Halse, were illegal in light of the German court's ruling in the *Llandovery Castle* case. Therefore, there could be no defense of superior orders for Weisspfennig, Hoffmann and Schwender. Eck's directives, he said, amounted to "cold blooded murder."[103] Halse also told the court that the case against Hoffmann had been fully proven. Hoffmann admitted firing the machine gun, and he said he was the only one who threw hand grenades. One of the three survivors testified in an affidavit that one of the men on a raft had been killed by a hand grenade.

The prosecutor made his strongest attack on Dr. Weisspfennig, saying that "his case is made the worse by reason of the fact that he is of the medical profession, and has no right to bear arms at all. . . ." Passing on to Lenz, he called his reason for taking the gun from Schwender "absurd." He allowed that Schwender was "in a curious position" because he was the only rating involved. But, argued Halse, "he must have known they were firing at human targets."

Colonel Halse's speech was the last made during the morning session. When the court reconvened at 2:15 p.m., the Judge Advocate began summing up the proceedings. He addressed each defense argument point by point in a manner more suited to a prosecutor's closing statement than an impartial jurist. He left the seven jurors no choice but to return a guilty verdict.

The seven members of the court took just forty minutes to reach a verdict of guilty on all counts for each defendant. There remained only the arguments for mitigation of the sentence.

Dr. Todsen made two points in his argument. The first was that the *Llandovery Castle* case and the *Peleus* case were considerably different. In the first case the sinking of a hospital ship was clearly a crime, and the captain was trying to hide his crime when he fired on the survivors. In Eck's case, he argued, the sinking of the *Peleus* was a legal act, and Eck's attempt to destroy the rafts was an "operational necessity."

Todsen's second point had to do with the testimony given by former U-boat ace Adalbert Schnee. Schnee was one of Germany's most experienced U-boat captains, argued Todsen, whereas Eck had little experience and was on his maiden patrol as a commander when *Peleus* was sunk. Schnee's statement about what his probable actions would have been had he found himself in a situation similar to Eck's represented Schnee's greater experience and confidence.

Thereafter, character witnesses were called on behalf of Weisspfennig, Hoffmann and Schwender. Dr. Pabst offered a statement on behalf of Weisspfennig and Schwender that stressed the requirement for unquestioning obedience in the German navy. He also cited the mutual dangers shared by a U-boat's crew, and the effect that had on binding the men together. "If the accused are sentenced," Pabst told the court, "they can only be sentenced on account of their faithfulness to their commander and on account of their comradeship to one another."

Major Lermon's attempt at mitigation on behalf of Lenz consisted of trying to convince the court that Lenz "did not commit this crime out of any sordid motives of gain, or any lust of cruelty." His actions were "certainly illogical, but not unchivalrous. . . ."[104]

The seven members of the court left the room to deliberate. Just fifty-eight minutes later they returned with their decisions: Heinz Eck, August Hoffmann and Dr. Walter Weisspfennig were condemned to death by firing squad; Chief Engineer Hans Lenz was sentenced to imprisonment for life, Wolfgang Schwender to fifteen years.

All five defendants stood stiffly at attention as the sentences were intoned, first in English by the court president, Brigadier C. J. V. Jones, and then in German by an interpreter. The faces of those condemned to death were as impassive as those who avoided a capital sentence. The sentences were confirmed up the line, with the last confirmation of them made by Field Marshal Sir Bernard L. Montgomery on November 12, 1945.[105]

On November 30, 1945, a cold gray morning in Hamburg, Heinz Eck, August Hoffmann and Walter Weisspfennig rose before dawn and put on their Kriegsmarine uniforms for the last time. The condemned men were marched across the Altona Prison exercise yard and down a tree-lined path to the prison firing range. Ahead of them were three posts side-by-side, all uniform in height. The prisoners were tied to the posts according to standard field regulations in such a way that after they were shot, the only visible changes in body positions would be a slight sagging at the knees and heads slumped forward. The officer in charge of the firing squad and his sergeant inspected the bindings and the latter pulled a hood over each man's head. At 8:40 a.m., all three were executed.[106]

Professor Wegner had told the court that "the passions of today will pass and be replaced by calmer and more peaceful judgment on war crimes and alleged German war crimes." For Eck, Hoffmann and Weisspfennig, that day would never come. But it did for Hans Richard Lenz and Wolfgang Schwender. After a series of reviews and sentence reductions, Schwender was released from prison on December 21, 1951; Lenz followed him to freedom on August 27, 1952.

*   *   *

Were Heinz Eck and his crewmen really war criminals? The peers of the convicted crew of U-852 argued then and still do today that they were victims of the victorious Allies' vindictiveness, or pawns in British-Greek relations. Eck's supporters speak darkly of the mysterious deaths of Dr. Pabst and Dr. Todsen shortly after the trial. Pabst allegedly committed suicide, while Todsen was killed when the car in which he was riding was hit by a British army truck. Both deaths were investigated by the British Military Police, whose reports still remain sealed and unavailable.[107]

A former senior German naval officer who commanded the German mine sweepers believed that Eck was guilty of an error in judgment. He added that many other actions in war killed defenseless people and are accepted as inevitable. Not all former German navy officers agree with that assessment. Some agree with the court's decision, describing it as harsh, but fair. Others believe Eck was simply not guilty of any wrongdoing whatsoever.[108]

Heinz Eck's act was atrocious. He clearly overreacted to the warnings he had received from Schnee in January 1944, and perceived a greater threat of discovery than actually existed. His decision to destroy "all traces of the sinking" was unrealistic. His prolonged and futile attempt to carry out his decision showed extremely poor judgment. But poor judgment, even when it results in manslaughter, does not necessarily rise to the level of a war crime. And a conviction for manslaughter does not carry with it a death sentence. Eck violated German military and municipal law and would probably have been convicted by a German court. But a probability is not a certainty, and the British did not want to take a chance on a repeat of the 1921 Leipzig Trials.

But the fact remains that, during World War II, the usages of war with regard to killing civilians and shipwrecked survivors changed. The American press openly reported the slaughter of thousands of Japanese survivors in the Bismarck Sea, evidence that—insofar as the Americans were concerned—the rules had indeed changed.

The British were less open than the Americans about the brutal acts they justified as "operational necessities." But the British government at least tacitly approved of killing German shipwreck survivors in certain circumstances. Many belligerents in World War II slaughtered civilians by the hundreds of thousands with massive air raids on population centers.

Allied loathing of Nazis atrocities, however, especially those in Eastern Europe, clouded their objectivity. All Germans were classed as Nazis, and everything the Germans did was seen as another example of Nazi barbarity. Acts committed with some regularity by virtually every army or navy in the world became war crimes when committed by Germans. For the British and their allies, these issues were seen in black and white. There was no middle ground.

Despite all the eloquent words written and spoken about the high standards and evenhandedness of the war crimes trials that followed World War II, Allied wartime propaganda and the excesses of the Nazi state made fair adjudications of the subject events virtually impossible. Before the war ended there was even serious discussion among the Allies about not holding trials at all. Former political leaders and soldiers charged with war crimes would simply be executed by executive action, "and those responsible for such action would answer for it at the bar of history."[109]

But such drastic measures, such a wholesale repudiation of western democratic principles, were impossible to carry out. The solution lay in holding trials that were ostensibly equitable judicial inquiries. All the elements for such "equity" were present: regulations governing procedures, attorneys for both the prosecution and defense, witnesses, a judge and a jury. And yet, it was under those conditions that Eck, Lenz, Hoffmann, Weisspfennig and Schwender were brought before a British military tribunal and tried for their crimes. Given the circumstances, it is doubtful that even the most aggressive, best prepared defense could have altered the outcome.

Regardless of whether or not Heinz Eck and the others were guilty of war crimes, poor judgment, or of just following orders, the outcome of the trial was *Siegerjustiz*.

*   *   *

Notes

In Memoriam Engelbert Endrass: Castor Mourns Pollux:

(pp. 1-17)

1. Both Erich Topp, born in 1914, and Engelbert "Bertl" Endrass, born in 1911, belonged to Crew 34, the group of 318 officer recruits who began their naval careers in 1934. Endrass was slightly older than most in his group because he had served in the German merchant marine before transferring to the regular navy. Topp wrote these pages while in command of *U-552* on his 15th war patrol in the summer of 1942. Endrass and his entire crew in *U-567* perished on December 21, 1941, while attacking the Allied convoy HG.76 north of the Azores. The sloop *HMS Deptford* and the corvette *HMS Samphire* were jointly responsible for the kill. *U-567* is credited with sinking the Norwegian steamer *Annavore* out of HG.76 but was itself destroyed before it could report this last success. Two days earlier, yet another member of Crew 34, Dietrich Gengelbach in *U-574*, had gone down under dramatic circumstances in the same convoy battle, the victim of *HMS Stork*, one of the most successful Allied U-boat killers. In all, four German boats were lost while chasing HG.76. For details on Crew 34, see Eric C. Rust, *Naval Officers under Hitler: The Story of Crew 34* (Praeger, 1991). The most reliable work on German submarine successes in World War II remains Jürgen Rohwer, *Axis Submarine Successes 1939-1945* (Naval Institute Press, 1983), while the fate of German U-boats is chronicled in several sources, including Erich Gröner, *Die Schiffe der deutschen Kriegsmarine und Luftwaffe 1939-45 und ihr Verbleib*, 7th ed. (Lehmanns, 1972), pp. 70-86, and Peter Cremer, *U 333: The Story of a U-Boat Ace* (Bodley Head, 1984), pp. 215-238.

2. For additional commentary on the symbolic meaning of Castor and Pollux and his friendship with Endrass, see Erich Topp, *The Odyssey of a U-Boat Commander: Recollections of Erich Topp* (Praeger, 1992), pp. 81-82.

3. "Group Endrass" engaged convoy HG.84 from June 12-21, 1942. It consisted of eight submarines, and no German boat was lost in this particular action. In two separate attacks in the morning hours of June 15, 1942, Topp is

credited with sinking five ships of nearly 16,000 tons combined. While he thought and reported that he had damaged a sixth vessel on this occasion, Allied records do not support his claim. Cf. Rohwer, *Axis Submarine Successes*, p. 103. For a more detailed account of his impressions of this encounter, see Topp, *Odyssey*, pp. 76-79.

4. Germany's naval academy, the Marineschule Mürwik, is located in Flensburg on the southern shore of Flensburg Bay just south of the Danish border. Topp, Endrass, and the rest of Crew 34 spent nine months together there in 1935-36. The third ensign mentioned was Klaus Pein, a native of Wilhelmshaven, Germany's major naval base on the North Sea. The described sailing trip led through the very restricted waters around the Holnis Peninsula to Sønderborg in Denmark on the island of Als over a distance of some 50 miles and back.

5. Weddigen, Saltzwedel and Emsmann (mentioned below) were German U-boat aces of World War I. When submarines were reintroduced into the German Navy in the mid 1930s, the new squadrons (or flotillas) of mainly coastal Type II boats were named after them. Later squadrons of larger boats (Types VII and IX) were simply numbered, such as the 7th U-Boat Flotilla based in St. Nazaire on France's west coast, to which both Topp's *U-552* and Endrass' *U-567* belonged. Friedrichsort is a suburb of Kiel, Germany's chief naval base on the Baltic Sea.

6. At the beginning of the war Endrass served as First Watch Officer on *U-47*, a Type VII boat commanded by Günther Prien, who would become one of Germany's most celebrated submarine aces of World War II. Topp held a corresponding position on *U-46*. Early on October 14, 1939, *U-47* made its way into the heavily guarded anchorage of Scapa Flow in Scotland and sank the battleship *Royal Oak* before escaping unharmed from the narrow waters. Prien, Endrass and their men became instant heroes. At the same time Klaus Pein, then First Watch Officer on the smaller *U-12*, undertook a diversionary mission into the English Channel. As Topp indicates below, *U-12* did not return from this patrol. Pein's boat probably struck a mine and sank with all hands on October 8, 1939, in the Straits of Dover.

7. Lacking independent means of verification, especially when attacking convoys at night, submarine commanders of all navies commonly overestimated the damage they thought they inflicted on the enemy. Endrass sank a total of 25 vessels of 137,860 tons and damaged four others of 25,209 tons while commanding *U-46* (eight patrols) and *U-567* (two patrols). Figures from Rohwer, *Axis Submarine Successes*. Topp, by comparison, sank a total of 181,754 tons of Allied merchant shipping, plus one destroyer. This earned him third place among World War II aces, according to Timothy P. Mulligan's careful compilation in *Lone Wolf: The Life and Death of U-Boat Ace Werner Henke* (Praeger, 1992), p. 220.

8. According to Rohwer, *Axis Submarine Successes*, Endrass reported torpedoing a tanker of 9,000 tons on June 6, 1941, in a position east of Newfoundland. Allied records do not indicate that a tanker was damaged in those waters at the time, nor does the tanker's crew appear to have noticed the collision with Endrass' boat, *U-46*.

9. Post-war analysis reveals that Endrass actually sank the British freighter *Trevarrack* (5,270 tons) in this attack with one torpedo while damaging the tanker *Ensis* (6,207 tons) with the other. See Rohwer, *Axis Submarine Successes*, p. 56.

10. Endrass engaged and sank the British freighter *Phidias* (5,623 tons) with gunfire after a torpedo failed to explode. Ibid.

11. The convoy in question was HX.156, guarded in part by U.S. Escort Group 4.1.3. in obvious violation of American neutrality. The destroyer Topp sank on October 31, 1941, was the *USS Reuben James* (DD-245), an old four-stacker first commissioned in 1920. For Topp's personal account and reflections on this episode, see Topp, *Odyssey*, pp. 1-8. Despite the long chase, Topp and Endrass failed to inflict additional harm on HX.156, even though each claimed to have damaged a freighter of 8,000 and 5,000 tons, respectively, before daybreak on November 1, 1941, in waters south of Iceland. Cf. Rohwer, *Axis Submarine Successes*, p. 71.

12. For more on Monique's background and her reaction to Endrass' death, see Topp, *Odyssey*, p. 81.

Karl-Friedrich Merten and the Prussian Tradition
(pp. 19-41)

1. Sketches of Merten appear in Karl Alman, *Ritter der sieben Meere* (Rastatt, 1963), pp.107-18, and the same author's (under the pseudonym Franz Kurowski) *Die Träger des Ritterkreuzes des Eisernen Kreuzes der U-Bootwaffe 1939-1945* (Friedberg, 1987), p. 45, translated as *Knight's Cross Holders of the U-Boat Service* (Atglen, PA, 1995), pp. 164-65, and Gordon Williamson, *Aces of the Reich* (New York, 1989), pp. 170-72. Merten's memoirs are discussed in footnote 4, below.

2. On the general history and significance of Prussia, see H. W. Koch, *A History of Prussia* (London, 1978), and E. J. Feuchtwanger, *Preussen. Mythos und Realität* (Frankfurt, 1978); Stauffenberg citation in Peter Hoffmann, *Stauffenberg. A Family History, 1905-1944* (Cambridge/New York, 1995), pp. 289-90. In the absence of memoirs or a biography of Lothar von Arnauld de la Perière, see Lowell Thomas, *Raiders of the Deep* (Garden City, 1928), pp. 126-31, 145-62.

3. Only as *Stadtrat* was the elder Merten popularly elected, mayors were usually appointed by city councils: See Frederic C. Howe, *Socialized Germany* (New York, 1917), pp. 270-71.

4. Personalakte (service record) Karl-Friedrich Merten, copy in the custody of the U-Boot-Archiv, Cuxhaven, Germany; and Merten's published memoirs *Nach Kompass. Lebenserinnerungen eines Seeoffiziers* (Bonn/Herford, 1994), pp. 15-18, 120. This carefully-researched autobiography is actually a condensation of nine volumes written by Merten after the war, which include copies of British, German, and French official records and postwar interviews/correspondence with other participants. An English translation was begun by Maj. Jack Gibbon. Copies of the complete memoirs are on deposit with the Bundesarchiv-Abt. Militärarchiv (Freiburg), the Bibliothek für Zeitgeschichte (Stuttgart), and libraries of military institutions.

5. Merten, *Kompass*, 15-18; on the Schichau yards see Gary E. Weir, *Building the Kaiser's Navy. The Imperial Naval Office and German Industry in the von Tirpitz Era, 1890-1919* (Annapolis, 1992), pp. 13-16, 40.

6. Quoted in Koch, *Prussia*, p. 286; see also, Corelli Barnett, "The Education of Military Elites," *Journal of Contemporary History*, II, 3 (July 1967), p. 25.

7. Merten, *Kompass*, pp. 18-27; Kurt Stöckel, "Die Entwicklung der Reichsmarine nach dem Ersten Weltkriege (1919-1935). Äusserer Aufbau und innere Struktur" (doctoral dissertation, Georg-August-Universität zu Göttingen, 1954), p. 94 and Anlage 7.

8. Merten, *Kompass*, p. 71; on the backgrounds of naval officers, see Eric C. Rust, *Naval Officers Under Hitler: The Story of Crew 34* (New York/Westport, 1991), pp. 9-28.

9. Merten Personalakte; Merten, *Kompass*, pp. 27ff., 322; identities of U-boat commanders provided in Jürgen Rohwer, *Axis Submarine Successes 1939-1945* (Annapolis, 1983), pp. 303-16, and Kurowski, *Knight's Cross*, pp. 213, 221, 299. The ten casualties were *Freg.kapt.* Rollmann (KIA South Atlantic, November 5, 1943); *Freg.kapt.* Schacht (KIA off the Brazilian coast, January 13, 1943); *Korv.kapt.* von Stockhausen (died in an automobile accident in Berlin, January 15, 1943); *Korv.kapt.* Werner Lott (captured November 29, 1939); *Korv.kapt.* Rolf Dau (captured October 13, 1939); *Korv.kapt.* Heinz Beduhn (KIA North Sea, August 3, 1940); *Korv.kapt.* Johannes Franz (captured September 20, 1939); *Korv.kapt.* Rolf-Heinz Hopmann (KIA North Atlantic, November 1, 1943); *Kaptlt.* Hans Spilling (KIA as commander-in-training, November 21, 1940); and *Kaptlt.* Ernst Raabe (KIA English Channel, March 29, 1945). See also Rainer Busch and Hans Joachim Röll, *Der U-Boot-Krieg 1939-1945. Bd. I: Die Kommandanten* (Hamburg/Berlin, 1996), pp. 26, 48, 70, 106, 149, 185, 196, 202, 235, 271. For information on the selection of officers

and their educational and training period, see Charles S. Thomas, *The German Navy in the Nazi Era* (Annapolis, 1990), pp. 111-16.

10. The significance of the different oaths taken by the Navy in 1933-34 is discussed in Karl Peters, *Acht Glas (Ende der Wache). Erinnerungen eines Offiziers der Crew 38* (Reutlingen, 1989), pp. 32-37.

11. Merten, *Kompass*, pp. 110-16, 122; Michael Salewski, "Das Offizierkorps der Reichs-und Kriegsmarine," in Hanns H. Hoffmann, *Das deutsche Offizierkorps 1860-1960* (Boppard/R., 1980), pp. 222-24. For Merten's subsequent observations on Hitler, see *Kompass*, pp. 144, 174, 346-47, 404-07.

12. These issues are discussed in Jost Dülffer, *Weimar, Hitler und die Marine. Reichspolitik und Flottenbau 1920-1939* (Düsseldorf, 1973), p. 279ff.; and Axel Schimpf, "Der Einsatz von Kriegsmarineeinheiten im Rahmen der Verwicklungen der spanischen Bürgerkrieges 1936 bis 1939," in *Der Einsatz von Seestreitkräften im Dienst der auswärtigen Politik*, ed. by the Deutsche Marine Institut (Herford, 1983), pp. 76-103.

13. See, Willi Schultz, *Linienschiff Schleswig-Holstein* (Herford, 1991), pp.163-97, and Bertil Stjernfelt and Klaus-Richard Böhme, *Westerplatte 1939* (Freiburg/Br., 1979), p. 39ff. Merten's personal experiences are described in *Kompass*, pp. 170-78. During this period Merten also met and influenced another future U-boat ace, Werner Henke. See Timothy Mulligan, *Lone Wolf: The Life and Death of U-boat Ace Werner Henke* (Westport, 1993), p. 37.

14. Admiral Raeder's comment is reproduced in *Fuehrer Conferences on Naval Affairs 1939-1945*, Introduction by Jak P. Mallmann Showell (Annapolis, 1990), pp. 37-38; Merten, *Kompass*, pp. 179-80.

15. Kommando 1. Unterseebootslehrdivision, "Zeugnis-Kaptlt. Merten," October 1, 1940, in Merten Personalakte (U-Boot-Archiv, Cuxhaven).

16. Merten's experiences are described in *Kompass*, pp. 192-97. The author's own research, based on the biographical data in Busch and Röll, *Kommandanten*, reveal casualty rates of 44%-46% for each of the three groups.

17. Author's interview of Merten, Waldshut, September 12, 1989; Merten, *Kompass*, pp. 198-209; for information on Liebe, see Busch and Röll, *U-Boot-Kommandanten*, p. 145, and Rohwer, *Successes*, p. 1ff.

18. Eberhard Rössler, *The U-boat. The Evolution and Technical History of the German Submarine* (Annapolis, 1981), pp. 103-05; Fritz Köhl and Axel Niestle, *Vom Original zum Modell: Uboottyp IXC. Eine Bild- und Plandokumentation* (Koblenz, 1990), pp. 5-8, 13-14.

19. Köhl and Niestle, *Original*, p. 13; Rolf Güth and Jochen Brennecke, "Hier irrte Michael Salewski. Das Trauma vom "Kinderkreuzzug" der U-Boote," *Schiff und Zeit* 28 (1989), p. 44.

20. *Kriegstagebuch* (KTB) U-68, February 11 through June 30, 1941, reproduced on National Archives Microcopy T1022, Records of the German Navy, 1850-1945, roll 3030 (hereafter cited in the format T1022/3030/PG

30065); Merten, *Kompass*, pp. 210-16; and Government Code & Cryptography Naval History, Vol. VII, "The German Navy—The U-Boat Arm," 72a, Item CBBD 53 in the NSA Historic Cryptographic Collection, Pre-World War I through World War II, Record Group 457, Records of the National Security Agency, National Archives. The author will review the variations of U-boat training in a future study.

21. KTB U-68, 30 June-1 August 1941, T1022/3030/PG 30065; Merten, *Kompass*, pp. 217-29; on the disputed claim of the corvette, see Rohwer, *Successes*, p. 60.

22. Cf. KTB U-68, 21-23 September 1941, T1022/3030/PG 30065; Merten, *Kompass*, pp. 236-42; Kurowski, *Knight's Cross*, p. 165; and Rohwer, *Successes*, pp. 66-67.

23. KTB U-68, 28 September 1941, T1022/3030/PG 30065; an account based on interviews is Jochen Brennecke, *Jäger-Gejagte. Deutsche U-Boote 1939-1945* (Munich, 1986), pp. 111-14; the British perspective is given in John Winton, *Ultra at Sea* (London, 1988), pp. 100-01.

24. Brennecke, *Jäger*, pp. 113, 203-05. The incident with the oilskins occurred on September 12, 1942, following the sinking of British freighter *Trevilley*. Merten, *Kompass*, pp. 320-21.

25. Brennecke, *Jäger*, p. 114.

26. Merten's factual account in the KTB of U-68 for 23 October 1941, T1022/3030/PG 30065, is supplemented by the vivid narrative in Wolfgang Frank, *Die Wölfe und der Admiral* (Oldenburg, 1953), pp. 251-55.

27. Merten's account of the sinking of the *Bradford City*, in KTB U-68, October 28 through November 15, 1941, T1022/3030/PG 30065, contradicts the more colorful version described by Brennecke, *Jäger*, pp. 205-07 (cf. also Frank, *Wölfe*, pp. 251-55); on British signal intelligence, see F. H. Hinsley et al., *British Intelligence in the Second World War*, Vol. 2 (New York, 1981), pp. 166, 172-73.

28. KTB U-68, 11 November-25 December 1941, T1022/3030/PG 30065; Merten, *Kompass*, pp. 259-79; Brennecke, *Jäger*, pp. 143-54; and Wolfgang Frank and Bernhard Rogge, *Under Ten Flags*, trans. by R. O. B. Long (New York, 1956), p. 134ff.

29. KTB U-68, 26 December 1941-6 December 1942, T1022/3030-31/PG 30065; *The U-boat Commander's Handbook* (U.S. Navy translation of German naval manual M.Dv. 906, 1943 Ausg.) (Gettysburg, PA, 1989), p. 63.

30. Ibid.; Merten, *Kompass*, pp. 297-306; Brennecke, *Jäger*, pp. 169-75. For German resupply operations in Spain, see Charles B. Burdick, "'Moro': The Resupply of German Submarines in Spain, 1939-1942," *Central European History*, III, 3 (September 1970), pp. 256-84. The verdict on Merten's success can be found in Gaylord T. M. Kelshall, *The U-Boat War in the Caribbean* (Annapolis, 1994), p. 108.

31. The deliberations of Dönitz and the Naval High Command are documented in the KTB of *Befehlshaber der Unterseeboote*, entries of 1-15 August 1942, T1022/3980/PG 30310a; for a general discussion of *Eisbär's* background and operations, see the South African official history by L. C. F. Turner et al., *War In the Southern Oceans 1939-45* (London, 1961), pp. 157-61. General data on signal intelligence is provided in Winton, *Ultra*, pp. 104-08.

32. KTB U-68, 20 September-30 October 1942, T1022/3031/PG 30065; Merten, *Kompass*, pp. 314-35; Turner, et al., *Southern Oceans*, pp. 166-82.

33. On September 12, 1942, U-156 (*Korv.Kapt.* Werner Hartenstein) sank the liner *Laconia* in the South Atlantic,only to discover that most of her passengers consisted of Italian prisoners of war en route to Canada. Hartenstein commenced a rescue operation for all survivors, ultimately albeit reluctantly supported by Dönitz with additional submarines. Four days later, an American bomber attacked U-156, despite its openly radioed intentions, crowded decks and lifeboats in tow. Hartenstein escaped, but a number of survivors were killed. As a consequence, Dönitz issued an order forbidding any rescue of survivors of torpedoed vessels, a directive that formed the foundation for one of the main war crimes charges against him at Nuremberg. For more information on this event, see Léonce Peillard, *The Laconia Affair* (New York, 1963).

34. Neither U-68's KTB nor Merten's *Kompass*, pp. 336-37, provides much detail. The best account is by survivor Ralph Barker, *Goodnight, Sorry for Sinking You. The Story of the S.S. City of Cairo* (London, 1984). Merten's *Kompass*, pp. 491-504, details his postwar contacts with survivors. The quotation appears in a newspaper article in the *Daily Mail* of September 15, 1984 (copy in the U-Boot-Archiv, Cuxhaven).

35. Most postwar publications, e.g., Kurowski, *Knight's Cross*, p. 165, still credit Merten with 29 ships totaling over 180,000 tons, but I am following the latest research by Jürgen Rohwer, *Successes*, p. 60ff.

36. Merten, *Kompass*, pp. 210ff., 280ff., 364, 369; Kurowski, *Knight's Cross*, pp. 158-59; Rohwer, *Successes*, pp. 157, 173-75.

37. Merten, *Kompass*, pp. 370-77; Fritz Brustat-Naval, *Unternehmen Rettung* (Bergisch Gladbach, 1970), pp. 30-31. Although no records of the 24th U-Flottilla are available for this period, some useful data is available in the KTB of the Kommandant im Abschnitt Memel, July 19 through August 5, 1944, T1022/4047/PG 39338-340.

38. The most extensive public documentation of these proceedings was collected by Merten as Teil V, Buch 9 ("Der Fall 'Frimaire'") of his complete "Lebenserinnerungen," only a summary of which appears in *Kompass*, pp. 307-09, 312, 459-70.

39. For a cogent discussion of this issue, see Michael Hadley, *Count Not the Dead* (Montreal/Kingston, 1995), p. 140ff., and especially pp. 163-64, 169, regarding Merten.

40. Karl-Friedrich Merten and Kurt Baberg, *Wir U-Bootfahrer Sagen: "Nein!" "So war das nicht!" Eine "Anti-Buchheim Schrift"* (Grossaitingen, 1985). Examples of his articles include "Betr. Film 'Das Boot' und Fernsehauftritt des Autors Buchheim," *Marineforum* 12 (December, 1985), pp. 17-18; "U 110 und die 'Gerechtfertigte Tötung. . .'," *Schiff und Zeit* 25 (1987), pp. 54-56. Examples of his correspondence, including typed notes of a telephone conversation with author Lothar-Günther Buchheim, May 22, 1985, are located in folder "Schriftverkehr Merten-Bredow," U-Boot-Archiv, Cuxhaven. The latter also contains copies of Erich Topp's critique of the Merten/Baberg book in *Marineforum* 11 (November, 1986), pp. 399-400, and Merten's letter to Topp, November 25, 1986.

41. For example, the author corresponded extensively with Merten from May 1987 to March 1992 in the course of his biographical research on Werner Henke.

Ralph Kapitsky: Battle in the Caribbean and the Death of U-615
(pp. 43-73)

1. Interview with Herbert Schlipper, U-615's First Watch Officer (IWO), who was on the conning tower alongside Kapitsky; Ralph Kapitsky's Diary, author's collection. According to Kapitsky diary: "Suddenly all hell breaks lose. Everything blows up. The sky is a sea of flames from which glowing parts are raining. I have been thrown into the back of the conning tower. I order everyone under deck and make off at full speed. Then up again, but there is nothing to be seen. The vessel and all lifeboats are gone. Only now I realize that my right arm does not move. My shoulder has been hit by a fragment."

2. Gaylord T. M. Kelshall, *U-Boat War in the Caribbean* (Naval Institute Press, 1994), pp. 380-381.

3. Essay on Ralph Kapitsky by Johannes Kapitsky, Ralph's brother, and Joachim Jaworski, translated by Hans Jurgen Steffen, September 1996. Author's Collection.

4. KTB U-615; U-Boat Command Diary. U-93 was sunk on January 15, 1943, by the British destroyers *Laforey* and *Hesperus*. Clay Blair, *Hitler's U-Boat War: The Hunters* (New York, 1996), p. 489.

5. Kelshall, *U-Boat War in the Caribbean*, pp. 299-301.

6. Ibid., pp. 301, 302.

7. Ibid., p. 416.

8. Ibid., p. 311. On June 14, 1943, U-134, U-415, U-68, U-155, U-159, U-564 and U-185 were under attack by Coastal Command aircraft in the Bay of Biscay.

9. Description of the operation was provided to the author by IWO Herbert Schlipper and U-615's Josef Faus, at the 1992 U-boat veteran's reunion at Trinidad. Konstantin Metz' tanker U-487 was sunk by aircraft from the *USS Core* 720 miles south-southwest of the Azores. Metz and several members of his crew went down with the boat; 33 others survived. William T. Y'Blood, *Hunter-Killer: U.S. Escort Carriers in the Battle of the Atlantic* (Naval Institute Press, 1983), pp. 70-73.

10. Description of the last cruise of U-615 in Schlipper letter to author, June 1993, and USN Interrogation Report on U-615 survivors.

11. Kelshall, *U-Boat War in the Caribbean*, p. 381; War Diary, Chaguaramas Naval Operating Base; U-Boat Command War Diary.

12. Schlipper letter to author, June 1993. One of the mistakes made by the Germans in the Caribbean was that they never grouped U-boats into wolf packs as they did in the Atlantic. Boats sent to the Caribbean always operated alone. Additionally they were assigned in a cluster around the major convoy terminals, which was where the strongest defenses were located. They might have achieved much more had they been grouped well away from the terminals in the wide open spaces between the various bases, where the defenses were not quite so strong and the combined strength of a wolf pack might have been able to break up a convoy.

13. Ibid.

14. Kelshall, *U-Boat War in the Caribbean*, p. 413.

15. Ibid., p. 383. IWO Herbert Schlipper does not remember this incident, but the War Diary of VP-204 details the attack and provides the explanation that U-615 was using the schooner's radar shadow. U-615 was on the surface at this time.

16. In 1943, Trinidad housed up to five flying boat squadrons at NAS Chaguaramas, together with four land-based anti-submarine squadrons at Edinburgh Field and one airship squadron, ZP-51. The Royal Navy at Piarco Field operated 300 training aircraft, many of which were used on anti-submarine operations. In addition, U.S. carrier-based aircraft used a dedicated runway for training. In total, the island had 16 runways, with at times up to 700 airplanes in operation. The Gulf of Paria, as well as being the terminus of the North Atlantic convoy route, was a major U.S. Navy work-up base for all classes of warships and operated alongside the dedicated anti-submarine destroyers stationed there. The TRNVR operated thirty anti-submarine vessels alongside Royal Navy MTBs and MLs and an ocean escort group. Canadian, Brazilian, Dutch and Free French anti-submarine ships also operated from Trinidad. Records indicate up to 250 warship movements each month during 1943.

17. Schlipper letter, June 1993.

18. Ibid.

19. Ibid.

20. Ibid.

21. U.S.N. Air Station, Chaguaramas War Diary.

22. Schlipper letter to author, June 1993; ibid., September 1996.

23. Crockett Attack Report, P-11, VP-204; VP-204/VP-205 and ZP51War Diaries. Although Horst Dietrichs managed to survive his ordeal in the Caribbean and return to France, his boat was sunk with all hands by *HMS Spey* on February 18, 1944, at 48-32N, 23-36W. Peter Cremer, *U-Boat Commander: A Periscope View of the Battle of the Atlantic* (Naval Institute Press, 1995), p. 226.

24. Ibid.

25. Ibid.

26. Ibid.

27. Kelshall, *U-Boat War in the Caribbean*, pp. 390-391.

28. Crockett Attack Report, P-11, VP-204; VP-204 War Diary.

29. This sequence of events and circumstances contained in Schlipper letters, June 1993 and September 1996, and confirmed by U-615's Josef Faus.

30. VP-204 War Diary.

31. Ibid.

32. Schlipper letter, June 1993.

33. VP-204 War Diary; U.S.N. Air Station, Chaguaramas War Diary. Lt. Cmdr. Hull's first name is not mentioned in either the squadron War Diary or in the NAS Chaguaramas War Diary.

34. Kelshall, *U-Boat War in the Caribbean*, p. 395. Airship K74 attacked U-134 on July 18, 1943, in the Florida Straits. The airship attacked unsupported and was destroyed. Ibid., p. 342.

35. Ibid., pp. 306, 320, 321.

36. Ibid., p. 396.

37. Kelshall, *U-Boat War in the Caribbean*, p. 398; ZP-51 War Diary. The airship crashed on Blanquilla Island, and although the machine was a complete wreck, her crew escaped injury. They were rescued from the deserted island the following day by a launch from Trinidad. The cabin of the airship was recovered several months later.

38. Descriptive essay by Cmdr. Robert Trauger, aircraft commander of VP-205, describing the squadron and some of the actions while based in Trinidad. Author's Collection; May 1994 letters from Robert Erskine, aircraft commander of VP-204, engaged in the action against U-615. Author's Collection; Schlipper letter, June 1993.

39. Schlipper letters, June 1993 and September 1996.

40. Ibid.

41. Ibid. This was also confirmed by Josef Faus at the 1992 U-boat veteran's reunion on Trinidad.

42. Schlipper letter, June 1993. There is little doubt that U-634 was well out of the area by this time and heading north for the Mona Passage. Orginally it was believed that U-634 was in the vicinity because U.S. Navy after-action reports stated there was definitely another submarine in the area.

43. War Diary, U.S.N. Operating Base, Chaguaramas. Although the U.S. Navy History of the Trinidad Sector states that the *Walker* attacked on a sonar contact, there was no other U-boat operating in that area. The destroyer may have been carrying out a depth charge attack on a whale or some natural anomaly. There is also the assumption that she may have launched her attacks on the direction of the aircraft.

44. Schlipper letter, June 1993.

45. U.S.N.A.S., Chaguaramas War Diary; Trinidad Command War Diary.

Fritz Guggenberger: Bavarian U-Boat Ace
(pp. 75-107)

1. The author's interview with Guggenberger was part of a larger project which has since been published as Eric C. Rust, *Naval Officers under Hitler: The Story of Crew 34* (Praeger, 1991). Unless otherwise attributed, all information in this study is drawn from that interview in July 1982, as well as related questionnaires and documents. Translations from German into English furnished by the author, except where indicated otherwise. This study was partially supported by a grant from Baylor University's Research Committee.

2. For a socio-geographical profile of Guggenberger's Crew 34, i.e. of those officers who began their naval training in 1934, see Rust, *Naval Officers*, pp. 19-36. Guggenberger's personnel records state that he left the Church in September 1937 for reasons no longer ascertainable. A complete copy of Guggenberger's service record with pertinent personnel data is contained in his "Personalnachweis," part of his "Personalakte" in Folder "RK-Träger der Kriegsmarine," U-Boot-Archiv Cuxhaven-Altenbruch. The Archiv is hereafter referred to as UACA. For a published summary of Guggenberger's service record through his reactivation in West Germany's Federal Navy, including promotions and decorations, see Manfred Dörr, *Die Ritterkreuzträger der U-Boot-Waffe*, Vol. 1 (Biblio, 1988), pp. 99-101.

3. Guggenberger and Crew 34 had taken the traditional oath to obey and protect the Constitution on May 1, 1934. See UACA, Personalnachweis, p. 1; further details in Rust, *Naval Officers*, pp. 39-40, 43-44.

4. Grades from "Zeugnis über den Besuch des Hauptlehrganges für Fähnriche zur See, Lehrgang 1935/36" in Guggenberger's Personalakte, UACA. Rankings from Ostseestationstagesbefehl (O.T.B.) as of 13 April 1937; copy in Bundesarchiv-Militärarchiv (BA-MA), Freiburg; cf. Dörr, p. 100. Of Crew 34's future U-boat aces, only Erich Topp ranked higher than Guggenberger as ninth in his Crew. Interestingly both would end their naval careers as rear admirals in the West German Navy.

5. One of the best sources on technical data and eventual fates of German submarines is Erich Gröner, *Die Schiffe der deutschen Kriegsmarine und Luftwaffe 1939-45 und ihr Verbleib*, 7th ed. (Lehmanns, 1976), esp. pp. 24-34, 70-87, 109-10. Jürgen Rohwer's *Axis Submarine Successes, 1939-1945* (Annapolis, 1983) remains the most detailed and reliable source of U-boat successes in all theaters of the war. U-boat allocations to particular squadrons and location of their bases in Bodo Herzog, *U-Boote im Einsatz* (Podzun, 1970), and Jak P. Mallmann Showell, *The German Navy in World War II: A Reference Guide to the Kriegsmarine, 1935-1945* (Naval Institute Press, 1979).

6. Data on U-28 successes from Rohwer, *Axis Submarine Successes*, p. 16.

7. See Rohwer, *Axis Submarine Successes*, pp. 18-21.

8. Information from Rohwer, *Axis Submarine Successes*, pp. 26-27, and letter, Gustav Hölterscheidt to Horst Bredow, dated 12 October 1986, in folder "U-28", UACA.

9. Hölterscheidt letter, p. 2.

10. Cf. *Rohwer, Axis Submarine Successes*, p. 35.

11. Hölterscheidt letter, p. 2; Personalnachweis in Guggenberger papers, UACA. Rainer Busch and Hans Joachim Röll in *Der U-Boot-Krieg, 1939-1945: Die Deutschen U-Boot-Kommandanten* (Hamburg, 1996) give the date of Guggenberger's takeover as U-28's C.O. as November 16, 1940, which would imply that Kuhnke stayed on board and in charge until the boat reached Stettin. U-28's transfer from the 2nd to the 24th Flottilla occurred on November 10. The boat performed faithful service for more than three years in the Baltic before it sank off Neustadt in March 1944 after a technical mishap.

12. Unless indicated otherwise, all data on U-81 and its patrols both in the Atlantic and the Mediterranean from documents in Folder "U-81" in UACA, from the Guggenberger interview, and from Rohwer, *Axis Submarine Successes*.

13. See illustration in Georg Högel, *Embleme, Wappen, Malings deutscher U-Boote 1939-1945* (Munich, 1984).

14. For the evolution of Hitler's naval strategy and the Kriegsmarine's opposition to the use of German submarines in the Mediterranean, see Gerhard Wagner, ed., *Lagevorträge des Oberbefehlshabers der Kriegsmarine vor Hitler 1939-1945* (Lehmanns, 1972).

15. The best book on German submarines in the Mediterranean, despite numerous inaccuracies, remains Karl Alman's *Graue Wölfe in blauer See* (Pabel, 1967), which deals with Guggenberger's exploits in considerable if sometimes inaccurate detail on pp. 26-33. Similar accounts in Jochen Brennecke, *Jäger—Gejagte: Deutsche U-Boote 1939-1945*, 5th ed. (Koehler, 1956), pp. 117-125, and Günter Böddeker, *Die Boote im Netz* (Lübbe, 1981), pp. 149-151. Further pertinent data in U-81's War Diary as well as Folders "U-81" and "Mittelmeer" in UACA. Statistics calculated by author using data from Rohwer and Groener, *op. cit.*

16. U-81 was preceded into the Mediterranean by U-371, 559, 97, 331, 75, 79 and 205, all commanded by experienced skippers, among them several of Guggenberger's Crew 34. Cf. Folder "Mittelmeer," UACA.

17. U-81 War Diary, UACA. Reschke made an attack on "Force K" at 0506 that morning, later claiming to have damaged the *Ark Royal* and a destroyer. Actually his torpedoes missed their targets.

18. U-81 War Diary.

19. Quotation and details from Corelli Barnett, *Engage the Enemy More Closely: The Royal Navy in the Second World War* (Norton, 1991), pp. 371-374.

20. Lothar-Günther Buchheim's novel and subsequent motion picture *Das Boot* provide a very realistic account of what could happen to U-boats trying to force the narrows at Gibraltar.

21. See Rohwer, *Axis Submarine Successes*, p. 230.

22. Rohwer, *Axis Submarine Successes*, p. 234; Folder "U-81," UACA. Guggenberger's unsubstantiated claims were relatively minor compared to those of some of his comrades in the Mediterranean. Fraatz and Guggenberger knew each other well, having been involved in several operations together, including the near-destruction of convoy SC.42.

23. Details from Guggenberger interview and John Hammond Moore, *The Faustball Tunnel* (Random House, 1978), pp. 17-19.

24. Guggenberger "Personalnachweis," UACA.

25. Peter Cremer, *U-333: The Story of a U-Boat Ace* (Bodley Head, 1984), p. 137.

26. For more on the mine incident and related information, see Edwin P. Hoyt, *The Death of the U-Boats* (Warner, 1988).

27. Ibid. Cf. Ladislas Farago, *The Tenth Fleet* (Obolensky, 1962), pp. 198-199.

28. Guggenberger interview and Folder "U-513" in UACA, especially "Bericht des Kommandanten Fritz Guggenberger über die Versenkung U-513." Helmut Schmoeckel in *Menschlichkeit im Seekrieg?* (Mittler, 1988), p. 148, indicates that as many as 20 men may have initially survived according to observations by American planes overhead. At any rate, five hours later only

seven were still alive. American sources, in contrast to Guggenberger's observations, claim that Whitcomb made two hits instead of only one. Farago, *The Tenth Fleet*, p. 199.

29. Moore, *Faustball Tunnel*.

30. Guggenberger was chosen over Topp because the former had sunk no Norwegian vessels during the war and thus was politically more acceptable for the post in Oslo.

31. Information from letter in UACA by Jürgen Heinze to fellow Knight's Cross holders, dated 29 August 1994, as well as Crew 34's Crew-Briefe (newsletters) Nos. 120 (3/88), 121 (1/89) and 127 (1/91), all in author's files.

Victor Otto Oehrn: The Ace With No Name
(pp. 109-135)

1. Victor Oehrn's surname is occasionally misspelled as "Ohrn," which is logical when the rules of the German language are followed. See, for example, Barrie Pitt, *The U-Boats* (New York: Time-Life Books, 1979). However, Oehrn himself uses the "oe" construction, and he traces his name not to German roots but to Nordic ones. Oehrn, he wrote, comes from the Swedish word Oern, which means "eagle."

2. Oehrn letter, August 23, 1992.

3. For a detailed discussion of the motives behind naval service in Germany between the wars, see Eric Rust, *Naval Officers Under Hitler: The Story of Crew 34* (Praeger, 1991).

4. Oehrn letter, March 18, 1992.

5. Ibid., letter, November 7, 1991. Oehrn is in error one one point: the *Karlsruhe* did not circumnavigate the globe in 1934-35.

6. Ibid., letter, July 17, 1991.

7. Oehrn, *Navigare Necesse Est*, unpublished memoirs.

8. There is evidence that morale wasn't as bad as many believe. "I don't think that there was a low morale due to the torpedo deficiencies," wrote Jürgen Oesten, who at that time was commander of U-61, "[but] we were furious and we did put the blame on that fat Admiral Goetting who was in charge of the 'Torpedo-Inspektion.'" Oesten letter, July 16, 1996. Oehrn agrees with Oesten's assessment. "Our torpedo problems were not easy, but I cannot say that in the submarine crews the morale was low." Oehrn letter, July 17, 1991.

9. Oehrn's first war patrol began on May 15, 1940 and ended June 9, 1940. During this patrol he sank the *Erik Frisell* (5,066 GRT), damaged the *Dunster Grange* (9,494), and sank the *Kyma* (3,994), *Sheaf Mead* (5,008),

Uruguay (3,425), *Brazza* (10,387), *Julien* (177), *Marie Jose* (2,477), *Telena* (7,406) [later salvaged], *Ioanna* (950), and *Snabb* (2,317). All tonnage data is taken from Jürgen Rohwer, *Axis Submarine Successes, 1939-1945* (Naval Institute Press, 1983).

10. Karl Dönitz, *Ten Years and Twenty Days* (New York, 1959), p. 102.

11. Oehrn's second war patrol began on August 1, 1940, and ended August 30, 1940. During this patrol he sank the *Upway Grange* (9,130 GRT), *Keret* (1,718), *Severn Leigh* (5,242), *Brookwood* (5,100), *HMS Penzance* (1,025), *Blairmore* (4,141), *Yewcrest* (3,774), and *Theodoros T.* (3,409). Rohwer, *Axis Submarine Successes*.

12. The sinking of the *Severn Leigh* is described by Oehrn in the first volume of his brief and as yet unpublished memoirs, *Navigare Necesse Est*. To this author's knowledge, Oehrn's version is not contradicted by any published source. Oehrn also claims that the *Severn Leigh* incident was used against Dönitz at Nuremberg.

13. Oehrn's third war patrol began on September 25, 1940 and ended October 22, 1940. During this patrol he sank the *Corrientes* (6,863 GRT)—credit for this sinking is shared with Hans Jenisch of U-32—*Georges Mabro* (2,555), *Samala* (5,390), *Heminge* (2,499), *British General* (6,989), and *Stangrant* (5,804).

14. Oehrn's combined total for his three patrols was just over 100,000 GRT. This qualified him for the Knight's Cross and also placed him in 28th place on the tonnage list for U-boat commanders in World War II. Rohwer, *Axis Submarine Successes*. As is the case with many commanders, these figures are sometimes misstated. Franz Kurowski, in *Knight's Cross Holders of the U-Boat Service* (NY, XXXX), p. XX, for example, states incorrectly that Oehrn conducted only two patrols and sank 108,000 GRT.

15. Oehrn, letter, July 17, 1991.

16. Oehrn has some interesting insights as to Hans-Joachim Rahmlow, a much-derided figure in the U-Bootwaffe community. According to Oehrn, Rahmlow was "two years younger than I, but we weren't really well acquainted. A classmate of his once told me that he was a most sensible and courteous man. Obviously Personnel made a serious mistake in assigning him as a U-boat commander, and Dönitz too, though he didn't know him. When we heard about the loss of the boat and the capture of the cypher equipment, we only knew what the enemy was reporting. We talked about it a lot, but Dönitz only said: we know too little about the circumstances of his loss. Without more information we cannot judge the commander.'" Oehrn, letter, October 11, 1991.

17. Ibid., letter, May 18, 1991.

18. Ibid.; Victor Oehrn, *Dönitz Nähe Gesehen* (*Dönitz Up Close*), unpublished memoirs.

19. Oehrn, letter, May 18, 1991.

20. "Rommel," wrote Oehrn in July 17, 1991 letter, "was a military commander gifted by God." In his memoirs and correspondence, Oehrn shows a great admiration for Erwin Rommel, and compares him on more than one occasion to Karl Dönitz.

21. Ibid., May 18, 1991.

22. Oehrn, *Navigare Necesse Est.*

23. The extent to which National Socialism permeated the German military is an explosive subject, although further examination of Victor Oehrn's politics is not within the purview of this essay. Two of Oehrn's statements are of interest on this subject. "Hitler would never have come to power (legally) without the Treaty of Versailles," he wrote in 1992. "Six million out of work. The merchant fleet taken away. Reparations without end. Finally the people just rebelled!" Oehrn letter, March 18, 1992. Later that same year, Oehrn wrote: "I am no blind nationalist; but I do know what is meant by language, culture, religion, and the blood in our veins!" Ibid., July 12, 1992. The idea of a war against Bolshevism was not uncommon in the U-Bootwaffe or in Germany: "I was convinced until the end of the war," wrote fellow U-boat ace Erich Topp, "that we were fighting for a just cause, for a united Europe and against Communism." Topp letter, July 8, 1991.

24. Oehrn did not know it then, but Renate had told Dönitz that she would wait ten years if necessary to marry Oehrn. It was something, Dönitz told them later, that helped him get through his own ten years in Spandau Prison.

25. The first stop for most U-boat crewmen captured by the British was the London District Cage (LDC) in Kensington. There the men were presented with encyclopedic accounts of their lives and interviewed by skilled interrogators who often succeeded in extracting something of value. After days or in some cases weeks, the men were sent to a POW camp in Britain, and eventually to Canada or the United States. Mahdi, which usually processed captured army personnel, was not as well equipped as the LDC to deal with U-boat officers.

26. Erich Topp, foreword to Jordan Vause, *U-Boat Ace: The Story of Wolfgang Lüth* (Naval Institute Press, 1990). It is tempting to speculate what would have happened to Oehrn had he not been captured in Africa. Rommel, of course, would have had little need of Oehrn's services, and it is more probable than not that Oehrn would have been back at BdU in time for the fierce winter fighting of 1942-43, during which many believe the Battle of the Atlantic reached its apogee. His record leads one to believe that Oehrn might have been able to plan more effectively some of the individual operations, although it is unknown whether his clear head and common sense would have led him to recognize that German naval codes had been compromised. His

presence, however, would not have altered the course of events. Given his continuing desire for sea duty and the lack of experienced commanders, he might have received his wish for a second boat (as he had been promised when removed from command of U-37). Many of the veterans Dönitz later returned to the sea themselves never returned, for the front in 1943 was far more dangerous than it had been in 1940, when Oehrn had earned his Knight's Cross.

27. Dönitz had become Kriegsmarine commander-in-chief (OKM) on January 30, 1943, after the fall into disfavor and gentle ouster of his predecessor, Erich Raeder.

28. One of Oehrn's temporary positions during this time was that of FdU-Mitte, based in Kiel and responsible for all "invasion reserve" boats. Subsequent events determined that this position was a useless one, but it may well have violated the terms of his repatriation. Peter Hansen letter, August 16, 1996.

29. Oehrn, *Dönitz Nähe Gesehen*.

30. Oehrn describes both the *Tirpitz* episode and his advice about Dönitz's messages in Oehrn, *Dönitz Nähe Gesehen*. Typical of these radio transmissions, which have long been a point of controversy, was the one Dönitz made on New Year's Eve 1944, in which he said: "The battle for freedom and justice for our peoples continues. It will see us pitted inexorably against our enemy. The Führer shows us the way and the goal. We follow him with body and soul to a great German future. Heil our Fúhrer!" Peter Padfield, *Dönitz: The Last Führer* (New York, 1984).

31. Oehrn, *Dönitz Nähe Gesehen*. Dönitz was arrested after this conversation. He was tried and convicted at Nuremberg as a war criminal and sentenced to ten years in prison.

32. These two volumes are *Navigare Necesse Est*, a short autobiography, and *Dönitz Nahe Gesehen (Dönitz Up Close)*, which describes Oehrn's work with the Grand Admiral in some detail. Because of a previous arrangement with Oehrn, this author is unable to quote from these documents at this time.

33. Oehrn, letters, January 15, 1992, and May 29, 1992.

23. Jürgen Oesten, letter, July 16, 1996; Otto Kretschmer, quoted in Peter Hansen letter, August 16, 1996.

Heinz-Wilhelm Eck: Siegerjustiz and the *Peleus* Affair:
(pp. 137-183)

1. "Bescheinigung," Eck, Heinz, Deutsche Dienststelle (WASt), Berlin.

2. Peleus Trial Transcript, Day 3, p. 7, WO235/5 (604), Public Record Office, London, and Bodo Herzog, *Deutsche U-Boote, 1906-1966* (Pawlak, 1990), pp. 255-257.

3. Peleus Trial Transcript, Day 3, pp. 6-7, WO235/5 (604), Public Record Office, London.

4. Ministry of War Transport, "Return of British Members of the Crew. . ." WO235/5 (604), Public Record Office, London.

5. Antonios Cosmas Liossis, Statement, September 1, 1944, and Roco Said, Statement, 16 August 1944, WO235/5 (604), Public Record Office, London.

6. Roco Said, Statement, August 16, 1944, WO235/5 (604), Public Record Office, London.

7. Antonios Cosmas Liossis, Statement, September 1, 1944, WO235/5 (604), Public Record Office, London.

8. Peleus Trial Transcript, Day 2, pp. 13-12; Day 3, p. 18, WO235/5 (604), Public Record Office, London.

9. Ibid., Day 1, p. 16, WO235/5 (604), Public Record Office, London.

10. "Officer-in-Charge, Naval Section, JICAME to Director of Naval Intelligence," Memorandum June 8, 1944, "U-852, Shooting of Survivors by," RG38, Records of the CNO, Records of ONI, National Archives, Washington, DC.

11 Peleus Trial Transcript, Day 3, p. 16, WO235/5 (604), Public Record Office, London.

12. Ibid., Day 2, pp. 7-10, WO235/5 (604), Public Record Office, London.

13. Ibid., p. 9, WO235/5 (604), Public Record Office, London.

14. Ibid., p. 17, WO235/5 (604), Public Record Office, London.

15. Ibid., Day 3, p. 18, WO235/5 (604), Public Record Office, London.

16. Ibid., pp. 3 & 13, WO235/5 (604), Public Record Office, London.

17. Ibid., p. 4, WO235/5 (604), Public Record Office, London.

18. Antonios Cosmas Liossis, Statement, September 1, 1944, WO235/5 (604), Public Record Office, London.

19. Ibid.

20. Roco Said, Statement, August 16, 1944, WO235/5 (604), Public Record Office, London.

21. Peleus Trial Transcript, Day 3, pp. 28-29, WO235/5 (604), Public Record Office, London.

22. Ibid.

23. Ibid., p. 24, WO235/5 (604), Public Record Office, London.

24. Ibid., pp.12 & 15, WO235/5 (604), Public Record Office, London.

25. Ibid.

26. "Officer-in-Charge, Naval Section, JICAME to Director of Naval Intelligence," Memorandum June 8, 1944, "U-852, Shooting of Survivors by,"

RG38, Records of the CNO, Records of ONI, National Archives, Washington, DC.

27. "Kriegstagebuch, BdU, 1-15 März 1944," Microfilm Publication T-1022, Roll 4065, PG30342, National Archives, Washington, DC.

28. "Kriegstagebuch, BdU, 1-14 April 1944," Microfilm Publication T-1022, Roll 4065, PG30344, National Archives, Washington, DC, and L.C.F. Turner et al., *War in the Southern Oceans* (Oxford University Press, 1961), p. 248.

29. J. Torrence Rugh, "Report of Prisoners' Interrogations," 26 July 1944, Josef Schilling Interrogation, RG226, Records of the OSS, National Archives, Washington, DC,

30. Turner, *War in the Southern Oceans*, p. 248.

31. J. Torrence Rugh, "Report of Prisoners' Interrogations," July 26, 1944, Esper Günter Interrogation & Alex-Heinz Rümmler Interrogation, RG226, Records of the OSS, National Archives, Washington, DC.

32. Antonios Cosmas Liossis, Statement, September 1, 1944, and Roco Said, Statement, 16 August 1944, WO235/5 (604), Public Record Office, London.

33. Turner, *War in the Southern Oceans*, p. 251.

34. Ibid.

35. "Miscellaneous Intelligence from Sundry Sources," July 26, 1944, RG226, Records of the OSS, National Archives, Washington, DC.

36. Ibid.

37. Ibid.

38. Ibid.

39. Turner, *War in the Southern Oceans*, p. 251.

40. Alfred M. de Zayas, *The Wehrmacht War Crimes Bureau, 1939-1945* (University of Nebraska Press, 1989), p. 321, note 58.

41. Turner, *War in the Southern Oceans*, p. 251.

42. "Officer-in-Charge, Naval Section, JICAME to Director of Naval Intelligence," Memorandum June 5, June 8 & June 9, 1944, RG38, Records of the CNO, Records of ONI, National Archives, Washington, DC.

43. Ibid.

44. Ibid.

45. Ibid.

46. Ibid.

47. Ibid.

48. Ibid.

49. Ibid.

50. Ibid.

51. Ibid.

52-53. "Charge Sheet," Peleus Trial Transcript, WO235/5 (604), Public Record Office, London.

54. de Zayas, *The Wehrmacht War Crimes Bureau, 1939-1945*, pp. 320-321, note 58; "Persönliche Akten Harold Todsen, Max Pabst, Albrecht Wegener, & Gerd-Otto Wulf," Bestand R22, Reichjustizministerium, Bundesarchiv Koblenz; and Peleus Trial Transcript, Day 1, p. 2, WO235/5 (604), Public Record Office, London.

55. Peleus Trial Transcript, Day 1, pp. 4-6, WO235/5 (604), Public Record Office, London.

56. "Warrant No. V.W.3/1945-46," Peleus Trial Transcript, WO235/5 (604), Public Record Office, London.

57-58. Peleus Trial Transcript, Day 1, pp. 4-6, WO235/5 (604), Public Record Office, London.

59. Ibid., pp. 9-14, WO235/5 (604), Public Record Office, London.

60. Zayas, *The Wehrmacht War Crimes Bureau, 1939-1945*, p. 320, note 58.

61. Ibid., pp. 250-253.

62. LCdr. Dudley Morton, "USS Wahoo, Third War Patrol, Report of," p. 5, RG38, Records of the CNO, U.S. Submarine War Patrol Reports, National Archives, Washington, DC; George Grider & Lytel Sims, *War Fish* (Little Brown & Co., 1958), pp. 100-101; and Richard H. O'Kane, *Wahoo: The Patrols of America's Most Famous Submarine* (Presidio, 1987), pp. 153-154.

63. Capt. Robert R. Buckley, Jr., *At Close Quarters: PT Boats in the U.S. Navy*, (GPO, 1962), p.181; *Newsweek*, March 15, 1943, p. 18; and *Life*, March 22, 1943, p. 28.

64. Peleus Trial Transcript, Day 2, p. 4, WO235/5 (604), Public Record Office, London.

65. Ibid., Day 1, p. 5, WO235/5 (604), Public Record Office, London.

66. Arno Spindler, *Der Krieg zur See, 1914-1918: Der Handelskrieg mit U-Booten* (G.S. Mittler & Sohn, 1931), pp. 250-255.

67. Oberleutnant z. S. Crompton, *U-41: Der Zweite Baralong-Fall* (Verlag August Scherl, 1917), pp. 47-54.

68. Peleus Trial Transcript, Day 2, p. 6, WO235/5 (604), Public Record Office, London.

69. Ibid., Day 1, p. 12, WO235/5 (604), Public Record Office, London.

70. Ibid.

71. Mauer Mauer and Lawrence J. Paszek, "Origin of the Laconia Order," *Air University Review* (March-April 1964), pp. 26-37. Eventually, the French rescued some 1,111 survivors from the *Laconia*. I. C. B. Dear, ed., The Oxford Companion to World War II (New York, 1995), p. 662.

72. Peleus Trial Transcript, Day 2, p. 12, WO235/5 (604), Public Record Office, London.

73. Ibid., p. 15, WO235/5 (604), Public Record Office, London.

74. Ibid., pp. 16-17, WO235/5 (604), Public Record Office, London.

75. Ibid.

76. Ibid., Day 3, p. 2, WO235/5 (604), Public Record Office, London.

77. Ibid.

78. Ibid., p. 4, WO235/5 (604), Public Record Office, London.

79. Ibid.

80. For an excellent history of the development of Bomber Command's strategic bombing offensive, see Max Hastings, *Bomber Command* (Dial Press, 1979). The de-housing decision is discussed on pp. 127-132.

81. Herzog, *Deutsche U-Boote, 1906-1966*, pp. 255-256; and Peleus Trial Transcript, Day 3, pp. 6-7, WO235/5 (604), Public Record Office, London.

82. Ibid., p. 7, WO235/5 (604), Public Record Office, London.

83. Ibid.

84. Ibid., pp. 8-9, WO235/5 (604), Public Record Office, London.

85. Ibid.

86. Ibid., p. 10, WO235/5 (604), Public Record Office, London.

87. Ibid., p. 14, WO235/5 (604), Public Record Office, London.

88. Ibid., p. 15, WO235/5 (604), Public Record Office, London.

89. Ibid.

90. Ibid., p. 24, WO235/5 (604), Public Record Office, London.

91. Ibid.

92. To get some idea of the social and cultural circumstances that may have played a role in forming Lenz's philosophy, see Eric Rust, *Naval Officers Under Hitler: The Story of Crew 34* (Praeger, 1991). Though not a member of Crew 34, Lenz was nonetheless a product of the same system.

93. Dr. Wegner's reference to his friendship with the Bishop irritated the Judge Advocate. It is interesting to note that Bishop Bell was Britain's most outspoken opponent to Bomber Command's area bombing policy. Peleus Trial Transcript, Day 3, p. 31, WO235/5 (604), Public Record Office, London, and Hastings, *Bomber Command*, p. 177.

94. Peleus Trial Transcript, Day 3, pp. 30-31, WO235/5 (604), Public Record Office, London.

95. John Cameron, *The Peleus Trial* (William Hodge & CO., 1948), pp. 167-183.

96. Ibid.

97. Peleus Trial Transcript, Day 3, p. 31, WO235/5 (604), Public Record Office, London.

98. Ibid., pp. 30-38, WO235/5 (604), Public Record Office, London.

99. Ibid.

100. Ibid., Day 4, p. 6, WO235/5 (604), Public Record Office, London.

101. Cameron, *Peleus Trial*, pp.183-187.

102. Peleus Trial Transcript, Day 4, pp. 9, 12-13, 25, 26, WO235/5 (604), Public Record Office, London.

103. Ibid.

104. Ibid.

105. *New York Times*, October 21, 1945.

106. "Death Warrant" November 12, 1945, and "Return of Warrant," November 30, 1945, WO235/5 (604), Public Record Office, London.

107. Karl-Wilhelm Grützemacher, Letter to the Author, October 17, 1996.

108. Rust, *Crew 34*, p. 106, and Horst Bredow, Letter to the Author, December 12, 1995. Because of the controversy over the trial and execution of Eck, few Germans are willing to take a public stand on the issue, and few were willing to speak with the author about this case. Those who wrote or spoke with me have insisted on remaining anonymous. The recent publication of Goldhagen's *Hitler's Willing Executioners* (New York, 1996), has not helped the situation—especially where an American researcher is concerned.

109. Cameron, *Peleus Trial*, p. xiv.

INDEX